ANOTHER SIDE OF THE COIN

*The Other Side
of the Controversy Surrounding
the Faith Message*

by

Gregg N. Huestis

Another Side of the Coin—
The Other Side of the Controversy Surrounding the Faith Message

Published by: Blessed To Be A Blessing Ministries
E-mail: **info@b2bablessing.org**
Website: **www.b2bablessing.org**
Blog: www.b2bablessing.org/htdocs/blog/

Published in the U.S.A. by
Blessed To Be A Blessing Ministries
Ft. Collins, CO 80524
All Rights Reserved

Printed In the United States of America

I dedicate this book to
Emily P. Huestis,
my beautiful wife and best friend,
who gave of her time and editorial talents.
Without her wonderful devoted support, this
book would still be just a manuscript.

Acknowledgments

To **the Holy Spirit** for His guidance and inspiration to write. To all the Word of Faith teachers who assisted and encouraged me in the writing of this book. Finally, to all those who are uncertain about Faith teaching: May the Spirit of Wisdom & Revelation be yours!

(Eph. 1:17-21 TAB)

PREFACE

Few have seen the books that have responded directly to Hank Hanegraaff's landmark book, *Christianity in Crisis*. Hanegraaff's book, according to him, exposes the Word-Faith Movement as a "cult" by quoting statements by its major leaders. Yet, many of the accused Word-Faith leaders have kept to an understandable policy to neither read nor respond to criticism. Nonetheless, many Word-Faith adherents have wanted someone to contend with Hanegraaff for what they believe to be out-of-context quotes, strawman arguments, false allegations, and bias theology.

One person attempted to answer that call. In 1994, Michael Bruno wrote *Christianity in Power*, responding to Hanegraaff using love, Scripture, and reason. We are thankful to God for Reverend Bruno's book, as it has restored the faith of millions of Christians. Though we laude Bruno's courage in responding to *the Bible Answer Man*, and his efforts were certainly blessed by God, Bruno's book did not address many of Hanegraaff's interpretations that make the faith teachers appear to be guilty of teaching heretical doctrine.

However, God has raised another author to take up where Bruno has left off. Gregg Huestis in his excellent book, *Another Side of the Coin*, not only answers Hanegraaff's literary investigation with scripture and reason, but he also takes the quotes that Hanegraaff used and places them within their contextual setting. By doing this, Huestis demonstrates to his readers that Hanegraaff *appears* to have put words into the mouths of the faith teachers that were not originally there.

Huestis also uses quotations by faith teachers that Hanegraaff did not cite since they would have proven counter-productive in painting them as "cultic" and "heretical." Many adherents to the Faith Movement believe that Hanegraaff has misinterpreted this teaching but cannot afford to purchase all of the books and tapes to investigate their position. Huestis, however, provides them with the necessary resource for this endeavor.

Huestis begins his thesis by citing a number of apologists, those in the same field as Hanegraaff, who disagree with how he has handled the Faith Movement. Afterwards, Huestis covers such subjects as the *Force of Faith*, the *Formula of Faith*, the *Faith of God*, the alleged *deification of man,* the alleged *demotion of God,* the *Jesus-Died-Spiritually* (JDS) *doctrine,* and other subjects of interest. You will find Huestis' handling of these controversial subjects done with care and precision?

If you have been questioning the genuineness of Hanegraaff's work, but have been waiting for someone to provide the needed answers, then your prayers have been answered in the form of *Another Side of the Coin.* You will find this to be a great resource for maintaining your faith as well as providing an accurate response to Hanegraaff's allegations.

Pastor Troy J. Edwards
Victorious Word Christian Fellowship

Table of Contents

A Personal Introduction From The Author

This book has not been written as an attempt to say, "**We** are right and *they* are wrong!" Rather, this is a prayerful effort at giving a proper answer to the critics of the Word of Faith. It is the desire of my heart that this writing be a tool to bring about *restoration* between both sides of this controversial debate.

This book was birthed within my spirit because I have encountered many believers caught up in confusion concerning the Faith message. Jesus said, "You shall **know** the truth, and the truth shall make you free." The purpose of truth *is not* to bring about confusion and disunity. As hard as it may be, we will have to get our doctrines and misunderstandings out of the way or we will *never* experience the freedom that Jesus referred to in this verse. Therefore, we will end up not really understanding the truth so that we can be made free.

In *Another Side of the Coin*, I intend to examine several portions of Hank Hanegraaff's 1993 book, *Christianity in Crisis*, and pay particular attention to quotations of the various Faith teachers used by Hanegraaff. However, I also plan to use other quotations, by these same people, *not* cited by Hanegraaff, in order to show the *true* meaning behind the message of most of today's Faith teaching.

Moreover, I am completely aware that many of the Faith teachers have a long standing policy by which they have chosen not to read, listen or respond to any public opinion *for or against* them and their teaching. I respect their decision and understand their reasons for choosing not to respond. If I had as much press as they have had, I probably would respond in kind. *Nevertheless*, the Lord has given me a clear directive to respond to and properly clarify various controversial teachings of the Word of Faith.

I further realize that this book may not "convert" those who are already opposed to the teachings of the Word of Faith. But I know that it will be an important source of help to many who are still *unsure* of their motives and teaching. I, too, was unsure until I began carefully listening to and researching various statements of the Faith teachers over the last 17 years, comparing them with the Word of God. *I do not agree with every word taught by the Faith Teachers. However, I disagree more so with methods of those attempting to correct them.*

I can say from my own *personal* experience with those who oppose the message of faith, that in those times of uncertainty I wished that I had had a book to assist me like *Another Side of the Coin*. My motivation **is not** to attack or slander Hanegraaff, but rather to clearly and openly show various misinterpretations so that one can properly decide for himself.

I pray that those who read *Another Side of the Coin* will take that which I have written, *plus* Mr. Hanegraaff's writing, and **compare both** in the light of the Word of God. I do not ask that anyone should read this book and base their beliefs *solely* upon what I have written. *More than anything*, I desire that the reader will thoroughly examine both sides of this debate to see how they line up with *God's Word*, and therefore form their own conclusion.

For so many thousands of years, people have *based* their whole belief system on what someone else has said or written, **without** taking the time to *research* the subject(s) in question for themselves.

The time has come for the Body of Christ to examine **both sides** of this coin, in order that the whole picture may come into focus.

—Gregg N. Huestis
Blessed To Be A Blessing Ministries

1

HANEGRAAFF'S CAST OF CHARACTERS & BEYOND

Before we begin to address Mr. Hanegraaff's book, I wish to make one thing **poignantly clear**—it has **never** been my intention to attack or defame Hanegraaff *in any way*. I simply want to accurately present his interpretation of the Word of Faith teaching found in *Christianity in Crisis*. It is important that one understands his line of logic in context. Many advocates of this book have felt I should have been more stringent in opposing Hanegraaff's remarks. Instead, I felt led of the Lord to be more polite and hospitable. That being said let us look into *Christianity in Crisis*.

Hank Hanegraaff opens his literary exposition on the Word of Faith with a reasonably detailed exposé of the Faith teachers who he intends to openly expose for promoting what he believes to be *unorthodox* doctrine. I was shocked by his *manner* of writing, in which he called them heretics and denounced their teachings as *cultic*.

> "Twisted text, **make-believe miracles**, and counterfeit Christs are common denominators of the Faith movement's cast of Characters."[1]

The first official chapter, "the Cast of Characters," opens with his interpretation of the origin and influence of each Faith teacher addressed in his book. Sadly, his language is cutting, much like that of a bullet. He proceeds by denouncing many of their private and personal spiritual experiences. Furthermore, he denounces many of them as frauds and thieves, claiming they televise "make-believe miracles"[2] and bilk the *unsuspecting* out of millions of dollars annually.

For example, Hanegraaff opposes the teaching of John Avanzini, who is considered a teacher of Biblical economics. In referring to Avanzini, he makes these unflattering comments:

> "John Avanzini is billed by his Faith peers as a recognized authority on biblical economics. The truth, however, is that he is

1

an authority at separating poor people from their money…Avanzini runs the gamut from teaching people how to get their hands on the 'wealth of the wicked' to what might best be described as his '***hundredfold hoax***.'"[3]

He continues by writing a few additional unflattering remarks about a man of God who has been a powerful influence in my own life and ministry—Dr. Morris Cerullo.

"He purports to have first met God at the age of eight. Since then his life has been one remarkable experience after another…On another occasion, Cerullo claimed God was directing him to say, 'Would you surrender your pocketbooks unto Me, saith God, and let Me be the Lord of your pocketbooks.'"[4]

I have been teaching the hundredfold return principle for several years hence; I understand this principle in great detail. I can assure you the Bible clearly affirms this teaching. Consequently, I can write with total confidence that the teaching of Dr. John Avanzini, regard this tenet, is in fact Scripturally sound. I have studied under his ministry since 1983, when I first met him in Chicago, IL at the Morris Cerullo *Chicago Partners Seminar*. I have examined Avanzini's teachings thoroughly and know them to be Biblically sound.

Concerning Morris Cerullo, I can say from ***personal experience*** with his ministry that he is a man of God of the **finest** quality that I have ever known. I have been blessed to meet Cerullo a number of times in person. I also worked for him for a short time in 1986 at Morris Cerullo World Evangelism. I know beyond a shadow of a doubt that the ministry of Morris Cerullo is not only doctrinally sound, but also financially sound. As for the other Faith teachers addressed in Hanegraaff's book, I haven't met them apart from their books, cassettes and videos. Still, I have examined their teachings thoroughly and have never found *anything* heretical in nature. I don't agree with all that they do or say, but I know their teachings to be Biblically unassailable. I must confess that I have seen some disturbing methods of fundraising by TV preachers that concerns me, but in recent years such emotional appeals are quickly fading away.

What Division?

"I have become both weary and wary of those who use the perversions of the Faith movement to drive a wedge between charismatic and noncharismatic Christians. Frankly, this is both counterproductive and divisive, for the Faith movement is not charismatic; it is cultic."[5]

Mr. Hanegraaff claims that the Faith teachers are promoting division between Charismatic and non-Charismatic believers. On the other hand, it was Hanegraaff who has written a book with a *"flare* of tabloid journalism," rather than Copeland, Hagin or Capps—we will address this issue in depth later in this chapter. Many advocates of the Word of Faith believe, as we will see later, that he has set his heart on tearing down the reputation and ministry of many great men and women of God within the Faith Movement. Hanegraaff's actions, like the ones previously mentioned, could be viewed as counterproductive and divisive. I find no credible evidence to infer that the Word of Faith teachers are causing division between Charismatic and non-Charismatic believers. In addition, Hanegraaff has also **publicly** denounced the teachers of the Word of Faith as cult leaders, and as teaching cultic doctrine. Rating them with the likes of the Mormons, the Jehovah's Witnesses, and the Christian Scientists.[6]

Further, many Christians believe Hanegraaff does not *seem* to show a spirit of love toward those mentioned in his book. This is a direct violation of what Jesus said to do with our enemies, Matthew 5:44: *"Love your enemies and pray for those who persecute you."* I ask the reader to continue and make that decision for one's own self. On the other hand, *most* of the Faith teachers continue to love Hanegraaff and pray for him, without demeaning, slanderous remarks against him or his ministry. The major portion of the Word of Faith teachers believe *he is a fellow believer* and would consent to discussions with him if they felt these issues would be resolved. However, based on his previous actions this doesn't appear to be likely (see quotes from *Charisma*).

It seems obvious, from *Christianity in Crisis*, that Hanegraaff's intentions for writing were not primarily for the **restoration** of these servants of God. According to the Word of God, the Biblical prerequisite for confrontation is **always** restoration of those in error. Love must *always* be the motivation for confrontation. When one confronts another out of love, restoration, peace, and spiritual growth will, *for the most part*, be the result. However, when one confronts another with improper motives, anger, or strife; then **division** will nearly always be the end result (See Proverbs 30:33c). I will not assume to understand Hanegraaff's intentions, but can understand why many have questioned his motivation.

Integrity Questioned In *Charisma*

I'm an avid reader of *Charisma* magazine, and one day I purchased their May 1995 issue where much to my amazement, I found an article titled, "Does the Church Need Heresy Hunters?" The content of this article was so stunning I felt the need to save it for use in this book.

"*Charisma* talked with people on both sides of this controversy to determine whether there is any hope of resolving it. What we discovered: Many Christian leaders, including some who represent cult-watching organizations, *think Hanegraaff is going too far.* 'The people I talk to don't appreciate the way Hank handles the Word-Faith movement', says Robert Bowman, a former CRI researcher who now works with the Atlanta Christian Apologetics Project. 'I refuse to put [Word-Faith churches] in the cult category. It's ridiculous [for Hanegraaff] to say that all these people are insincere hucksters.'"[7]

"Ron Enroth, a cult watcher and author of the book *Churches That Abuse* (Zondervan), takes exception to Hanegraaff's strident tone. '*Christianity in Crisis* is an important book, but I think Hanegraaff has gone too far in some of his statements,' Enroth says. 'I consider [Word-Faith] people my brothers and sisters in Christ, so it is difficult for me to put them in the same category as cultists.'"[8]

"The Group for CRI Accountability, organized last year, includes some 30 former CRI staff members who are **publicly demanding Hanegraaff's resignation**. They say Hanegraaff does not have the theological training, the communication skills or the ethical standards to lead CRI."[9]

Having read the previous three excerpts from *Charisma* magazine, it is easy to see that Hanegraaff's views and methods are particularly questionable. It is also clear that his own ministry peers have questions about his ability to confront other members of the Body of Christ in the Biblical manner. Again, I ask the reader to consider these quotations and come to their own conclusion. These questions have raised a red flag in the minds of many concerning Hanegraaff's motivation, as well as his qualification as a cult-researcher. It also seems hard for one trust his allegations against the Faith teachers when his ministry peers are unable to trust him?

Problems With Accountability?

"His most vocal critics are former CRI staff members including one who sued him 14 months ago. Brad Sparks says he filed his lawsuit **after** Hanegraaff **refused** to agree to Christian arbitration. Sparks claims he was wrongfully terminated from CRI because he spoke out against **ethics violations at the ministry**. He alleges, among other things, that Hanegraaff receives an 'excessive six-figure annual income'...Sparks believes there is 'a serious lack of accountability' at CRI, especially since 1993 when CRI withdrew from the Evangelical Council for Financial Accountability...Sparks alleges that CRI pulled out of ECFA so the ministry wouldn't have to comply with an ECFA conflict of interest clause, which states that ministry personnel cannot receive royalties from sales of books that are used for fund-raising purposes."[10]

"The Group for CRI Accountability...also want to know why Hanegraaff lives in a $731,000 house in Coto de Caza, an exclusive, gated community in Orange County, Calif."[11]

I cannot prove whether or not these claims against Hanegraaff are true. Still, the fact that they have been raised publicly causes many to question the Bible *Answer* Man's integrity and accountability. Concerning his six figure salary and $731,000 house, one could have assumed that *Charisma* had confused Hanegraaff with Dr. Frederick K.C. Price, one of the Faith teachers who Hanegraaff berated for driving a Rolls Royce. If one didn't know, one could have thought that Hanegraaff is now a prosperity preacher? As to whether or not Hanegraaff should be prosperous, there is nothing wrong with him making a large salary and living in an exclusive area of Southern California. **Every** Christian worker is worthy of his wage. However, many see a problem when he accuses others of being in it for the money when he too could be accused of a lifestyle similar to those of the Word of Faith. Many find his accusations hypocritical when considering his own financial status.

Furthermore, it is interesting that when Brad Sparks, a former CRI staff member, went to him with Christian arbitration, Mr. Hanegraaff *refused*. His actions with Sparks appear to show why *he* hasn't initiated Christian mediation with the members of the Word of Faith. This further leads one to believe that even if Christian mediation were attempted—Hanegraaff would still carry on opposing the Faith teachers?

Hence, many feel he does not *appear* to desire restoration, but rather the destruction of the reputation of those who oppose his methods?

Christ's Solider or Assassin?

> "James Spenser, a former Mormon who has written several books on how to share Christ with members of cults, says he's been on the receiving end of that hateful attitude. He thinks cult-watchers like Hanegraaff actually are involved in **character assassination**. In a book published in 1993, *Heresy Hunters: Character Assassination in the Church* (Huntington House), Spencer says cult watchers are too zealous. 'They are on a high and holy crusade to rid the church of heresy,' he says. 'But modern apologists are *too reckless*—they're **doing their work by fax machine**, and they're not being careful about what they say and write.'"[12]

According to the previous article, Hanegraaff has committed character assassination. *Charisma* points out that his methods *seem* to have little love or concern for correction of error. For this reason, his technique, for the most part, has proved to be fruitless. Godly correction in love bares fruit and the restoration of our brother and sister in Christ. *Charisma* maintains that Hanegraaff's methods of correction are merely driving the assumed erroneous person away into alienation, instead of embracing them into restoration.

In addition, in the August 1993 issue of *Charisma*, Stephen Strang had some **important** comments to make about Hanegraaff's assessment of the Faith movement.

> "I've prayed and worshipped side by side with many of these folks in the Faith movement, and Hanegraaff's depiction of them as heretics flies in the face of what I've seen with my own eyes…Everyone I know in the Faith movement proclaims Jesus Christ as Lord and would die for the fundamentals of the faith listed in the Apostles' Creed or the Nicene Creed. (At Rhema, for example, they affirm the 16 'fundamental truths' of the Assemblies of God). Interestingly Strang suggests several points to evaluate charges of heresy, among which are:
>
> Is the point of the criticism correction or restoration? Or is it to sell books and attract listeners and donors?

Has the critic tried to determine what the speaker meant? Or is he quick to at tribute beliefs to a fellow Christian that he may not even hold. Has the critic made an effort to confront fellow Christians in love? Or has he alienated his brother with a derisive tone and caustic charges of heresy, blasphemy, scam and worse.

Has the critic given his errant brother ample opportunity to change? Or is he in a rush to nail his victim."[13]

Charisma On the Radio?

In June 1995, Stephen Strang, founder and publisher of *Charisma* magazine, was faced with a rather remarkable opportunity to run an ad submitted by the Christian Research Institute (CRI).

> "...a situation occasionally comes up that seems *less than black-and-white*. One such incident arose **after** we ran a news story about the legal battle between Hank Hanegraaff of the Christian Research Institute and one of his former staff members. Last month we published a feature story about so-called heresy hunters and quoted some of Hanegraaff's critics. **The next thing we knew**, we had been **added to the list** of people and ministries Hanegraaff *regularly* attacks on his radio program. So you can imagine our surprise when an ad for his ministry arrived *via Federal Express*! Because Hanegraaff has been no fan of ours, we wondered why he chose to advertise in *Charisma*. A few skeptics in the office assumed he was setting us up—maybe expecting us to turn down the ad so he'd have ammunition with which to attack us. After consulting with several national Christian leaders, we decided to run the ad in this issue...*we certainly believe he is part of the Christian community*...Besides, we want to make a statement that we are **neither for nor against** Hanegraaff or his ministry."[14]

Did Hanegraaff really attempt to set-up the staff of *Charisma* magazine for public ridicule? The skeptics mentioned by Strang in the above quotation seem to think so. Why would a man who previously disliked their magazine, all of a sudden, desire to place an ad with them? Additionally, to my knowledge (being an avid *Charisma* reader), I haven't seen another advertisement in *Charisma* from the Christian Research Institute (CRI) or *the Bible Answer Man* since. His previously mentioned conduct appears to further demonstrate why one would assume that

"Hanegraaff is a maverick outlaw who enjoys chasing his Christian brothers with a branding iron."[15] I am **not** judging Hanegraaff but his actions cause one to question his motivation and integrity.

Is Restoration In Sight?

According to the May 1995 article of *Charisma* (mentioned previously), many observers believe that restoration is possible, but only if the Word of Faith preachers will voluntarily come together and have a meeting of the minds with Hanegraaff. However, *is this really reality?* Hasn't this been tried once before? Pastor/evangelist Benny Hinn thought along those same lines and discovered that he was *sincerely* mistaken. He relates his experiences with Hanegraaff in the August 1993 issue of *Charisma.*

> "**Charisma**: Hank Hanegraaff has used actual statements you made in sermons to base his claim that you are teaching error. Do these statements accurately reflect your current teaching?
> **Hinn**: Not at all but the sad fact is that CRI continued airing my old tapes for months *after* I made the changes. When I met with Hank Hanegraaff in August last year, I said, 'Hank, I no longer believe this and I don't teach it anymore.' I thought he understood, but he continued rehashing the whole thing until recently."[16]

Despite Hinn's efforts to make adjustments on portions of his teaching and crusade presentation, Mr. Hanegraaff continued to denounce Hinn's teaching after they met (August 1992) to explain his ministerial revisions. This speaks loud and clear that meeting with Hanegraaff to discuss doctrinal differences would most likely prove to be *a fruitless effort*. In spite of Benny Hinn's attempt to rectify their disagreements, Hanegraaff chose to continue airing Hinn's former teaching on his radio talk show, *The Bible Answer Man*—which is broadcasted nationwide in the United States. Hence, it is understandable why many believers in *Charisma* feel Hanegraaff is guilt of character assassination?

The Footnote

In 1994, Hanegraaff wrote and released a companion to his 1993 book which he titled the *Christianity in Crisis Study Guide*. In the beginning of this study guide, Hanegraaff writes a brief footnote concerning the previously cited revisions by Hinn's ministry, claiming that Hinn had made his theological changes **shortly after** the release of *Christianity in Crisis.*

> "*Shortly after the publication of *Christianity in Crisis* in 1993, Benny Hinn stated that he has revised his views on certain aspects of his teachings. However, Hinn's views as articulated in the latest of his works, including *Good Morning, Holy Spirit*, are presented in this study guide until material to the contrary is available."[17]

In spite of all of the retractions and theological revisions conducted by Hinn, Hanegraaff did not seem to be convinced of his truthfulness. This conduct should unquestionably answer any observer's thoughts concerning intentions for restoration. He acknowledged that Hinn stated he made these changes; however, instead of *acting in good faith* toward him, he decided to include Hinn (and his old material), in his follow-up study guide. Shouldn't Hinn have been given the benefit of the doubt? I ask the reader to form their own conclusion!

Based on the quotations from *Charisma* many believe Hanegraaff's motivation is actually two fold. First of all, he *literally* believes he is called by God to extricate (that which he has deemed to be) heresy from the Body of Christ. Second, they also see his motivation as a subconscious desire for prominence, prosperity and an odd yearning to be in the center of controversy. Thus, he has created a large audience for himself and his radio program. Where there is much controversy, there will also be an open door for fame and affluence. If you don't believe this look at some of today's sports heroes and movie stars for example.

Perhaps some might be thinking, "*You're just as bad as he is. All you've done is to divisively question Hanegraaff's reputation and integrity.*" I can understand why some might think this. *However,* I did not make any negative statements concerning Hanegraaff's integrity. These statements are direct quotations from *Charisma* magazine—I have merely researched and compiled what is **already public knowledge**. I have left it up to the reader to consider this information and make a decision for one's self. *Hanegraaff's style of writing* has placed his character and motivation on suspicion more than anything I or anyone else has said concerning him thus far.

Some might wonder further, "*Do you believe that he is a brother in the Lord?*" **Yes!** Without a doubt! I have made this question *perfectly clear* in prior statements. However, many view him as a *misguided* brother in the

Lord who sees things from his *perspective* only. I believe his **predominate motive** is to extricate (what he considers) heresy from the Body of Christ. However, in his attempt to do this he has nearly destroyed the reputations of many.

A *Very* Important Statement

The Bible is **very** clear that every born-again believer has an important roll in the Body of Christ. Mr. Hanegraaff has a significant job as a counter-cult researcher and Christian leader. Whether we agree with his interpretations, motivations or actions, does not change the reality that he has **a vital part** in the Body of Christ.

We need people who monitor cultic activity **and challenge error** if it arises in the Church. His methods may be disturbing to many *but he is still a brother in the Lord* who needs our love and prayer support. We must **always** do our best to respond in a loving manner to the critics. We are all one Body—attached to Christ. If we attack one another then **we are ultimately opposing Christ!**

Toronto & Florida Revivals Questioned

In order to further illustrate why many question Hanegraaff's *character* and *motivation*, it is important to note that he seems to be repeating the same mistakes made with *Christianity in Crisis* (1993). He does this by questioning the genuineness of the revivals that took place in Toronto, Canada and Pensacola, Florida, in the writing of *Counterfeit Revival* (1997).

"We can only imagine how Hanegraaff would react to these types of behavior [*shaking, trembling, falling*] if they were to appear today. He seems to assume that **Christian orthodoxy is a rationalistic, sterilized Calvinism** that functions entirely on an **intellectual** level—devoid of the subjective spiritual dimension. Scholars today who accept the authority and inerrancy of Scripture **are challenging the view** that miracles and gifts of the Spirit ceased after the apostles died…Pentecostals and charismatics do not advocate the present move of God because of experience alone…Hanegraaff, on the other hand, **believes reason is altogether superior to spiritual experience**…The position was championed during the Enlightenment (circa 1650-1790), when revelation, enthusiasm or religious experience was denied *in favor of the rational processes of* **scientific method**. Rational 'certainty' **replaced** faith as the way of truth. The rational approach influenced Christian theologians, and **intellectual understanding of doctrine eventually became their goal—not the biblical 'knowing' of God *by revelation of the Holy Spirit.*** (See 1 Cor. 2:14). Hanegraaff's *disdain* of charismatic gifts, experiences and manifestations flows from this perspective. By criticizing charismatics, he ridicules the Father's lavish gifts of joy and playfulness…A true encounter with God does not produce *a* **sour rationalism**, but life-changing fellowship with God and an exuberant desire to spread His love to others."[18]

The above observation made by Jon Ruthven, PH. D. in *Charisma*, was in reference to Hanegraaff's book, *Counterfeit Revival*. Based on this comment it appears that Hanegraaff has not learned from the negative fall-out from *Christianity in Crisis*. Furthermore, from the quotation above, we have also seen that others are aware of Hanegraaff's fondness for intellectualism and the scientific method. Ruthven believes Hanegraaff's interpretation of traditional Christian Orthodoxy appears to be purely unemotional *intellectualism*; hence, his opposition toward the Word of Faith and the various revivals. For many it is difficult to comprehend his viewpoint of Biblical "orthodoxy." In many ways, Hanegraaff is reaping what he has sown. He has accused others of acting improperly and now he too is being accused of similar improper actions by his peers.

I realize this chapter **is not** easy to read, *nor was it easy for me to write*. Nevertheless, the harsh realities that it covers are worthy of our examination. **Again**, the purpose of this book is not to slander or defame Hanegraaff, *in any way*, but merely to demonstrate the questions raised by prominent leaders in the Body of Christ regarding his character, motivation and Biblical interpretation. I have not made up these statements, but rather have pointed one to that which is already public knowledge. The reader is now asked once again **to form one's own conclusion!**

2

THE "FORCE" OF FAITH

Spiritual principles are often times extremely difficult to illustrate because human language cannot properly clarify spiritual understanding. The language of the Holy Spirit (tongues) is the only *language* capable of verbally expressing the deep and profound revelations of God. However, *tongues* are not understandable without the Anointing or someone with the interpretation.

Due to the fact that human language is so limited, many times an alternative style of expression is needed in order to convey spiritual truth. Therefore, I believe this is *one of* the main reasons why Jesus always used parables in order to address the multitudes. He knew that if He wanted to be **remotely** understood, He would have to relate spiritual truth as compared to the multitude's *previous* knowledge. Thus, Jesus used these earthly comparisons to illustrate the awesome principles of the Kingdom of God.

How does this apply to the *force* of faith? This applies aptly to our topic at hand because the term *the "force" of faith* is simply an earthly illustration used to describe a spiritual principle. Some traditional *religious* people believe that this terminology is just an impersonal depiction of an impersonal God. However, is their interpretation valid and accurate? To answer this question, we will need to first of all define the term *force* in relation to *the force of faith*.

May His Force Be With You

The dictionary defines *force* as: "strength or energy...*active power*...moral or mental strength...."[1] My computer's thesaurus gives these words for *force*: energy, intensity, might, power. Thus, the term *the "force" of faith* is, in fact, an accurate description of faith's *active* abilities. So, the use of the word "*force*" is nothing more than a metaphorical way of describing faith's active abilities in straightforward language that even the unschooled Bible student would be able to understand.

Despite the fact that we have clearly covered the use of such terminology, we will nevertheless continue in our investigation of the "*force*" *of faith*!

In *Christianity in Crisis*, Hanegraaff penned a chapter called *Force of Faith* in which he tends to drift on to several other areas of the teaching of Faith. In his chapter he confesses that he has researched for many hours on this subject, and that "the significant theme" of Faith teaching is that *faith is a force*. He attempts to prove this assumption by *quoting* Kenneth Copeland's book—*The Force of Faith*.

"Faith is a power force. It is a tangible force. It is a conductive force."[2]

I am confused as to why Hanegraaff believes this statement is so strange. Jesus Himself made a statement very much like Copeland's that can be found in Matthew chapter 21, verse 21 (*the Amplified Bible*).

"...Truly I say to you, **if** you have *faith* (a firm relying trust) and do not doubt, you will not only do what has been done to the fig tree, but even if you **say** to this mountain...."

It seems quite obvious that Jesus specified that faith was the key ingredient (*power*) that caused the fig tree to wither and die. Jesus wouldn't have said we had to have faith in order for this to take place, *if* faith was not the key **active force** (power) that brought this manifestation to pass. We must, first of all, have His faith *living in our hearts*, which will in turn build confidence in God and His Word to do exactly what Jesus previously said. An unbeliever cannot do these same types of things and get the same results. Why? *No faith, no life force*!

Faith Filled Words

The previous verse of Scripture also brings us to another hot topic of conversation. *Is faith released in our words?* Remember that Jesus said "if you have faith...even **if you say** to this mountain." Jesus was literally telling us that faith is the key **force** or *active power* that *works* in all situations.

Also, He said we must **speak** to something in order for the *force* of faith to be released. Jesus is illustrating for us the principle of releasing faith *through the words that we speak*. Our faith is founded in God. We have His faith living in us. However, faith will **only** be released to work *in our own lives* when we determine to speak *God's Word* believing He will do the rest. Why argue with God's Word? Let's humble our pride *and do it* (speak) in obedience to His Word!

Faith v. Fear

"God cannot do anything *for you* apart or separate from faith, any more than Satan cannot do any thing *to you* apart from fear...Fear activates Satan, the way faith activates God."[3] Hanegraaff contests such statements from Copeland feeling they are in error.

Let's examine this statement according to Scripture.

James 1:6-8 (NKJV): "But let him ask in faith, with no doubting...For let not that man suppose that he will receive **anything** from the Lord; he is a double-mind man, unstable...."

According to the apostle James, any one who comes to God not asking *in faith* will receive absolutely nothing. The book of James confirms that God *cannot* do anything for the one who **is not** asking in faith. God wants to do it, but actually He **cannot** do it because of our lack of faith. Why did I say God cannot do it? I said this because God's Word clearly states that without faith, it is **impossible** to please Him. If we aren't pleasing to Him, then He cannot intervene in our lives. If we have resisted His Spirit by disobeying His Word, then that disobedience (sin) hinders us from receiving from Him.

Consequently, *we* are in sin and God *cannot* look upon, nor have anything to do with sin. **We** are the ones who block His hand from moving in our lives in the same way that the Israelites did in the desert. God told them in Malachi chapter four that their words were "**stout** against Him." Today, our words are still, often times, our greatest hindrance in life? We are the ones who are failing, **not God**! God does not fail! Human beings fail!

How Fear Activates Satan In Our Lives

Job 3:25 (NKJV): "The thing I **greatly** feared has come upon me, And what I *dreaded* has happened to me."

Many anti-faith folks literally go into hysterics when their *idol* of pain and suffering (Job) is addressed. As painful as it may be, Job is a perfect example of how someone can *ignorantly* open the door of his life to Satan.

I do not believe Job ran around and boldly shot off his mouth; however, he **still** lost everything he had and *thought* God had taken it away. It is obvious that Job's words (**before** he lost everything) were not words of faith and trust in God. Job said, "...the thing I feared the most came upon me, and that which I dreaded [was nervous about the most] happened to me." To me this clearly shows that Job was worried and nervous about his life long **before** he experienced tragedy. Therefore, his fear of loss was Satan's open invitation!

As of this moment, I have never met a fearful, worrisome person who was not *constantly* talking about the things they fear and worry about the most. Why? This is because they are consumed with the fear of loss, and they focus on their previous losses, instead of acting in faith on God's promises to protect them. Consequently, I see no reason to believe Job was any different from others I have known. Human nature has not changed since Adam's fall into sin. We must remember Job **was not** born-again—he was Spiritually Dead!

The Origin of the Modern Faith *Movement*

There is a concrete idea in the mind of Hanegraaff that tells him that the Faith *movement* **ultimately** began with E.W. Kenyon. "Kenyon, the real father of the modern-day Faith movement, 'majored' in metaphysics."[4] Hanegraaff is consequently saying E.W. Kenyon brought ungodly metaphysical New Thought into the Church, which is a perversion of traditional **systematic** theological interpretation.

However, did E.W. Kenyon *really* intermingle metaphysical New Thought into Christian doctrine and establish the so-called "modern-day Faith movement"?

In *Quenching the Spirit*, William DeArteaga affirms that E.W. Kenyon did indeed attend a metaphysical college in Boston, Massachusetts. However, DeArteaga continues by sharing some commonly missed details of Kenyon's life.

> "Yet by the time he published his **first** theological work, *The Father and his Family* (1916), he had discerned **and rejected** the core of Gnostic beliefs in metaphysical philosophy. His writings consistently show that he considered himself **strongly opposed** to the whole Metaphysical movement, from Unity to its most extreme form as in Christian Science."[5]

DeArteaga includes an excerpt from Kenyon's book, *Two Kinds of Faith*, in order to prove this point.

"Christian Science, Unity, and the other Metaphysical and philosophical teachers of today do not believe that God is a person.

They will tell you that He is perfect mind, but He has no location. It is just a great universal mind which finds its home in every individual. He has no headquarters...

They do not believe in sin as Paul taught it in the Revelation given to him.

They do not believe that Jesus died for our sins, but that He died as a martyr.

They do not believe He had a literal Resurrection, a physical Resurrection, but put it as, 'a metaphysical resurrection.' (**whatever that means**).

If God is not a person and Jesus did not put sin away, then who is Jesus and what is the value of our faith in Him?"[6]

The words of E.W. Kenyon cited here certainly do not sound, by any stretch of the imagination, like a man who is deceived by and endorsing metaphysical New Thought. It is strange to me how Hanegraaff could accept and embrace a former cult group like *the World Wide Church of God*, and yet completely disregard all logical proof of Kenyon's rejection of the metaphysical New Thought idealism that was being taught at Emerson College. Kenyon's statement above **clearly** shows that he did not endorse such heretical teaching.

In all fairness, I believe that we need to take some time to address where E.W. Kenyon and *most* of the other Faith teachers originally found their ideas about the Biblical concepts of faith.

The *Biblical* Origin of Faith Teaching

This is a very lengthy endeavor; therefore, I will only be able to give a few *brief* Scriptural examples of faith teaching found in the Word of God. Paul writes in Galatians chapter three verse eight, "And the Scripture, foreseeing that God would justify the Gentiles by faith, **preached the gospel** to Abraham before hand, saying '*In you all the nations shall be blessed*'" (NKJV). God the Father was the *first* Faith preacher. God Almighty preached **the Gospel** of faith to Abraham *many years before* any Faith teachers were in existence. His Gospel included His promise to Abraham and what He told him to do to receive it. Plus, He also included the foretelling of an Anointed Savior Who would come. God the Father was the first to preach the Gospel, and it was the Gospel of how to receive from Him by using the faith that He imparted to us.

Jesus Is A Faith Preacher

Mark 11:22b-24 (NKJV): "…Have faith in God. For assuredly, I say to you, whoever says to this mountain, 'Be removed and cast into the sea, and does not doubt in his heart, but believes that **those things he says** will be done, he **will have** whatever he says. Therefore I say to you, whatever things you ask *when you pray*, **believe** that you receive them, and you **will** have them."

This may be a revelation to some, *but* E.W. Kenyon and Kenneth Hagin are not the authors of Mark11:22-24. Jesus *Himself* is preaching the Gospel of faith to us in Mark 11:22-25. The requirements He laid down for our receiving are: to have faith in God, **speak** to the mountain (*circumstances*), believe *when* we pray, and forgive.

These are the secrets to receiving *any* prayer of petition that we pray from God. So, why would one want to argue his point *for another way*, when our Lord Himself told us what to do? The Word of Faith (WoF) teachers have simply discovered and followed God's example (Eph. 5:1). They are merely teaching that we should pray according to God's Word instead of by a **man-made systematic method** of prayer.

Paul Was A Faith Preacher

Romans 10:8 (NKJV): "But what does it say? [*the righteousness of faith*]? 'The word is near you, **in your mouth** and *in your heart*' (that is, *the word of faith* which **we** preach):"

Paul's words here are a confirmation of Jesus' words in Mark 11. He, too, states *the Word of faith* is in our mouths and hearts (our spirits) which brings about our receiving. *God* implants His desires into us *from His Word*, we confess His promises, and through our obedience **God** brings the result!

Many critics would say, "These are just a few isolated verses of Scripture taken out of their context." To some, this may be true! However, to discerning Bible students, who carefully read the teachings of Jesus and Paul, faith (trust) in God & His Word are their central themes. Remember, without faith, it is *impossible* to please God because we must believe that He exists **and** that He is a *rewarder* of those who diligently seek Him. We *can not* be rewarded by God, **unless we believe it is His will to reward us!**

Hebrews Chapter Eleven Verse One

Hanegraaff also seems to have a thorn in his side concerning the use of the terminology: "...the substance of things hoped for...." He believes the Faith teachers are basing their whole doctrinal teaching on *one* verse of Scripture, namely Hebrews chapter eleven verse 1 *the Amplified Bible.*

Now Faith is the assurance (the confirmation, **the title deed**) of the things [we] hope for, being the *proof* of things [we] do not see *and* the conviction of their reality [faith perceiving *as real fact* what is *not revealed to the senses*].

First of all, Hebrews chapter 11 verse 1 defines faith as *assurance*. However, it also goes on to define faith as the *confirmation* and *the title deed* of the things we hope for. What is a title deed? A title deed is a legal **tangible** document which displays ownership of something, such as a piece of property or a car. In other words, faith **is** our *assurance* that we *have* received. It is our *literal* titled deed to those things that we have believed God for.

Spiritually speaking, we have **a tangible title deed** showing ownership of the things that we have believed God for (*when we pray*)! This entire argument about substance and tangibility is **foolishness**. The tangibility that is in question is in **the realm of the Spirit** and Hanegraaff *seems* to think of it as referring to *the realm of the senses*. Hanegraaff is thinking in the natural; however, faith is *active* in the Spirit.

"Now faith is the substance of things hoped for, the evidence of things not seen."

I would like to point out that in the *Kenneth Copeland Reference Edition* Bible, Copeland has added in a number (5) by the word *substance*. This note is given for clarification concerning the meaning of the word *substance*. In his reference edition, *substance* has been defined as: "*ground, or confidence.*"[7]

Thus as a result, this clearly shows that Copeland is not attempting to distort the true meaning of *substance* as *The Bible "Answer" Man* claims. The previous statements clearly illustrate the viewpoint the Word of Faith teachers hold when it comes to defining what faith is.

19

Faith Defined In Their Own Words

"Faith, in other words, is grasping the *unrealities of hope* and bringing them into the realm of reality. And faith **grows** out of the Word of God."[8]

"It is more than just believing. You have to ACT on what you believe. You have to take what you believe and then do something about it. That's what faith is. **Faith is doing something about what you believe.**"[9]

"Faith is not a natural force: it is supernatural. It is God-given, God-imparted, and God implanted...God the Father is the source of faith. God the Son is the word of faith. God the Holy Spirit is the substance of faith."[10]

"Inward confidence, inward assurance, inward trust...to have faith in God simply means that **we trust Him**."[11]

"...you must have the substance, or **assurance**. 'Substance' in the Greek language is *hupostasis*. In the English language this can be translated '**title deed**, or *legal paper*'. When you have a clear goal, **and** you have the desire burning in your heart to a boiling point, *then* you should kneel down and pray until you receive the substance, the **assurance**."[12]

"Just as faith is **confidence** in God's ability to protect you, fear is confidence in Satan's ability to hurt you."[13]

"Why is it so important for you to develop your faith? Because faith *is what connects you to the blessings of God*. It's the force that gives those blessings *substance* in your life (see Hebrews 11:1)...It's faith that reaches into the realm of the spirit, grasps the promise of God and brings forth a tangible, physical fulfillment of that promise.[14]

"God is wanting the church to bring forth great things in prayer and it requires faith for us to do that. You see, in prayer we always travel by faith. It [*faith*] is like a vehicle that takes us from where we are to where we want to go. And **the size of our faith determines** whether we travel by Concorde or by pony express."[15]

"There is a big difference between *believing* and having faith. Faith is imparted—*a gift of faith*—**God's faith**...Faith is a spiritual resource that comes from God. It is given to the believer as a 'sixth sense'...It is knowing what God knows."[16]

According to the above cited quotations, one can clearly see that each Faith Teacher's definition of faith corresponds with that of Scripture. Consequently, not one of these definitions by the teachers of faith is heretical. To assume heresy from these definitions is inconceivable and reckless. Yet, Hanegraaff *still* proclaims their view of faith as heretical.

The Amplified Bible's definition of faith

"Now Faith is the **assurance** (the confirmation, *the title deed*) of the things [we] hope for, being the **proof** of things [we] do not see *and* the **conviction** of their reality [faith perceiving **as real fact** what is not revealed to the senses]."

As a result, one can see that all of the previously cited definitions of faith all flow in line with Hebrews 11:1, according to *The Amplified Bible*.

Substance: Hanegraaff's Conclusion!

"Therefore, according to Faith teaching, the book you're reading is made out of molecules, which in turn are made out of atoms, which are composed of subatomic particles, which are comprised of this thing called "faith." According to Faith theology, virtually everything is *made out of faith!*"[17]

Since we have already dealt with this subject previously, we won't take a long time to clarify. Hanegraaff seems to truly believe that when a Faith teacher says something like "*All material matter was created by the faith of God*", they are actually insinuating that everything is *literally* made of "*faith*." Then, I bet he thinks they still believe in *the tooth fairy* as well. Wood **is** wood, but faith was God's tool to bring the wood into **material existence** or reality, everything exists by or because of faith. Faith, released from God's Words, caused everything to come into physical manifestation.

The Faith teachers *are not* saying that everything is made out of *faith*. What they are saying is that faith is the spiritual *substance* that God **used** to create all physical matter, and the entire world is held together by

21

the force of faith which God put into motion. This is a Spiritual Law that He set in motion. The Word of Faith teachers are in no way attempting to say that everything is **literally** made out of "faith." Rather, they are saying that faith released in God's words caused everything that we can see to come into material existence. In addition, this *does not* mean that these things didn't exist prior to the human eye perceiving them.

In other words, God *used* faith to bring these unseen things into the realm of the natural, so that natural man could see and use them. The Faith teachers are speaking of *spiritual* substance, but Hanegraaff, for *some* reason, keeps hearing *natural* (carnal) substance. Perhaps this is the reason he *struggles* to understand the Faith teachers and their message.

Consequently, the existence of so-called heresy remains strictly *within the imagination* of Hanegraaff and his associates. Therefore, it appears that Hanegraaff defines "heresy" as anything that does not fit into his own interpretation of *traditional Systematic Theology*, more accurately known as **the scientific method** of studying the Bible. Since when is God our personal science project, and who are we to think that we can "intellectually study Him" the way we would *a bug!*

Fortunately, traditional interpretations and creations of men can in no way determine what true biblical theology is. God cannot and will never be understood by the intellectualism of mere men. Faith and an open heart to the movement of the Holy Spirit (Rhema—revelation) are the *main* keys to understanding and learning more and more of God Almighty. Man will never know *all there is to know* pertaining to God on this earth. Revelation by the Spirit God is His way of opening our understanding of His Word. This is also called revelation knowledge. Without this revealed knowledge by the Holy Spirit, we could never comprehend even the simplest concepts of God and His Kingdom. Studying and becoming educated isn't a terrible thing, providing that we recognize its limitations. Hence, we must depend on the Holy Spirit for knowledge and not *merely* upon our limited human abilities, such as Systematic theology.

3

THE *FORMULA* OF FAITH?

Are the teachers of the Word of Faith teaching that the secret to receiving all one has ever lusted after lies within ones confession of a so-called faith *formula*? Likewise, are the Faith teachers attempting to downgrade God to nothing more than the believer's *spiritual bellhop*?[1]

Unfortunately, this is the rendering that *Christianity in Crisis* endeavors to transfer into the minds of Christians today. Is this really what the WoF teaches? Exactly how would one go about demoting **God** to their own level or below? In this chapter we will answer these questions and a few more.

Hank Hanegraaff sarcastically comments on the power of confession by saying, "Positive confessions activate the positive side of the force; negative confessions activate the negative side."[2] His comment was one of criticism; however, that statement pretty much sums up how our confessions either make or break us. Hanegraaff even uses a small quote from E.W. Kenyon to prove his viewpoint: "*it is our confession that rules us.*"[3]

The book of Proverbs, for example, is abounding with passages affirming the power that our confession has over the destiny of our lives.

Proverbs 18:20, 21 (TAB): A man's [moral] self **shall** be filled with the fruit of his mouth; and with **the consequence** of his words he **must** be satisfied (whether good or evil). Life and death *are in the power of the tongue*, and they who indulge in it shall *eat the fruit* of it [for death or life].

The Amplified Bible has a cross reference in the New Covenant that refers to (Prov. 18:21):

Matthew. 12:35-37 (TAB): The good man from his inner good treasure flings forth good things, and the evil man out of his inner evil storehouse flings forth evil things. But I tell you, on the day of judgment men will have to give account for **every** idle (*inoperative, nonworking*) word they speak. For **by your words** you will be justified *and* acquitted, and by your words you will be condemned *and* sentenced.

Both of these passages of Scripture explain that our justification or condemnation is measured back unto us *in proportion* to our own words. In reality, we are reaping that which we have sown. A sinner *by his words* of repentance is made just in Christ. In contrast, by his words this same sinner can reject Christ and seal his own condemnation. This is the **crucial** point that Kenyon and the Word of Faith teachers have desired to get across to the Body of Christ!

What Is *Faith* In *Faith*?

Hanegraaff claims that, "Hagin teaches people to have faith in their faith *as opposed to* having faith in their God." In reality this topic is not even worthy of discussing, nevertheless, for the sake of misinterpretation we will briefly address it. Kenneth Hagin is in no way attempting to teach people to have faith in their own faith, *as if* their faith was their god. He is *only* teaching people to have *confidence* in the measure of faith that **God** has given them so that they will be unhindered in using *their* faith. Note the following comment:

> "The dictionary says that to confess means 'to acknowledge or to own, to acknowledge faith in.' To confess...[it] means to make confession of one's faults, but it also says it means to make confession of one's faith. There are four kinds of confessions: (1)...confession of sins of the Jews; (2) the confession of the sinner today; (3) the believer's confession of his sins when he is out of fellowship with God; and (4) **the confession of our faith in God's Word.**"[5]

According to this quotation, one can clearly see that Hagin is indeed teaching people to have faith in God and His Word. Why? This is because Jesus is the Word of God *made flesh*. Hence, one cannot separate God from *His Word*. Thus, Hanegraaff's claims are totally out of line. Hagin is simply teaching the Church to have confidence (faith) in the measure of faith that they've received at salvation. According to the Word of God, the believer is *expected* to have confidence, assurance, and trust that one's salvation is secure in Christ!

Consequently, why shouldn't a believer have faith (confidence) in the measure of faith that he or she has *received*. Our faith *is* His faith because we received it from **Him**. As a result, we *are* to have confidence (faith) in *all* the gifts and fruit of the Spirit within us. Hagin clearly illustrates this point in his mini-book, *Your Faith In God Will Work* [a revised edition previously entitled, *Having Faith In Your Faith*].

> "Why don't some people believe that their faith in God will work? I know from experience that a lot of people have faith in my faith and the faith of others. *But they do not have confidence* [faith] **that their own faith in God will work**—They feel their faith is not strong enough."[6]

Writing Your Own Ticket with God

Hanegraaff writes as if he has a predominate difficulty with Kenneth Hagin's mini-book, *Writing Your Own Ticket With God*. By his choice of words he seems to feel as though Hagin made up a vision in order to *validate* his teaching. This is shown to be evident by the following comment, "Either Hagin is dreadfully deluded or else he had a conversation with *another* Jesus...."[7] According to all the misinterpretations we have uncovered thus far, it would appear rather that Mr. Hanegraaff is somewhat on the ignorant side of this issue.

Did Hagin really have a vision with *another* Jesus, as Hanegraaff has supposed, or was this vision in line with sound Biblical doctrine? You be the judge! After having read *Writing Your Own Ticket With God*, I realized a few fine points that *the Bible "Answer" Man* seemed to overtly miss. I truthfully wonder if we read the same words because Hagin's message was crystal clear.

> "Anything **that the Bible promises** you now, you can receive now by taking the four steps." "1. Say it. 2. Do it. 3. Receive it. 4. Tell it."[8]

Hagin was not attempting to say that Jesus told him we can have just *whatever* our little hearts lusted after. Notice the words of Hagin "*anything that the Bible promises*."[9] He most assuredly was talking about our using the prescribed four steps in order to possess *the promises* that are already made known to us in the Word of God. Here, Hagin was actually referring to Mark 11:22 and 23. In addition, I believe Hagin was also talking about those promises that God has made to us personally within our hearts. This means those things that are not necessarily spelled out in the Word, but have been deposited in our hearts by God. In other words, the things that we have believed for **must be** in line with God's Word or will. God's promises **are** His will.

2 Corinthians 1:20 (NKJV): For **all** *the promises* of God in Him are **Yes**, and in Him **Amen**, to the glory of God through us.

There is much debate concerning the above Scripture, however, this should not be. God has given me an infallible way to quench this heated debate. Please allow me to ask you a question. What am I if I made you a promise and failed to keep that promise? The answer is quite simple, *I'd be a liar*! Likewise, if God were to make promises in His Word and He did not keep them, He too would be a liar. On the contrary, we all know God does not make promises that He cannot or will not fulfill. God is not a liar! For this reason, we **can** believe God will fulfill the promises written in His Word.

How can I be so sure that Hagin isn't writing about man's own *selfish* desires? First of all, he already said, *"Anything that the Bible promises."*[10] Also, consider another quotation from Hagin's own writing.

"Well, He will do everything He said He would do, and He will do everything you believe Him for...Are you ready to write your ticket? If you need healing or victory over the world, the flesh, or the devil, **say** and **act** on **God's Word**."[11]

In the previous quotation, everything that Hagin was addressing pertained to the promises *already given to us* in the Word of God. He was not writing of a God who will give us every selfish lust that the heart may desire. In reality, a born-again believer should not be longing for selfish, evil desires because we have received a **new** nature. The *nature* of Jesus, which is *righteousness*, now lives in us. He also said that God will do everything that He said He would do. Hence, God has enclosed His will for us in the form of promises in the Word of God. Bottom line, Hagin is simply teaching every believer to take God at His Word and believe what God **has** said.

What promises has God made to us? According to Dr. David (Paul) Yonggi Cho, there are *over* **8,000** promises in the Word of God.[12] Therefore, we could not possibly list them all. God has promised healing (Ex. 23:25, 26), prosperity (Mal. 3:9-12), salvation/healing (Rom. 10:9, 10), authority over the enemy (Matt. 16:19/18:18-20) and the list goes on and on. I suggest that if you want to know more about the promises of God, then sit down with a concordance and research these topics on your own. The point I am trying to make is this: God intends to do **all** that He has promised us in His Word, and also the personal promises He has given us, if we'll stand on (hold on to) the promises that He has given.

Thou Art Snared With The Words of Thy Mouth

Hanegraaff continues his accusations by opposing Hagin's and Capps' interpretation of Proverbs 6:2, *"Thou art snared with the words of thy mouth."* He contests that this passage is simply referring to a literal interpretation concerning our making pledges rashly to others, and later having to pay for the rash commitments.[13] I must agree with Hanegraaff that this passage is *literally* referring to our making rash pledges. **However**, I also see an important spiritual principle being established here. Rash pledges (confessions) of any sort are extremely dangerous to our physical as well as spiritual well-being.

Positive and negative confessions may not be the literal interpretation of (Prov. 6:2), but it does establish an important principle concerning the power of our words. Solomon is teaching us to be careful with the words that we speak, not just our pledges. He is establishing a spiritual principle concerning the power of our confessions (words), both negative and positive. One could be just as easily *snared* into a verbal and written commitment of marriage without thoroughly considering all that is involved before making the commitment. In this section of Proverbs, God is reestablishing the Spiritual principle keeping a watch over the tongue. *It is that simple*!

In *Christianity in Crisis*, Mr. Hanegraaff attempts to defend his technique of writing which reads much more like a tabloid with the following anxiety-filled outburst:

> **"Why Be So Harsh?** At this point you may be thinking, *Well, maybe Hagin, Hinn, Hickey, Hayes, and the other Faith teachers are dead wrong. But do you have to judge their words so harshly?* My answer is a resounding 'Yes!' When the core of the Christian faith is imperiled, strong measures are necessary."[14]

Hanegraaff's statement appears to be one of intensive fear and anxiety concerning the *imperilment* of "the core" of the Christian faith. Hank, I would like to add this insight comment, **God is not *nervous*!** God also has not given us a spirit of fear or anxiety, but one of power, love and of a sound (disciplined) mind (2 Timothy 1:7). God is not anxious or fearful that **any** particular doctrine is going to destroy His plan. So, why, in the Name of Jesus, are you, Mr. Hanegraaff?

I believe Hanegraaff, in reality, is anxious and fearful that *his interpretation* of the core of the Christian faith is now **imperiled** by the teachings of the Faith message. The number one traditional doctrine that is threatened by the Faith message is the doctrine of *Systematic* (scientific) *Theology*.

In short, this teaching implies that God and His Word can be studied in a scientific method. *The Scientific Method* is a creation of man. God **cannot** and will not be understood by the mere pretenses of man through the understanding of his natural (*unrenewed*) mind. The things of God are *spiritually* understood. People of God—God is not apprehensive! His eternal plan will still be carried out into fulfillment. Put your faith where your mouth is and dominate your fear, Hank!

Visualization: Is It Scriptural?

Hanegraaff is *vehemently* opposed to the thought of a Christian using visualization in any form whatsoever. He cites the occult with the use of visualization, attempting to "prove" that this practice is of the devil. He cites three principle beliefs of the occult: "the power to create their own reality lies within themselves…these people believe that words are imbued with creative power…and finally, occultists believe they can use creative visualization…."[15]

Nevertheless, Jesus also said the world is sometimes smarter than the Church!

However, is visualization an evil, forbidden practice according to the Bible? Regardless of what people think about it, what does God's Word say about it? [*See also my book: *When The Holy Spirit Reveals*, for more details].

Visualization And The Apostle Paul

2 Corinthians 5:17: Therefore if any man be in Christ, *he is* a new creature: old things are passed away; **behold** (see, realize), all things are become *new*.

Romans 6:11: Likewise **reckon** ye also yourselves to be dead indeed unto sin, but alive unto God through Jesus Christ our Lord.

Was Paul telling us the truth in these verses of Scripture? If so, and if we really are new creatures, why is it that so many of us live as if we are *not?* I believe the answer is found in the book of Romans chapter 6 verse 11. The majority of believers *do not* see (visualize) themselves as new creatures, victorious **over** sin, sickness, the devil and fear. Most born-again believers spend their time trying to kill some old man (carnal nature) that has already been crucified with Christ (Rom. 6:6). Hence, most do not walk in victory because they cannot **see** victory. The Bible tells us, "Where there is no vision [no redemptive revelation of God], the people perish…."

Paul tells us to reckon ourselves dead to sin, but alive to God in Christ Jesus. What does he mean when he says *reckon?* The concordance defines *reckon* as "to esteem, reckon, suppose, think (on)."[16] Paul was saying visualize (think of) yourselves as being dead to sin but alive to God in Christ Jesus.

Therefore, unless we think in this way, we will *never* be able to walk in the reality of these verses. Thus, in the Church, the majority of believers have **no vision** or *no redemptive revelation* thus they live in defeat (Proverbs 29:18).

Visualization Kept Jesus On The Cross!

Hebrews 12:1, 2: Wherefore seeing *we also are compassed about with so great a cloud of witnesses*, let us lay aside every weight, and the sin which doth so easily beset us, and let us run with patience the race that is set before us, *Looking* unto Jesus the author and finisher of our faith; who *for the joy that was* **set before him** endured the cross, despising the shame, and is set down at the right hand of the throne of God.

In Hebrews chapter 12 verse 2 the words *"set before him"* are defined by the concordance as "to lie before the view, to be *present* (**to the mind**)."[17] Therefore, while Jesus was hanging on the cross, there was a joy *set before His mind*. The joy that Jesus pictured in His mind was His people being made completely free from the enemy's attacks and control. He *visualized* our freedom through His sacrifice, and that visual picture gave Him overwhelming joy!

Why? This is because He visualized the dominion of the enemy being removed from the human race. This revelation also strengthened Him to endure **separation** from His Father in hell on the behalf of a race of unworthy sinners (Acts 2:22-27 NKJV). Without a doubt, the Bible is clear that the Apostle Paul and Jesus Himself utilized the practice of visualization and encouraged others to use it also. I have not merely given my opinion concerning this subject, but I have also given clear **irrefutable proof** that the Bible supports the use of the practice typically known to us as visualization.

Hanegraaff is openly critical of ministers such as Dr. Cho and Benny Hinn for their teaching about the power of words. He criticizes Cho especially for his use of the terminology *"the fourth-dimensional power."*[18]

This term simply symbolizes the *active-power* of the Spirit world itself. Hank further brings Cho to task for his method of counseling a woman on how to find a man to marry. The follow quotations are from Cho's book *The Fourth Dimension Vol. 1* and they address the situation in question.

"God is within you. God never works anything independently of *you* **that concerns your life**. God is only going to work through your thinking, through your beliefs; so, when ever you want to receive answers from the Lord, bring out that clear-cut objective."[19]

"When you have a clear goal, **and** you have this desire burning in your heart to a boiling point, **then** you should kneel down and *pray until you receive* the substance, **the assurance**."[20]

In the first quote cited above, Cho explains to this woman that God will not do anything "that concerns *her* life," independently of her desires. In other words, God will not force His will on us. This is because we possess a free-will. He wants us to willingly accept His direction. See, God imparts us the desire to desire that which is right and good for us. Proverbs 16:3, in *the Amplified Bible*, confirms this fact:

"Roll your works upon the Lord [commit and trust them wholly to Him; He will cause *your thoughts* **to become agreeable** *to His will*, and] so shall your plans be established and succeed."

Concerning the next cited quote, Cho told this woman that she was, first of all, to have a clear goal (from God and His Word). Also, she was to have a burning desire (from God's heart) for that thing. Once all of this was present, she was to kneel down and pray until the substance (assurance) of receiving that thing was imparted into her spirit. Why did he tell her these things? This woman was sitting around waiting for "God" to bring some man (any man), to her door step and say, "Here he is; come and get him." Cho was simply pointing out that this isn't the way that God operates in our lives. *God puts His desires* into us (desires which *do not* contradict Scripture), but the rest is up to us whether or not we partake of the desires that He has placed within us.

Dr. Cho continued by explaining that God uses words spoken in faith *from Him* and creates the desired realities, **according to** His Word spoken to us. Thus, we are to speak His Word *after Him,* and faith released in His Word will create the physical manifestation according to His Word/will.

> "Claim and speak the word of assurance, for your word actually goes out and creates. God spoke and the whole world came in to being. Your word is the material which the Holy Spirit uses to create."[21]

Furthermore, Dr. Cho makes an extremely important distinction between the *written* Word of God and the *Living* (spoken) Word of God. This is important because words are *only* creative when they are released in **faith**. In other words, we can release faith toward God concerning His promises; or we can release "faith" *(fear)* in the destructive ability of the devil's words. God has given us the ability to choose our destiny by our words. Hence, we should be speaking **His** Word!

> "The spoken word has powerful creativity, and its *proper usage* is vital to a victorious Christian life. This spoken word, however, *must have a correct basis* to be truly effective. The principle for discovering the correct basis for the spoken word is one of the most important portions of God's truth...People think that they can believe on the Word of God. They can. But they fail to differentiate the Word of God which gives *general knowledge* about God, and the Word of God *which God uses to impart faith* about specific circumstances into a man's heart...there are two different words for 'word,' *logos* and *rhema*...Here is my definition of **rhema**: **rhema** is a *specific word* to *a specific person* in a *specific situation*. Rhema brings faith. Faith comes by hearing, and hearing by **rhema**."[22]

> "Rhema is produced *out of logos*...but rhema is not given to everyone. Rhema is given to that **specific person** who is waiting upon the Lord until *the Holy Spirit quickens logos into rhema*...When you receive rhema faith given is not your own; **it is imparted faith** that God has given you. After receiving this imparted faith,

then you can command mountains to be moved. *Without receiving God's faith you cannot do this.*"[23]

The Power of Words

William DeArteaga gives us some powerful insight into the Evangelical line of reasoning concerning its opposition on the teaching of the *power* of words.

"Evangelicals have a difficult time facing the issue of the power of words and thoughts to influence the natural world…This theology of total depravity of the soul has been updated by the influential Chinese theologian Watchman Nee, who died in 1972. In his works, especially *The Latent Power of the Soul,* he elaborated on Calvin's suspicions and concluded that the fall caused the powers of the soul to become tools for *demonic use* **only**. Thus, words and thoughts have no legitimate power over natural circumstances. There seem to be biblical and practical exceptions to this theory. In the Bible both believers and heathen are shown to have quite legitimate and God-directed 'soul' experiences. Pharaoh's prophetic dream…or the dream of Pilate's wife that Jesus was a just man are but a few examples. It may be true that the soulish powers of man were *damaged* at the fall, but there is no evidence that this damage was so total that God does not speak to man through them or that their use is *only* for witchcraft."[24]

"Certainly words and thoughts have more legitimate power than Calvin-Nee (materialist-realist) theology understands. Scientific research has proven, for instance, that the mind can be trained to stimulate the body's immune system and help in the healing process. Yet it is also obvious that the belief of the idealist cults, that powers of mind were god-like and needed only cultivation, were a gross exaggeration…America was not transformed by positive thinking into a paradise on earth…Yet the biblical promises that Jesus made in regard to faith and its ability to move mountains and uproot mulberry trees (Luke 17:6) by verbal command are even more incredible than any New Thought claims of business success. Herein lies the core issue. If the power of the mind (through thoughts and word confessions) is only very limited by itself, then the real power of the mind comes through making the choice of faith. By faith the mind acts in the power of God and can move mountains. Thus we should be cautious in judging the Metaphysical movement's techniques of positive thinking, visualization and affirmation. Certainly all those activities are capable of demonization and witchcraft, but they are not, as Calvin-Nee theology holds, *necessarily witchcraft*. They all may have a legitimate place in the uses of thoughts and words as God originally intended."[25]

I sincerely believe that DeArteaga's comments give one a precise understanding of where Hanegraaff and other typical *traditionally minded Christians* get their understanding, and hence opposition to the teaching that human words have power for good as well as evil, *similar* to that of God's words. *Especially*, when we speak God's Word **in faith!**

In some of my earlier writings, the Holy Spirit stirred within me some powerful revelations concerning the power of the spoken word, and I would like to share some of these insights with you.

"Words are very creative tools. They can be used to paint a mental picture of love and peace or one of *fear* and *abuse*. Verbal abuse is one of the most common forms of abuse in relationships today, and a leading cause of divorce. Countless relationships are damaged beyond *human* repair simply because of the way someone used words to destroy another person's self-esteem. On the other hand, words can also be used to paint mental pictures of good things. If I were to say 'flower,' instantly a picture of a flower would form in your mind. As I defined that picture further, your mind would create a similar kind of picture that I perceived. Thus if I said 'long stemmed flower' or 'long stemmed red flower' or even more detailed, 'a long stemmed red rose,' then you would know exactly what kind of flower I was thinking about. Can you see how words create mental images?"[26]

Moreover, I've always loved the words of the centurion to Jesus in Matthew 8:8, 9.[27]

"The centurion answered and said, Lord, I am not worthy that thou shouldest come under my roof: but **speak the word only**, and my servant shall be healed. For I am a man under authority, having soldiers under me: and I say to this *man*, Go, and he goeth; and to another, Come, and he cometh; and to my servant, Do this, and he doeth it."

This centurion realized that Jesus was a man under God's authority, as *he* also was. He also understood the power of the spoken word (verse 9). He knew when Jesus spoke *the Word all* power and authority in heaven (and earth) was behind the Word that He spoke. This is the reason that Jesus was so amazed when He heard what the centurion said. Jesus then replied with: "I have not found **so great faith**, no, not in all of Israel." Jesus was amazed that the centurion understood the authority of the spoken word and that he also had *the faith to believe* that his servant would be healed even though he couldn't physically see him. The book of Revelation also firmly reinforces this same Scriptural principle.

> **Rev. 12:11**: And they overcame him (Satan) by the blood of the Lamb, **and** *by the word of their testimony*; and they loved not their lives unto the death.

Please notice there are **two keys** given to us in the Word God from the book of Revelation to enable us to live the life of an overcomer. The first and most important key, *the blood of the Lamb*, and the second key which is also **vitally** important: *the word of our testimony*. These life changing keys are *inseparable* when they pertain to living a victorious overcoming life. Without both of these keys used together, we will **never** live the life of a victorious Christian.

Despite Jesus' words in (Matt. 8:8&9) and the writings of John the revelator, the vast majority of the Body of Christ has *greatly ignored* the power of the spoken word. Proverbs clearly says that <u>life and death</u> **are in the power of the tongue** (Prov.18: 21). Also, the *entire* book of James further supports this statement concerning the power of the spoken word addressed in Proverbs. James says if one can control the tongue, then one can control **the whole body,** as in the case of a horse's bit or a ship's rudder. Seeing that these statements must be true (since God is not a liar), why is it that so many "believers" still fail to acknowledge the power of the spoken word? **God only knows!**

The *only* possible explanation is that Satan knows the power of the blood, *coupled together* with God's Word as our testimony, and he will use *any method possible* to try to keep God's people in bondage so that they will not be victorious, like the Word says we are. He has used the *"theologians"* of the past 150 yrs. to convince us that if we use God's Word as our confession of faith, we are participating in mind sciences and **so-called** occult practices (such as *Positive Confession or Visualization*).

Please understand Satan has **never** created anything. All he has ever done is to **try** to copy, distort, and pervert that which **God** has already created. It is time that the children of God begin to rise up, in

Jesus Name, and use both keys God has given to us in (Rev. 12:11), and become the victorious Christians that God's Word says we are. In order for us to walk in victory, we must speak God's Word into our lives.

Whether we like *this* truth or not does not change the fact that words (all words) clearly have power to influence the quality of our lives. Words are our basis for government. Words are our basis for faith in God. Without these written words in the Bible, we would not have anything to guide us, set our standards or base our faith upon. God's Word is the **main** source by which we *know* His will for all of creation. We know Him *predominately* by His Word! We are to speak God's words and He is the One Who brings His *repeated* words to pass in our lives.

Consequently, Hanegraaff poses only a one-sided view of the Word of Faith teaching concerning the power of words and of the fourth-dimension (the spiritual world). For some strange reason he seems to only see this issue from the view point of its use in *the occult.* In his mind, words do have power *but **only** for those of the occult world.* When has the devil been able to "create" anything? Satan is merely a **counterfeiter** of that which God ordained before the foundation of the world. I have already shown that Hanegraaff has a typical Calvinistic viewpoint when addressing the power of words.

Hanegraaff would argue that Proverbs 18:20, 21 has little or nothing to do with man having power within his words *like* God.[28] Unfortunately, he sees these verses of Scripture as only addressing our personal relationships in which we have power to harm someone with whom we encounter. But if words have enough power to *harm* another person, which would *affect* the emotional or *soulish* part of them, then why couldn't our words have power to affect the realm of the spirit as well, which is far more sensitive?

Still, we can only affect that which we have been given power to influence by God Himself because He **is** sovereign—*supreme* in authority. According to Hanegraaff, if our words had power *like* God's, then we would be able to *manipulate* God.[29] How could we **ever** accomplish this?

"If God could be controlled through positive confessions, He would be reduced to the status of a cosmic servant subject to the formulas of faith. You would be God and He would be your bellhop! You would sit on the throne of a universe centered around your own ego."[30]

I want to remind Hanegraaff that God, indeed, **is not** controlled by our confessions in the sense that we are able to *dictate* to Him as if He is under *our* control. However, our words do have power to resist His will. For example, one can resist His will concerning salvation if one refuses to confess Him as Lord and Savior of his life. God **is not** our bellhop, and we don't sit on the throne. We simply obey His Word and do what He told us in (Mk. 11:22-25).

Charles Capps wrote in one of his books of an experience he had with the Lord about the power of words. Hanegraaff challenged this experience in *Christianity in Crisis.*

"You are under an attack of the evil one and *I can't do anything about it. You have bound me* by the words of your own mouth."[31]

I am extremely confused when it comes to Hanegraaff's contention with Capps' cited statement. Especially when God's Word clearly says that *only* those who *call upon the Name of the Lord* will be saved. In other words, all other people will be lost for eternity regardless of God's love and compassion for them. Those who refuse to accept Christ into their lives have bound (**tied**) the Hand of God as far as their lives are concerned, for eternity!

Furthermore, God sternly addresses this point very clearly in the book of Malachi:

Malachi 3:13, 14: "Your words have been **stout** against me, saith the LORD. Yet ye say, What have we spoken *so much* against thee?"

In Malachi chapter three, God addressed *the words* of the people who were speaking against serving Him because they could not *see* any profit in serving the Lord. He said that their words were "stout" against Him. The Strong's Exhaustive Concordance defines *stout* as:

"[*Stout*] a prim. root; to fasten upon; **hence to seize**, be strong (fig. courageous, strengthen, cure, help, repair, fortify), obstinate; **to bind**, *restrain*, conquer:...constrain...(lay) hold (fast)...behave self valiantly, withstand...."[32]

If the words of the people in Malachi three could "*seize, be strong, obstinate, bind or restrain*" God **in their own lives**, then one can see that Capps' words or even our words could also do the same. That **is not** to

36

say that God is *"powerless* without people," but simply that people have the authority to restrain or hinder God's hand from moving **in their own lives**. This is a harsh reality because we have been given a <u>free will</u> to choose life or death, blessing or cursing!

Moreover, John Garlock in the Biblical masterpiece *The Spirit-Filled Life Bible* shares some insightful comments concerning the power of our words. He comments regarding Proverbs 18:21:

"A person's life largely reflects the fruit of his tongue. <u>To speak life is to speak God's perspective on any issue of life</u>; to speak **death** is to   declare life's negatives, to declare defeat, or complain constantly."[33]

Hanegraaff continues with his odd line of reasoning by addressing the issue of men having "control" over God by quoting Dr. Frederick K.C. Price out of context on the subject.

"Now this is a shocker! But God has to be given *permission* to work in this earth realm on behalf of man....Yes! *You are in control!* So, if man has control, who no longer has it? God....When God gave Adam dominion, that meant God no longer had dominion. So, God cannot do anything in this earth unless *we let* Him. And the way we let Him or give Him permission is through prayer."[34]

Now, if one were to read **only** the previous *out of context* quotation, then one would naturally get the same sort of interpretation as Hanegraaff. I must admit when I read *Christianity in Crisis*, I, too, was shocked and confused concerning the legitimate meaning behind Dr. Price's cited quotation. However, once I read Dr. Price's comment, in its entirety, the confusion I experienced dissipated.

"There is a common consensus that God can do whatever He wants to do, but that is not *exactly* correct. *He can do anything He good well pleases from the standpoint of having ability* — **because He is God**. However, based upon the way *He* has designed this system to work — the world, man, the planet, the universe — He has built into it *certain laws that govern and control it.* **So, in that sense**, He cannot do anything *that violates <u>that law that He has set in motion</u>*...Now this is the shocker! But God has to be given permission to work in this earth realm *on the behalf of man*. And we give Him permission through prayer...And the reason why can be

37

found in Genesis 1:26…What does dominion mean? It means **'control, rule,** *reign,* **authority,** *possession.'* Yes! *You are in control!* So if man has control, who no longer has it? God…Do you honestly think **God** has this world messed up the way it is? The earth is messed up **because of us.** *We* have been given the con- trol!…When God gave Adam dominion, that meant God no longer had dominion…."[35]

Price is merely speaking from the premise that God of His own sovereign will gave man control (dominion and authority) over all the works of His hand. **Man** has messed up all that God had set in order. Therefore, God chose to send His Son to redeem man *back* to his (man's) original position of authority. Then Jesus handed that authority back to man in order that man could finally subdue the earth and have dominion over it, which was God's original plan for man. Price's point is plain! God gave man authority to rule the earth and man's Sin is **the cause** of the confusion we now see on earth.

Please notice that Price said *"He can do anything He good well pleases…because He is God…He has built into it certain laws that govern and con- trol it.* **So in that sense,** *He cannot do anything that violates that law* that He set in motion…."[36] Dr. Price is in no way denying that God cannot do whatever He chooses because He is God.

However, He has **voluntarily** and sovereignly <u>limited Himself</u> by setting up certain laws which govern this planet, including the Law of dominion. God put limits upon Himself rather than man usurped control over God! God sovereignly chose to give man dominion and He still ex- pects man to follow His original commandment: *"subdue the earth and have dominion…"* Each of us, as individuals, must give God permission to oper- ate *in our lives* (on this earth) because man has been given a free will by God Himself. We have the power of a free will that can and will hinder the will of God in our own personal lives *if we rebel* against His direction.

Israel is a perfect example of man's free will in action. That's not to say that God's eternal plan for "man" will be controlled by rebellious human nature, *no way!* God's will for all men is that they be saved, but if all men do not repent, then those who are unsaved will remain unsaved *for eternity.*

God did not make us a bunch of *"remote-control"* robots. He only has *Lordship* (complete sovereign control) of those who surrender the throne of their hearts to Him. We're *lord* of our lives *until* we give our hearts to Him. Jesus is a gentleman He will not force Himself on anyone!

At this point, let's look at man's dominion of the earth from a little different perspective. Who, would you say, is responsible for holding the Body of Christ together? Most likely, Hanegraaff, as well as many others, would say, *"Jesus is the One Who is holding the Church together."* Oh really! Is that why the Body of Christ is in such disunity and remains powerless against many satanic attacks? Could we be saying that Jesus does not know how to care for His Body? If Jesus is **solely** responsible for holding the Church together, then something is extremely wrong!

We are The Joints And Ligaments

Ephesians 4:16 (TAB): For because of Him the whole body (the church, *in all its various parts*), closely joined and firmly knit together **by the joints** and **ligaments** *with which it is supplied*, when each part [with power adapted to its need] *is working properly* [*in all its functions*], grows to full maturity, building *itself up* in love.

Paul illustrates the type of unity that the Body of Christ *should* function in by comparing it to the way the human body is held together (*unified*) by its joints and ligaments. The sad commentary to all this is that **we** are the very joints and ligaments holding the Body of Christ together; hence, we now know why the Church is in such *disunity*.

Most believers think Jesus *alone* holds the Church together, but that is not what Scripture teaches. Of course, the Lord *holds* the Body together, *but* He does this **through** His children. Recall the verse that speaks of the Lord working *with* them. That verse doesn't say *for them*, but *with* them. **We** are the ones to blame for the Church's disunity.

In verse sixteen of Ephesians four it says; "...when each part is working properly...[the Body] grows to full maturity, *building itself up* in love." If every part is working properly, then we will have an efficiently running "machine." But what if all the parts aren't working properly, what do we have then? We end up with the Church of Jesus Christ in its present condition. Paul tells us that the Church is to build *itself* up in love. Notice this doesn't say, *"Jesus will build it up in love."* We are responsible for strengthening the Body!

Like it or not, **we** are ultimately responsible for holding together the Body of Christ. Jesus *is* capable and will do *most* of the work. Nonetheless, we are the ones who must be obedient **to do what He said** so we will be able to love and live in the unity of the Spirit through the bond of peace. If *we refuse* to start functioning in our proper places, there will be no authority or principle of dominion put into affect on earth. And we will be held responsible for our disobedience to God's command to live in love and unity.

Ephesians four verse sixteen plainly states that we are the joints and ligaments that strengthen, or weaken, the Body of Christ. There is a wise saying that I've heard that says: *"A chain is only as strong as the weakest link."* This cliché aptly describes the condition of the Church today. This is positive proof that Jesus alone *is not* holding the Body of Christ together. Jesus is the Source of our strength, but **we** are the ones who must stay connected to His life force in order for us to have dominion and be effective witnesses.

Again, we are *ultimately* responsible for holding together the Body of Christ. This is only one part of our role in taking dominion over the earth. Jesus rules the earth, this is true. But today, He enforces the mandates of His Kingdom **through** His Body. We have been given His authority as well as His *power to enforce* that dominion here on this earth. Our power of enforcement lies **exclusively** within the Name and blood of Jesus.

The book of Psalms plainly communicates that God's authority and power was unreservedly *and sovereignly* invested in all of man-kind by crowning "man" with honor and dominion over this earth.

Psalm 115:16: "The heaven, even the heavens, *are the Lord's:* **but** the earth hath he **given** to the children of men."

In closing, the Strong's Concordance defines, *given* has having many meanings. Below are only a few of its many denotations.

[Given] a prim. root; *to give*, used with great latitude of application...*appoint, ascribe, assign...***bestow**, bring (forth, hither), *cast*, cause, **charge**, come, *commit* consider, count...**deliver** (**up**), direct, distribute...**give** (**forth, over, up**), grant, hang (up)...*lend*, let (out)...**yield**."[37]

We have been given authority by God to take dominion (control) over this earth and all that God has placed on it. The Church must start obeying Jesus' final command.

Matthew 28:18-20 (NKJV): "...**All** authority has been given to Me in heaven and on earth. *Go **therefore** and make disciples* of all the nations, baptizing them in the name of the Father and of the Son and of the Holy Spirit, teaching the to observe all things that I have commanded you...."

4

THE FAITH OF GOD

Hank Hanegraaff wrote in his book, *Christianity in Crisis*: "God doesn't *have faith* He is the object of our faith."[1] At first glance his statement *seems* to make perfect sense. On the other hand, if one were to say, "Have the peace of God—Have the joy of the Lord," or even "Walk in the love of God;" most would not think to question what had been said. God has peace, joy and love—does He not?

> **Galatians 5:22, 23**: But the *fruit* of the Spirit is love, joy, peace, long-suffering, gentleness, goodness, **faith**, meekness, temperance: against such there is no law.

So here we see that God, in fact, does *have* peace, joy and love (etc.); they're His nature. However, the Scripture also says "God *is* love." Does this mean God is *submissive* to His peace, joy, or even love? Certainly not! In Galatians chapter five the qualities mentioned are simply a part of God's nature. These godly attributes do not necessarily "dictate" to Him, but He rather employs them. This could be compared to the way a man determines what his hand does, rather than vise-a-versa. Consequently, a man is in control of his actions; but, his hand is still part of his total physical make-up.

Now let's look at another aspect of the fruit of the Spirit. Does God have faith? According to Hanegraaff, God **doesn't** have faith; He is *just* the object of our faith. But what does Galatians 5 have to say about faith? The apostle Paul was directed by the Holy Spirit to include *faith* in the fruit of the Spirit. Thus, the Spirit *must* have faith, and the Holy Spirit is God, isn't He? And since the Godhead is equal in all qualities, then it would be logically correct for one to say that Jesus and the Father have faith as well. His fruit is a part of His character! One might say, "Faith is not translated in modern translations of Galatians 5." This is correct; however, faith and faithfulness both come from the same Greek root word and hence *both* words apply.[2]

Please also notice that in this passage of Scripture the word **fruit**, rather than *fruits*, is used to describe these **virtues** of God. In other words, *man* has all of God's character (fruit) imparted into *his* spirit at conversion. It also indicates that God's fruit *cannot* be divided but is rather imparted as a complete component. He *infused* His character into each of us when we became born-again!

Patience Is A Virtue

It has also been said, "*Patience is a virtue.*" Scripture in turn says patience is a fruit of the Spirit. Yet, what exactly is a virtue? According to the Bible dictionary, *virtue* is defined as "strength, ability, often involving moral worth, any excellence of a person or thing; power, influence."[3] According to another Bible dictionary, *virtue* also means "any particular moral excellence where virtue is enjoined as an essential quality in the exercise of faith."[4] God and His virtue are **one**! His excellence of virtue is seen in the unveiling of His character, which is revealed *in us* by the fruit of the Spirit.

Consequently, these qualities are the very essence of God Himself. The fruit of the Spirit (**God**) derive from God Himself; therefore, they are *part of* His excellent nature. However, these all function under the direction of love (God). The Word also says, "Faith which worketh by love" (Gal. 5:6). Love is the primary element which causes all of His fruit to produce in our lives. Mr. Hanegraaff also contests the Faith teacher's rendering of Mark 11:22: "Have faith in God or have the faith of God." All right! Who is the author or originator of faith? Most intelligent people would naturally respond, "*God is!*" Now, since God is the Author or Originator of faith, then all faith must belong to Him because He is the Source of all things.

This is much the same way as a child belongs to and receives the characteristics of his parents. Thus, the parents are his *source* of **physical** life because a material part **of** them, called genes, was engrafted into him at conception. In the same manner, the fruit of the Spirit is God's *spiritual genes*, God's engrafted character (*His features*), which are birthed into the born-again human spirit. Let us examine Ephesians chapter two verses 8 and 9:

> For by grace are ye saved through faith; and that not of yourselves: *it is the gift of God*: Not of works, lest any man should boast.

When most believers read this passage, they seem to always focus on "*it is the gift of God*" as referring to God's grace. However, they ignorantly overlook the fact that *the faith* in which we received to become saved was also *the gift of God*. We didn't even have the faith to become saved. In other words, we received God's gift of faith or **God's faith** so that we could be saved. God is the Origin of the faith which He gave to us to become born again. Consequently, it was *His* faith before it became *our* faith.

Moreover, having faith in God and having the faith of God are one in the same because God and His virtue are inseparable. He is the Source of all faith, and in turn all faith belongs to Him. For this reason, we believe and trust Him, but on the other hand, we are also using His faith (which He deposited **in us**) in order to believe and trust Him. He is the Origin of the very faith which we *use* to fellowship with Him every day. If He had not given us the gift of faith, we would never be able to believe or receive from Him. Faith is the condition that is needed to receive anything from God.

Why does God's Word say, "without **faith** it is *impossible* to please Him..." (Heb. 11:6)? Is it possible that the faith which God gave us was to be the fruit of the Spirit that spiritually connects man to Him? According to Ephesians 2:8 & 9, the first **virtue** (fruit) that man received was **faith**.

For example, if I do not believe (have faith or trust) in someone, then I will never trust them enough to act upon their word. We deal with God in this same manner. If we do not trust Him enough to obey His Word and receive His promises, then we live a life long existence of sin, sickness and lack; hence, always thinking that God has given us these torments to make us stronger. God wants us to have and use faith in all that we do.

Thus, *faith* (or trust) is the virtue that God has engrafted into us to connect us up to Him, so that the rest of His fruit can be *stirred up* in us. Without trust (faith), His virtue can not work in our lives, **because** we must believe that He is, **and** that He is a Rewarder of those who diligently seek Him. Jesus is not only our Source of faith, but He is also the Developer of the faith He has given.

In addition, I decided to use the thesaurus check on my computer for the word *virtue*, and I discovered some interesting words, such as chastity, purity, virginity, decency, morality, goodness, integrity, uprightness, justice, prudence, temperance, rectitude, quality, attribute, merit, excellence. These words describe the fruit of the Spirit (God) which is born into the reborn human spirit taking place at conversion.

These qualities are "the spiritual genes" of our Father, which He implanted into us at salvation.

> **Galatians 5:22, 23**: But the fruit of the Spirit is love, joy, peace, long-suffering, gentleness, goodness, faith, meekness, temperance: against such there is no law.

> **Galatians 5:22, 23 (TAB)**: "But the fruit of the [Holy] Spirit [the work which **His presence within** accomplishes] is love, joy (gladness), peace, patience (an even temper, forbearance), kindness, goodness (benevolence), faithfulness, gentleness (meekness, humility), self-control (self-restraint, continence). Against such things there is no law...."

Scriptural "Food" For Thought

> **Ephesians 2:8, 9**: For by grace are ye saved through **faith**; and that not of yourselves: *it is the gift* of God: not of works, lest any man should boast.

> **Galatians 2:16**: Knowing that a man is not justified by the works of the law, but **by the faith of Jesus Christ**, even we have believed in Jesus Christ, that we might be justified **by the faith of Christ**, and not by the works of the law: for the works of the law shall no flesh be justified.

> **Galatians 2:20**: I am crucified with Christ: nevertheless I live; yet not I, but Christ liveth in me: and the life which I now live in the flesh I live **by the faith of the Son of God**, who loved me, and gave himself for me.

We have already established the fact that God gave us the gift of faith, as well as grace, in order to become saved. Therefore, the faith that we received at conversion was the part of God Himself that gave us the ability to believe the Word of God which we heard. Please notice the other two verses from Galatians chapter two, which contain the phrases *"the faith of Jesus and the faith of the Son of God."* I'm fully aware that the more modern translations do not use this terminology. Nonetheless, in order for us to have faith **"in"** Jesus, we must first have faith *living* in us.

Accordingly, since all faith comes from God, we not only have faith in God, but we also have His faith living in our spirits. Thus, we have the faith of God Himself living and moving in us! If it were not for God giving us His faith, we would not have even been able to get saved. Our merciful heavenly Father has given us everything we need to overcome in an evil society, and it's about time we started living that way!

In *Christianity In Crisis*, a small portion of *God's Creative Power*, by Charles Capps, was quoted: "A more literal translation [of Mark 11:22] is 'Have the God kind of faith or faith of God…God is a *faith* God.'"[5]

Let's examine Capps' statement in important detail from its original format:

> *"God never does anything without saying it first. God is a faith God. God released His faith in Words* (Mark 11:22). A more literal translation of the above verse says; 'Have the God kind of faith, or faith of God."[6]

It appears that Hanegraaff's integrity may be in crisis. I say this because he *seems* to be doing the very thing that he accuses the Faith teachers of doing. He has quoted Capps in such a way as to make his statement *appear* heretical. Therefore, he has taken Capps' quotation completely *out of* its context in his attempt to use it to *prove* his point. Had Hanegraaff quoted Capps according to the original context he could have prevented anyone from being able to question his integrity.

What Did Charles Capps *Really* Say?

First of all, "God **never** does anything without saying it first." God's Word confirms this, "Surely the Lord God does **nothing**, Unless He reveals His secret to His servants the prophets." "Then God *said*, and there was…." (Amos 3: 7 & Genesis 1: 3 NKJV). According to the Bible, God **always** declared (spoke) His decrees before He acted.

"God is a faith God. God released His faith in Words." God *released* faith in and by the Words that He spoke, **knowing** that what He said would come to pass. No matter how we look at this, faith was being put to work, even if only at the minimum of His expectation of the end result. When God spoke He was releasing faith in and through His Words. God had faith, *assurance*, that what He said would come to pass. Faith is the substance (*assurance*) of the things we hope for, *is it not?*

"A more literal translation of (Mark 11:22) is Have the God kind of faith, or the faith of God."[7] Hanegraaff stated something similar in

Christianity In Crisis. He mentioned that if one was to use a Greek-to-English New Testament, one would find that it says: "echete '**have**,' pistin '**faith**' and theou '**of God**.'"[8]

Consequently, this **is** a *more literal* translation of the original Greek text as Capps originally stated. Capps' statement is still true regardless of which **case** it was written in. Our faith is part of God's gift that He gave us at salvation. The faith that we use to believe God with originally came from Himself—He is the Source of all faith.

Therefore, Capps *has not* twisted God's Word with his statement. In reality, no heretical teaching exists in Capps' statement of obvious fact. The implied perversion lies solely within the mind of Hanegraaff and his associates.

Hanegraaff continues in this questionable line of logic with another defamatory comment against Kenneth Copeland.

Faith God's *Source* of Power?

"Copeland, for example, insists that 'God cannot do anything for you apart or separate from faith.' The reason is that '*faith is God's source of power*.'" [9]

I, too, was a bit puzzled the first time I read Hanegraaff's version of Copeland's statement, and even after reading the original quotation from Copeland. *However*, upon reading a page *before* and a page *after* the original quotation in question, the picture became considerably clearer.

As with Capps, Hanegraaff quoted only the portions of Copeland's mini-book that *seemed* to fit into his own line of logic. He would call this "*quoting out of context*." I can't say if he has *deliberately* quoted them out of context. On the other hand, he has either purposely done so or perhaps he was *visually* impaired; thus, unable to discern the true meaning of their words (Hosea 4:6).

Kenneth Copeland's Original Words

"Fear is a satanic force that works against you at every opportunity. Faith is **a** creative force *that God* **uses** to build and uplift. Faith helps; fear hurts...Satan knows that he cannot do anything to you apart or separate from fear, just as God cannot do anything for you apart or separate from faith. Satan can't touch you as long as you stand on the Word of God. Fear is Satan's source of power the way faith is God's source of power. Satan has people *operating in fear* and they don't even know it...Faith is the upholding force of God. He upholds all things by the Word of His power (Heb. 1:3)...Faith power is not produced in your head; it is produced in your heart. It is produced by the Word of God being fed into your spirit."[10]

In reality, there is no reason for me to explain this quotation, but for the sake of misinterpretation I will. First of all, Hanegraaff has implied that Copeland and other Faith teachers believe God Himself *depends* on faith in order **to live**—as if faith was God's *god!*[11] However, faith in God is the key to His work *and* our being able to receive.

However, Copeland makes himself very clear concerning this by saying, "Faith is a creative force **that God uses** to build and uplift."[12] This is much different from the way that Hanegraaff portrayed his statement. Copeland *never* said that God is *obedient* to the force of faith. Rather, he said that faith is a creative force that God **uses** to accomplish His plans and purposes **in the lives of humans**.

Faith is the creative force that connects us to God, *so that* He can work in and through our lives. This is because man has a free will and the right to tell God *not* to work in one's life. Faith **is** the key force (active power) that we accept from God, and it is this faith that allows us to open ourselves up so that He can work in our lives, and so that we can trust His Word. God *can not* work **in our lives** apart from faith, because Hebrews 11:6 says, "*Without faith it is impossible to please God: for he who comes to God must believe that He is, and that He is a rewarder of those who seek Him.*" If we don't have His faith working in us, then we will never be able to please Him or trust Him; therefore, we will not be able *to receive anything* from the Lord (See: James 1:5-8). God **utilizes** faith, and man is created in His image after His likeness.

Thus, man can not help acting like his Creator. However, God is not subservient to His own faith. Faith is God's source of creative power, which allows Him to work *in us*, but He is not dependent upon *faith* to exist.

Faith is the source (*well spring*) of power that God **uses** to operate in the lives of His creation. God has and will always continue to exist (live perpetually) **independent of faith**. However, He has chosen faith to be the *spiritual umbilical cord* between Him and His creation. Faith is the spiritual life line that connects us to God, and supplies us with *everything* that we need.

God upholds and builds up all things by the Word of His power, and faith is the upholding force that He **uses**. If God didn't have faith that what He said would come to pass, then nothing would be upheld or built up. Furthermore, if we didn't have faith of and in God, then we would never be able to receive (from, nor trust in), anything that He said. God chose to use faith as His way to connect, and have free course in our lives. Faith is the active power (force) that brings the unseen things into the natural realm.

In Jesus' Own Words

Matthew 17:19, 20: "Then came the disciples to Jesus apart, and said, Why could we not cast him out? And Jesus said unto them, Because of your **unbelief**: for verily I say unto you, If ye have faith as a grain of mustard seed, *ye shall say* unto this mountain, Remove hence to younder place; and it shall remove...."

Mark 11:13, 14, 20, 22-23: "And seeing a fig tree afar off having leaves, he came, if haply he might find any thing thereon: and when he came to it, he found nothing but leaves...And Jesus answered and **said unto it**, No man eat fruit of thee hereafter for ever. And his disciples heard it. And in the morning, as they passed by, they saw the fig tree dried up from the roots...And Jesus answering saith unto them, Have faith in God. For verily I say unto you, That **whosoever shall say** unto this mountain, Be thou removed, and be thou cast into the sea; and shall **not doubt** in his heart...."

In these two portions of Scripture, what was the ingredient that Jesus highlighted as the *secret* to His success? Jesus pointed to the *Supernatural* virtue of faith, which was in operation in His life and ministry. Jesus literally told His disciples that if they had *faith*, they would be able to cast out demons and command mountains to move. But, because the disciples were in unbelief (or not *walking* in faith), they could not cast out that demon. He told them they must use their faith without doubting to see the *same results* that He did.

Consequently, we can discern from Jesus' own words that He had and used faith in order for these miracles to take place. Jesus *had* to have faith. Why? Because without faith it would have been *impossible* for Him to please His Father and He **always** pleased His Father. Simply stating it, Jesus was telling them; "Once your faith is *mature* like mine, then you too will experience the same results, and greater works than these...."

Have The Faith *of* God

"Hanegraaff goes into great detail concerning the translation of Mark 11:22. He points to scholars who render the verse as 'Have faith in God.' Whether it is translated that way or rendered 'Have the faith of God' would make no difference to the verses following in regards to having faith. Hanegraaff is arguing a small point, and as I understand his own reasoning, it could be translated *either way*. **It's strictly an opinion of the translator.** How in the world can Hanegraaff say that either rendering affects the sovereignty of God?...If faith is believing, would it really limit God to say that He had faith that what He spoke into being would come to pass?"[13]

Robert W. Tozier brings up an important point. With all the different Bible concordances and dictionaries that are in print today, one could easily find several different interpretations of the same Greek or Hebrew word. Hence, we must prayerfully decide which definition is most appropriate *based on the context* **of the whole Bible**. Moreover, as Tozier points out, many of these disputes, including this one, are merely splitting spiritual hairs. We have the faith of God in us so that we can have faith in God and His Word, and so that we can use God's faith to bring to *nought* anything that opposes the will/Word of God in our lives.

It's time for the people of God to dare to deny their *own* way of doing things and begin to use their faith and speak the Word of faith to their circumstances. When we do this, we will see the same powerful results as Jesus experienced in His ministry.

5

THE HEBREWS HALL OF FAME

Hank Hanegraaff addresses the eleventh chapter of the book of Hebrews, which I refer to as "The Hebrews Hall of Fame," in a rather unusual manner. He opens his chapter, *The Faith Hall of Fame*, with a few irrational questions that have absolutely no bearing upon what God wanted recorded in the Hebrews Hall of Fame.

"Well, how about it? Who do you think should be **inducted** into the Faith Hall of Fame?...Does Job indeed belong in the Faith Hall of Fame along with such luminaries as Abraham, Isaac and Jacob? Or was Job carnal and faithless...."[1]

What in the Name of Jesus does Job have do with the Hebrews Hall of Fame? **Nothing**! I trust you can see what I mean. With this illogical line of reasoning, Hanegraaff attempts to build a case for "inducting" Job into some new *faith* hall of fame. I must agree that Job was a man who was *faithful* to God, in that he never cursed God *despite* all that he went through.

However, Job's faithfulness to God was *a far cry* from the kind of faithfulness that's portrayed through the lives of the patriarchs of the faith. Job was faithful *in the sense* that he refused to curse God, but *that in no way* implies that Job was a man who walked and lived by faith as 2 Corinthians 5:7 & Romans 4:16,17 define the lifestyle of faith:

(TAB): For we walk by faith [we *regulate* our lives and conduct ourselves by our conviction or belief respecting man's relationship to God and divine things, **with trust** (faith) and holy fervor; thus we walk] **not by sight** *or* appearance.

(NKJV): "Therefore, *it is* of faith that *it might be* according to grace, so that the promise might be sure to all the seed...(as it is written, 'I have made you a father of many nations') in the presence of Him whom he believed—God, who gives life to the dead and calls things which do not exist [in the nature realm], as though they did...."

53

I intend to *scripturally* prove that Job, indeed, *was not* one who lived his life in the exact manner of 2 Corinthians 5:7—meaning Job did not walk and live *by* faith. He did not curse God, but this doesn't mean he lived *by faith*. He lived his life only *by* those things that he could encounter with his five (natural) physical senses. He was unable to *see* who was really behind the attack that was coming against his life.

Hanegraaff continues to denounce the Word of Faith teaching about Job's trials, while at the same time he attempts to *over-inflate* his case, in order to "prove" Job to be a prime candidate for *his* new faith hall of fame. Again, if one were to *only* read that which Hanegraaff has written on the subject, one would receive an extremely different viewpoint. However, upon reading Job's story simply from the Word of God, one can easily see the *actual* Scriptural perspective.

What you are about to read is the true, *unadulterated* story of the life of Job. This is the account of Job's trials which Hanegraaff and the rest of traditional Christianity wish we were unable to comprehend![2]

What Can Happen When *Ignorance* Talks?

I desire to continue with a practical example of what can, *and often times* does happen to us when we let our ignorance do the talking. I realize for many this illustration may be a bit painful. However, I ask you to endure the pain, because this example *may* save your life from many devastating attacks of the enemy. "*He who has an ear to hear, let him hear.*"

I want you to join me on a Scriptural investigation of the life of Job. We've heard so much opinion and theological debate concerning his life, but I believe it is time for us to *really* see what the Bible has to say about Job's trials. Tradition has made Job appear to be *the model* of Christianity, but was he? Was Job truly a model of New Testament faith as some claim?

Job 1:8-12 (NKJV): "Then the Lord said to Satan, 'Have you *considered* My servant Job, that *there* is none like him on the earth, a blameless and upright man, one who fears God and shuns evil?' So Satan answered the Lord and said, 'Does Job fear God for nothing? Have **You** not made a hedge around him, around his household, and around all that he has on every side?'...'But now, stretch out *Your* hand and touch all that he has, and he will surely curse You to Your face!' And the Lord said to Satan, '**Behold**, all that he has is in your power; only do not lay a hand on his person...."

Let's examine what we have just read. God makes a statement to Satan about Job: "Have you considered my servant Job?" *The Spirit Filled Life Bible* uses a side note which says, "Lit. set your heart on."[3] Thus God literally said, "Have you **set your heart on** My servant Job?" Here God is showing us that Satan had *already* set his heart on destroying Job, thus destruction was *the will of Satan* for Job's life. Satan, therefore, was *attempting* to deceive God into giving him what he wanted (Job's life) and God exposed Satan's motive before he was even able to open his mouth. Satan goes as far as trying to get God to stretch out His hand *against* Job to destroy him, fulfilling *Satan's will* and *purpose* for Job's life.

However, what was God's response to Satan's attempt? He replied, "**Behold**, all that he has is in your power..." To some this is proof of God giving His *stamp of approval* upon Satan's deceptive plan to destroy the life of Job. Unfortunately, some sincere believers see this as God partnering up with Satan to make Job (*us*) miserable. This couldn't be further from the truth. God and Satan are not allies.

God told Satan "Behold," but what does *behold* mean, and why would God use this sort of wording? According to the concordance, the word *behold* means, "lo, see."[4] Despite this concordance definition, I was still kind of out in the dark as to how *lo* and *see* were being used in this passage. Researching further, I determined how the words *lo* and *see* were used in other portions of the book of Job.

The word *Lo* is defined as "lo!, behold."[5] Similarly, the word *see* means "advise self, behold, consider, discern; gaze, take heed; lo, look; perceive, regard; cause to or let see, look, think, view."[6] God told Satan to *see* (perceive, understand) that something had happened to the hedge around Job.

I finally realized what God said to Satan that day: "And the Lord said to Satan, 'Behold (lo, see, advise yourself, consider, discern, gaze; take heed, perceive, think) all that he has is within your power....'" God did not take heed to Satan's *challenge* of lowering His hedge of protection; *no, no, no!* God was literally saying to Satan, "Behold, see, look; perceive, *understand*, all he has is **already** within your ability to attack, but do not harm his life." God didn't lower His hedge around Job so that Satan could torment him. God Himself called Job righteous. Then why would our loving Father bring torment on a righteous servant? Such logic is mere foolishness and ignorance of God's character and nature.

Think about this for a moment from an earthly parents' position. How many *decent, godly* parents would take their child and voluntarily put that baby out in the open where wild animals could come in and destroy that child? I can say this with 100% confidence that there *isn't* a **decent,** godly parent in this world who would commit such a foolish act. Therefore, *why* in the Name of Jesus would the church try and make our heavenly Father *appear* to be so cruel and insensitive? Why would He do something so appalling that even decent human parents would never do?

Trimming Off Traditional "Hedge" Work

Job 1:10: Hast not thou made *an hedge about him*, and about his house, and about all that he hath *on every side?* thou hast blessed the work of his hands, and his substance is increased in the land.

Ecclesiastes 10:8: He that diggeth a pit shall fall into it; and **whoso** *breaketh an hedge*, a serpent shall bite him.

Ezekiel 13:4, 5: O Israel, thy prophets are like the foxes in the deserts. Ye have not gone up **into the gaps**, neither *made up the hedge* for the house of Israel to stand in the battle in the day of the LORD.

Ezekiel 22:30, 31: "And I sought for a man among them, that should **make up the hedge**, and *stand in the gap* before me for the land, that I should not destroy it: *but I found none.* **Therefore** have I poured out mine indignation upon them; I have consumed them with the fire of my wrath...saith the Lord GOD."

In every verse of Scripture cited here, the hedge that is referred to is *a spiritual hedge* of protection. In addition, Ecclesiastes 10:8 refers to our own *willfulness* in breaking the hedge of protection; thus allowing *a serpent* access to bite us. Please notice closely Ezek. 13:4, 5 & Ezek. 22:30, 31. Both passages of Scripture overtly state that God **desired** that someone would *stand in the gap* and **make up** *the hedge.* What gap was God talking about? I believe He was referring to gaps *that* **the people** had made in their spiritual hedge, thus causing the hedge to be lowered and to acquire holes of vulnerability to attack which is how *a serpent* can get in and bite!

Who Lowered Job's Hedge?

Having just read all of the Scriptural evidence concerning God's will on the subject of *hedgework*, if God didn't do it, then who did? To answer this question we need to look at the words of Job himself.

Job 3:25: For the thing which I *greatly* feared is come upon me, and that **which I was afraid of** is come unto me.

Job 1:20-22: Then Job arose, and rent his mantle, and shaved his head, and fell down upon the ground, and worshipped, And said, Naked came I out of my mother's womb, and naked shall I return thither: the Lord gave, and *the Lord hath taken away*; blessed be the name of the Lord. **In all this** Job *sinned not*, nor charged God foolishly.

Referring to Job chapter three verse 25, Job openly states that the very thing he *feared* the most (losing everything) has come upon him. Job said that he received **what he believed** for. That may sound strange but it is the truth. Fear is faith *in reverse*, it's perverted (twisted) faith. Job had more "faith" (fear) in the *reality* of losing everything than he did in God's ability to protect him and all that he had. Job had "*faith*" in his ability to lose all. Faith in a thing's ability to harm is called **fear** or *twisted faith*.

Here is the key to how Job lowered his own hedge of protection. Job was *living in great fear* of losing everything, and, without a doubt, he was **verbalizing** his fear where everyone, *including* the devil, could hear him. How can I be so certain that Job was verbalizing his fear of losing everything that belonged to him?

First, I've never met anyone who did not talk about what they *feared* as well as what they *enjoyed* the most. This is just part of human nature. We all tend to talk about those things which are strongest on our hearts. Since *unregenerate* man has always been subject to fear and bondage, I believe it is precise to say that Job talked a great deal about his fears **prior to** his loss. Jesus also made this principle clear in Matthew twelve.

"O generation of vipers, how can ye, being evil, speak good things? for *out of the abundance* of the heart **the mouth speaketh**...For **by thy words** thou shalt be justified, and **by thy words** thou shalt be condemned." (Matthew 12:34, 37)

Job's confession of fear, instead of faith in God's protection, gave Satan an opening to walk in and take everything Job had. Job spoke fearfully *until holes* in his hedge came into existence, thus leaving *himself* open to Satan's attack. Satan heard all Job said, and he authorized him to come in and destroy all that he has by his own fearful words.

Did Job Sin With His Mouth?

*"**In all this** Job sinned not, nor charged God foolishly."*

The above verse of Scripture says that Job did not charge God *foolishly*. I agree that Job did not *knowingly* shout off his mouth against God and sin by cursing God. That's what God meant when He said Job sinned not. Hence, I *don't* believe that he did anything like this during his entire ordeal.

However, I do believe, as I said earlier, that Job spoke words of fear **in ignorance**. For example, in verse 21, Job says "the Lord gave *and the Lord* hath taken away...." We can read the verses prior to verse 21 and see that the Lord wasn't the One Who caused Job's problems. Satan was the one who took away Job's possessions. Job's words were **false** and were spoken in his *ignorance* of the situation, rather than in foolish disobedience. Job spoke without full knowledge of the situation because he couldn't *see* his enemy.

"Did Job sin with his mouth?" In order to answer this question, I want to pose another question: *What is sin?* Is living and walking in fear sin? Is speaking falsely in ignorance sin? I ask again: *What is sin?*

Romans 14:23: And he that doubteth is damned if he eat, **because** *he eateth* not of faith: *for whatsoever is not of faith* **is sin**.

Anything that we do that is not done in faith (confidence, trust) in God and His Word *is sin*. Thus, from the words of Job's own mouth we can see that he did indeed sin with his mouth. Recall how God spoke of him as being perfect, *but* He **did not** speak of him as being some **sinless** icon of perfection as the traditional church has portrayed him.

Moreover, God also sees the redeemed of the Lamb (us) as perfect, but our perfection is through the blood of Jesus. We must *never* forget that Job *was not* spiritually reborn. God in His mercy saw Job as a man who loved Him, but due to ignorance, he experienced a temporary setback. It is sad but true that we all experience spiritual & physical setbacks from time to time. However, God *is not* the cause of or an **accomplice to** these setbacks.

What *NOT* To Do In Trials!

Job 7:11 (TAB): Therefore I *will not* restrain my mouth; I *will* speak in the anguish of my spirit, I *will complain* in the bitterness of my soul [O Lord]!

Job 9:20-22 (TAB): Though I am innocent *and* **in the right**, my own mouth would condemn me; though I am blameless, **He** would prove me perverse. Though I am blameless, I regard not myself; I despise my life. It is all one; therefore I say, **God** [*does not* discriminate, but] *destroys the blameless* and the wicked.

In ignorance, Job says some pretty strong things against the Lord. Job attempts to justify himself and makes God *seem* to be the One in error. Job was not only living in fear, he was also living under the influence of a *self-righteous spirit*. Job was *unwilling* to believe that *he* could have done anything to bring this trial upon himself. This reminds me of many well meaning believers who **insist** they have done everything right and think that God *has not* honored His Word. We must hear the wake up call: **We are, many times, the makers of our own demise!** Until we humble ourselves and get off our self-righteous high horses, God cannot intervene on our behalf. Yes, I meant what I said God *cannot* help us if we live in fear and self-righteousness. **Why?** It is because, God will *respect* our right to continue in our own will! Finally God intervened in Job's situation.

Job 38:1-3; 40:1, 2; 8 (TAB): "THEN THE Lord answered Job out of the whirlwind and said, Who is this that darkens counsel *by words without knowledge*? Gird up now your loins like a man, and I will *demand* of you, and you declare to Me...MOREOVER, THE Lord said to Job, Shall he who would **find fault with the Almighty** contend with Him? He who disputes with God, let him answer it...Will you also annul (set aside and render void) My judgments? Will you *condemn Me* [your God], that you may [**appear**] **righteous** *and* justified."

Reading the above passage, I find it **hard to believe** that anyone would argue for Job's side of *this* debate. It is obvious that God was *somewhat* upset with Job's conduct. In fact, God even referred to Job's words as *words without knowledge*. The Lord continued by addressing the self-righteous spirit that was influencing Job. God told him, "Who are you to make yourself appear to be righteous and Me your Creator to be unrighteous?" Basically He said: "Who do you think you are condemning **Me** with all these ignorant confessions of yours?" Finally, *the light* dawned somewhere within Job's spirit. Miraculously, he was able to see *the evil* behind his own words.

> **Job 42:1-3; 10 (TAB):** "THEN JOB said to the Lord, I know that You can do all things, and that no thought *or* purpose of Yours can be restrained *or* thwarted. [You said to me] Who is this that darkens *and* obscures counsel [by words] without knowledge? Therefore [*I now see*] I have [**rashly**] uttered **what I did not understand**, things too wonderful for me, which I *did not* know...And the Lord turned the captivity of Job *and* restored his fortunes, when he prayed for his friends; also the Lord gave Job twice as much as he had before."

Here we note that Job's restoration did not come *until* he did some things first. What did Job do? First, he *repented* of self-righteousness and his words without knowledge. Then, he also *prayed* for his friends. Repentance and prayer were **the keys** to Job's breakthrough, just as they are for each of us. Repentance and prayer are two important things that we all should take part in when experiencing tragedy in life. Job is a *perfect example* of how one **should not** speak to or about God when in a crisis. Without a doubt, this crisis would have turned into Job's restoration much sooner, had he looked more closely at his own weaknesses.

Moreover, to this day, many still believe that Job's crisis was a *lifelong* experience. However, many Bible scholars say that it actually lasted only approximately nine to twelve **months**. Whatever the length of time was when Job's temptation *by the enemy* was completed, **God** restored double of what he had before his crisis began. Repentance & prayer caused Job's restoration of double. In reality, Job's restoration was, the whole time, only a repentant breath away. He could have stopped this trial sooner if he had only thought to *examine his own life and words*.

At this point, perhaps you're wondering, *"What is the difference between Job and the people addressed in the Hebrews Hall of Fame? Didn't they fail too?"* The main difference should be clear! The Spirit of God obviously did not consider Job's lifestyle as an example worthy of mentioning in Hebrews chapter 11; otherwise, He would have acknowledged Job's faith. Job was dominated his by circumstances! However, He did find Job worthy of acknowledgment for his patient endurance during his trials.

James 5:11: "Behold, we count *them* happy *which endure*. Ye have heard of the **patience of Job**, and have *seen the end of the Lord*; that the Lord is very pitiful, and *of tender mercy*."

The Spirit of God, who had pity and mercy, said Job endured, and thus Job saw the end of the Lord (restoration of double) *despite* his weakness and ignorance. How can I be so sure this is what the Holy Spirit desired to communicate through the apostle James? Please notice the next verse in James chapter five.

James 5:12: "But *above all things*, my brethren, **swear not**, neither by heaven, neither by the earth, neither by any other oath: but let your yea be yea; and your nay, nay; *lest ye fall into condemnation*."

Here, the Holy Spirit is endeavoring to communicate that if we do not watch our words (swearing, confessions) in the same way that Job failed to do, then we *too* will fall into *condemnation* from Satan. We must be diligent to watch the words we speak. Our words open us to either God or the enemy. What's more, the word *condemnation* in James chapter five is defined by the concordance in such a way that it supports the notion of our words cause a form of condemnation to come upon us.

"[*Condemnation*]…to decide (**speak or act**) *under a false part*, i.e. (fig.) dissemble (*pretend*)"[7]

The condemnation of the devil mentioned in James will strive to destroy our lives. However, *we* are the ones responsible for giving him a foothold in our lives by the false proclamations, *anything* contrary to the Word of God, that we allow to come out of our mouths.

Thus as a result, we now know the main reason why the Spirit of God chose **not** to include Job within the Hebrews Hall of Fame! He acted in fear, not in faith. He had more "faith" (fear) in impending destruction than he did in God's ability to protect him. It amazes me how Hanegraaff and those who embrace *his* version of orthodox Christianity seem to always *over-emphasize* the righteousness of Job, but at the same time fail to see that God Himself rebuked Job for his "*words without knowledge*." Hanegraaff states that God **commends** Job for his speaking right words in Job chapter 42 verses 7, and 8.[8] **However**, did this take place before or *after* Job repented?

Job 42:1-3 (TAB): "THEN JOB said to the Lord, I know that You can do all things…[**You said to me**] *Who is this that darkens* *and obscures counsel [by words] without knowledge?* **Therefore** [*I now see*] I have [**rashly**] uttered what I did not understand, things too wonderful for me, which I did not know."

God was not commending Job for his words without knowledge; rather he was commending him for his **words of repentance** once he was able to see the error of his ways. Why would God commend Job for speaking "right words" when prior to Job's repenting He openly rebuked him for speaking *words without knowledge* **and** self-righteousness. It seems that either God *or* Hanegraaff is a bit confused!

Job 38:1, 2; 40:1, 2; 8 (TAB): "THEN THE Lord **answered Job** [*not his friends*] out of the whirlwind and said, Who is this that darkens counsel by *words without knowledge?*...MOREOVER, THE Lord said to Job, Shall he who would **find fault with** the Almighty contend with Him?...Will you also annul (*set aside and render void*) My judgment? Will you **condemn Me** [your God], that **you** may [appear] *righteous and justified?*"

The Word of God makes it **extremely clear** to whom God was speaking with. He *was not* directing this discourse to Job's friends, but rather to Job himself. God is not the author of confusion, and He would **never** commend someone for speaking *false words*, especially when He had **previously** rebuked that person for those very same erroneous words.

Therefore, God's endorsement of Job's words could **only** refer to *his words of repentance* which caused the Lord to be pleased with him once again. God does not take pleasure in us when we speak and act *contrary* to His Word. The Bible calls these actions *faithless* and double minded!

In addition, Hanegraaff claims that in order for the Faith message to *flourish*, Job has to fall.[9] In his opinion, the Word of Faith teachers are responsible for his fall. On the contrary, the Word of God is crystal clear concerning who was responsible for Job's "fall from grace." Job, **and Job only**, was responsible for uttering fearful words. Job's words opened the door to Satan to waltz in and destroy everything that Job possessed. His story should be an example for all *believers* of how we shouldn't speak rashly to or about the Lord. This is a prime example of how one should never blame God for one's trials. God is not and never will be our problem. He's for us...not against us!

We must always remember that the subject of emphasis in Hebrews chapter eleven was the God-kind of faith, which all of those mentioned in that chapter walked in. On the other hand, as we have seen from the book of Job, Job, in fact, *did not* live and walk in the same dimension of faith as those mentioned in Hebrews chapter eleven. The "heroes" of Hebrews chapter eleven were radical servants of God. They were not perfect, in the sense of never failing, but they were people who lived and *acted* in faith upon the Word of the Living God. However, Job acted upon his *life long* fear of losing all, rather than acting upon his faith in God's ability to protect him from all loss.

Now **you** *decide whether or not Job should have been included in the Hebrews Hall of Fame!*

6

WHO'S DEIFYING MAN?

There is absolutely no question that the enemy is attempting to sell his long circulating lie of man becoming "God." Since the fall of Lucifer with his self-deluded "*I will*" speech, man has been foolishly convinced by him that he too can become "God." According to Hank Hanegraaff, the leading proponents of the Faith message are presently attempting to peddle this ancient deception.

"It is no surprise that such blasphemy should spew forth from witches...What is shocking, however, is that *similar* statements are now being voiced by some of the biggest names in the church."[1]

Is this statement really true? Are statements made by various Faith teachers as similar to the occult as Hanegraaff would lead one to believe? Could this be just another case of "*guilty by association?*" Let's look beyond mere surface "evidence" for answers to these questions!

Kenneth E. Hagin, as usual, took the brunt of this accusation when Hanegraaff quoted him as saying, "Man...was created on terms of equality with God, and he could stand in God's presence without any consciousness of inferiority...God has made us as much like Himself as possible...He made us the same class of being that He is Himself...Man lived in the realm of God. He lived on terms equal with God. *The believer is called Christ...That's who we are; we're Christ!*"[2]

According to *Christianity in Crisis*, those were the exact words of Kenneth E. Hagin. However, upon deeper examination one finds that the above quotation is not completely accurate. I returned to the original cited text:

"[Born-again] man has received the life of God and has come into a kingly state. We are accepted by God to reign as kings in the realm of life. We are no longer servants in the realm of spiritual death, but have passed out of death...Man was never made to be a slave. He was made to reign **under** God...He was created *on terms of* equality with God, and could stand in God's presence without any consciousness of inferiority [*Psalm 8:4, 5]...In some translations there is a number or letter by the word "angels" in the this text*. If you look in the margin you'll find that the Hebrew word here is *Elohim* — the same word or name for God...That means God has made us *as much like Himself as possible*. He made us in His image. He made us in His likeness. He made us **the same class of being** that He is Himself...God took something of Himself, which was spirit, the life of God, and put it into man...*Man was made His* **understudy**, so to speak...Man lived in the realm of God...We know this then: Man is a spirit. We know he is in the same class with God, because God is a Spirit and because man was made to have fellowship with God."[3]

As I returned to the original quotation, I was frustrated as well as amazed. Hanegraaff included statements in his quotation of Hagin that did not appear in Hagin's writing. I realized I was reading the sixth printing of *Zoe: The God-Kind of Life*, printed in 1995, and Hanegraaff quoted him from the 1989 printing. However, I find it very unlikely that there would be such an extreme difference between printings. One might say, "Perhaps Hagin revised the text after the 1989 printing?" Perhaps! **Nonetheless**, the 1995 printing does not give one any impression that the text has been altered from the 1989 printing, has his revisions in other books have noted. *Nevertheless*, the word Christ means "anointed," and since Jesus lives in us we are "*Christ*-ened" (anointed) as is He. Also, he who is joined to Christ is one spirit with Him (1 Cor. 6:17 NKJV).

Let's examine the original quotation. Hanegraaff leaves one with the impression that Hagin assumes he is an **exact equal** with God Almighty. However, Hagin, in fact, *never* made such a foolish statement. To the contrary he said, "He [man] was made to reign **under** God...Man was made His **understudy**, so to speak...." With statements such as these, Hagin could not possibly assume that he is equal with God. One could not be an exact "equal" and yet under complete subjection at the same time. Even Jesus Himself said "*It's not Me, It's the Father within.*" For one to be an equal with God, he would have to have *every* advantage and gift that God the Father has at his *own* disposal. Even Jesus the Son of Man did not do any mighty works *until after His baptism.* Thus, beyond doubt, Hagin **is not** insinuating that he lives in **exact** equality with God Almighty. God could never sin and still remain holy where as Hagin was once a sinner!

Furthermore, Hagin states that "God has made us as much like Himself *as possible*," denoting that there are obviously *some things* that man

does not possess in himself, thus, showing that Hagin doesn't think he's an *exact* equal with God. Nevertheless, he does say, "He [man] was created *on terms of* equality with God...*the same class of being*...."

What was Hagin attempting to say? First of all, being on terms of equality and an *exact* equal are extremely different ideas. For example, I associate with my parents on an *equal level* (as an adult); however, I am not an exact equal with them. Why? They are my source of creation. I will always in some ways be subordinate to them. I can relate to them on terms of equality (being an adult), but I could never be their equal because I am *only a part* of each of them.

Our terms of equality with God is not in the fact that we are all-powerful (deity), but rather that we are able to come to Him in Christ Jesus as though we had never sinned. This is because we have the privilege of Him living in our hearts, which causes us to be transformed into the image of Christ—a representation of Jesus to the world. We are also created in His image after His likeness. God, **Himself**, was the *pattern* for our creation. Hagin & I both understand that we will **always** be *subordinate* to our Creator. Hagin *is not* saying that we are exact equals, or that we have the right and power to do whatever **we** so desire as God the Father does. We act according to God's will. He *is* Lord!

Finally, it is extremely amazing to me that Hanegraaff somehow still seems to not understand what Hagin means when he says, "[we are in] the same class of being [as God]." If he had thoroughly read the book in question, he would have seen the following explanation of this term.

> "We know this then: *Man is a spirit*. We know he is in the same class with God, **because God is a Spirit** and because man was made to have fellowship with God."[4]

This is his answer on how we could be in the same spiritual class of being as God. God is a Spirit—man is a spirit. God is a three fold Spiritual being—man also is a three fold being—*spirit, soul and body* (1 Thess. 5:23). God is a triune being and man was created after that pattern.

In my opinion, Kenneth Copeland describes this same principle in much more explicit detail:

> "You are a spirit. You don't have a spirit—you are a spirit being created in the likeness of God...As a spirit being you were created

in the same spiritual class with God. The difference between you and God Himself—It's a very important difference…The difference between you and God—even though you were created in the same class with God, cause your created in Him image. You're not created below angels you were created above the angelic class. *Angels don't have the same rights that you have with God*…Now, the difference between you, me or any other human being and God is this—**He is sovereign**. He's the Creator. No body created Him. He does not have a spiritual head. He **is** *THEE* spiritual Head. Are you listening to me now? I've had people carry signs and advertise my meetings for me—You know?…And most of them, the sign that they carry said, *'Kenneth Copeland says he's God.'* Now look—I was born at night, but it wasn't last night. **I am not that stupid.** I don't even look that stupid…Anybody who thinks he's God—*It don't take but a second to prove that he's not.* Amen! Now, we are created in the same class   with   God, **in the fact that** we have the spiritual capacity…to be called His own sons and daughters. We are born of His Spirit."[5]

I dare say that if one were to ask Hagin if he agreed with the above quotation, he would, without a doubt. say, "Yes!" This sums up the *true* meaning behind the Faith teachers' statements about our being on terms of equality with God and being in His class of spiritual being. It also answers any questions one might have concerning Copeland's thoughts on this subject. We *are not* God or a god. We're His children. He is sovereign and we are not.

As we continue, Hanegraaff quotes evangelist Morris Cerullo as saying, "Who are you? Come on, *who are you?* Come on, say it: **'Sons of God!'**…And when we stand up here, brother, you're not looking at Morris Cerullo; you're looking at God. You're looking at Jesus."[6]

At *face value*, one could easily form the opinion that Cerullo thinks he's Jesus. *However*, this is very doubtful. Having met and worked for Morris Cerullo and having sat under his ministry since 1983, I can say with total confidence that Dr. Cerullo in no way believes he is *thee* "Christ." How can I know this for sure? First of all, I know his heart. He loves and serves Jesus closer than just about any person I know. He would never be so foolish to imply such idiocy. Also, the Word of God clearly tells us, *"We are dead and our lives are hidden with Christ in God."*

Hence, when one looks into our eyes they *should* not see us, but rather Jesus in Whom we are hidden. The Bible also says, *"He who is joined to Christ is one spirit with Him.*" That is not to imply that we are **sovereign equals** with the Almighty, instead it shows the closeness we have with and in Him as children of God.

Hanegraaff continues his allegations that the faith teachers believe they are exact equals with God or a god by opposing Charles Capps. "God duplicated *Himself* in kind!...*Adam was an exact duplication of God's kind!*"[7]

Seeing that we have already addressed this area we will not take a great deal of space to discuss it. Capps is actually saying the same thing that we have previously examined. God's kind (image) is spirit. His likeness in us is that He made us a Three-fold being. This is evident from the next quotation:

> "God created man after His likeness, an exact duplication *in kind*. Then, what *kind* is God? Jesus said, *God is a Spirit*. **You aren't God.** *You aren't equal with God* in His divine attributes, but you are a spirit being **under authority.** You are able to partake of God's divine nature: **righteousness.** Adam *was subordinate* to God."[8]

I don't believe Capps could make himself any clearer than with this statement. We are **not** God or a god. We are God's highest creation, but we are still under the Supreme authority of our Creator. Again, the words of Copeland echo this same thought:

> "Now, God is sovereign. He doesn't have any head over Him. *There's nobody that God has to answer too.* **There's no such thing as a sovereign human being.** No such thing as that. **God Almighty is the only sovereign being there is.** Jesus, by coming *as a man,* called the Son of Man, making Himself **obedient** *unto death,* and then submitting Himself to the Father, gave up *a part* of His sovereignty and handed it to the Father."[9]

As a result, I dare say that none of these ministers cited believe that they are *a sovereign equal* to God—Father, Son or Holy Spirit!

Little *Gods*—Hanegraaff's Affirmation

"First, it should be pointed out that the phrase 'little gods' may be unfortunate, but it is not necessarily heretical in and of itself, as long as it is not intended to convey that man is equal with or a part of, God."[10]

Hanegraaff affirms that the term "little gods" is, in fact, depicted in Scripture, and he says in and of itself it is not heretical. As we have seen from the beginning of this chapter this is exactly what the Faith teachers are trying to convey. Hence, his accusations are, in reality, absolutely unwarranted. I know he means well, but I wish he would think and research more before he's so fast to pick up his pen in judgment.

Psalm 82:6: I have said, **Ye *are* gods**; and all of you *are* children of the most High.

According to this passage of Scripture, God is saying that we are "gods" with a little "*g*," hence the terminology "little gods." In the Hebrew concordance, the word *gods* is:

"*'elohiym, el-o-heem'*; plur. of H433; gods in the ordinary sense; but spec. used (in the plur. thus, esp. with the art.) of the supreme God; occasionally applied by way of deference to *magistrates*; and sometimes as a superlative:--angels, X exceeding, God (gods) (-dess, -ly), X (very) great, *judges*...."[11]

This verse is not saying that we're little *exact* copies of the Almighty—sovereign to *our own* will. It's merely telling us that God has called us into a ministry of dominion and authority—under His leadership. The term "gods" literally implies a magistrate (ruler), or judge (one with authority to make certain decisions). However, our decisions must not be made without consulting with our Commander and Chief—*Jesus Christ!*

Again Copeland makes a *clear* statement concerning the controversy surrounding the idea of men being "gods."

"He [Adam] had given Satan *authority* over this earth as *far as mankind is concerned*. He **didn't** have authority over this earth as a planet, *but he had the use of it*...God told Adam to subdue the earth...Now in that he's created in God's class...God gave man authority—that put him in the same class with God. Now you take the word 'god' with a little 'g' just simply means author-ity. It also means *provider*...In that sense—the fact that God gave man a free will to make choice...In that way we're created in God's class. Now when I originally started talking about that I didn't take time to explain that. I thought Ned and the third primer could understand that. But I forgot about how ignoramus religion can be and how blind it can be...*In that sense* you're created in God's class...**Man is not a sovereign being.** You're subject to something. *You can't be sovereign* and I don't care how hard you try. You are either subject to God, or...to the devil."[12]

Copeland clearly states that men *are not* sovereign and that we will **never** be a sovereign "god." Consequently, Copeland and the rest of the Faith teachers do not believe that they are gods or that they will become a god. No matter what Hanegraaff has tried to perpetrate, the evidence is clear from the words of those he has accused, therefore, proving that his accusations to be without a doubt totally unfounded.

Partakers of The Divine Nature?

Hanegraaff continues his assault against the Word of Faith by accusing them of using (2 Pet. 1:4) as evidence to bolster their so-called "little gods doctrine."

Whereby are given unto us exceeding great and precious promises: that by these ye might be *partakers* of the *divine nature*, **having escaped the corruption that is in the world** through lust.

Hanegraaff says, "In no way can this text be twisted to mean that believers actually take on the essence or nature of God."[13] But, are the teachers of the Word of Faith literally saying such nonsense? Are they teaching that we're partakers of **all** the attributes of God? In reality, we've already answered these questions; nonetheless, it's important to thoroughly examine 2 Peter1:4, in order to clarify its actual meaning and stop of the endless speculation. For the sake of deeper understanding, I performed a word study from three different sources on three important words found in 2 Pet. 1:4: *partakers*, *divine* and *nature*. At this point, I wish to share the results of this word study.

Partakers: "a sharer, i.e. associate: -- companion, fellowship, partaker, partner."[14]

Partakers: "To give or have in common."[15]

Divine: "Theios 'nature' (from theos God) is used of the power of God, 2 Pet. 1:3, and of His nature v.4, in each place, as that which proceeds from Himself."[16]

Divine: "godlike (neut. as noun divinity): -- divine, godhead."[17]

Divine: "Divine, godly, god-like, theios."[18]

Nature: "'to bring forth, produce,' signifies 'the nature' of a person or thing, ('kind')...."[19]

Nature: "growth (by germination or expansion), i.e. (by impl.) natural production (lineal descent)...a genus or sort...natural disposition."[20]

According to the following word definitions, we (the church) are *partakers* (a sharer, associate, have in common), the divine (godly, god-like), *nature* (spiritual germination, *lineal descent*; natural disposition) of Jesus Christ engrafted into us when we became born-again. In other words, we have been born into the Super-natural family of God. Because of the redemptive work of Christ, we have received the nature of Jesus Christ infused into our hearts. What do I mean by the nature of Jesus?

First of all, the primary characteristic that we have received is right standing with God or **Righteousness**. Moreover, we now have the ability to live and walk in the Holy Spirit. Meaning, God birthed within us His fruit when we became born-again. I am not, *in anyway*, saying that we have **all** of the godly attributes (omniscience, omnipresence, omnipotence). However, we do have the same spiritual characteristics (genes) of our Father. Those spiritual *genes* are primarily righteousness and the nine fruit of the Holy Spirit. Through these god-like qualities, we are able to escape from the moral decay that is in this present world. Thus, we are able to "be holy, even as He is holy." The holiness of God is infused into our spirit man.

Moreover, Kenneth Copeland makes the spiritual limitations of Christian believers plainly clear with the following eye opening statement.

"I'm talking to you about the Super-natural world. And we were born-again to live in it. There's coming a time very soon where your body will be full of it. A glorified body with the glory of God flowing in your veins. Every cell of your body permeated with it *to the point that it has absolute law over the natural physical world.* Right now we *don't* have absolute law over it, **God does but we don't**. We exercise our faith, we release it in the Word of God and then we are connected to the Anointing and the Anointing or the Holy

Ghost Himself moves in the Super-natural world on the natural world…that's the way we function today."[21]

With a quotation like this, how could anyone insinuate that Copeland or any other Faith teacher could believe that they are exact *equals* with God Almighty? Whether Hanegraaff wants to admit it or not, God created man in His image (a spirit being) after His likeness (a three fold being: spirit, soul, and body). He gave him dominion or authority to rule and reign over this earth as His under-lord. Jesus Himself, after His resurrection, reinstated the believer's dominion over this earth by saying:

Matthew 28:18, 19 (NKJV): "…All authority has been given to Me in heaven and on earth. Go therefore and make disciples (believers) of all the nations…."

Hence, we have all the available God-given authority and power that we will every need in this life. Jesus re-instituted the God given dominion that we lost through man's fall into Sin. Hence, we have available all the God given authority *and power* that we need to complete **any** spiritual task we're given!

Nevertheless, we need to be totally dependent upon God the Holy Spirit, in order that we can live an authoritative life over Satan, and be able to perform the works of God. Unless we cast off our doctrinal differences and simply rely on the Comforter, the Counselor, the Advocate and Strengthener (the Holy Spirit), we will **never** be able to do anything that will affect this world for eternity. My friends that is our commission!

7
HOW WOULD SOMEONE
DEMOTE GOD?

According to *Christianity in Crisis*, the Faith teachers are not only deifying man, but they are also demoting God Almighty,[1] whatever that means! How could the *creation* ever be able to demote or downgrade his Creator. That is absolutely impossible. Such a notion is totally ridiculous, literally or figuratively. Hanegraaff takes Copeland, Savelle, Cerullo and Hinn to task for saying that the Father, Son & Holy Spirit have some sort of spiritual form. Copeland is the first to get "the ax" when Hanegraaff quotes him as saying:

> "Kenneth Copeland claims that God is 'not some creature that stands 28 feet tall, and He's got hands, you know, as big as basketballs. That's not the kind of creature He is...A being that is very uncanny the way He's very much like you and me. A being that stands somewhere around 6'-2", 6'-3", that weighs somewhere in the neighborhood of a couple of hundred pounds, little better, [and] has a [hand] span of nine inches across."[2]

I realize that Copeland's words begin to appear as if he was referring to *God the Father*; however, I also believe that the rest of the context of his statement should easily reveal that he was actually speaking of *Jesus the Man*. How can I be so sure? Well, first of all, Jesus Christ was **God** in flesh, and so is referred to by all believers as *God*. Next, Copeland's depiction of "God" was almost identical to the way most theologians and historians describe Jesus of Nazareth—between 6 feet and 6 feet 3 inches tall.

Moreover, chances are **very good** that Jesus' hand "span-width" is approx. 9" wide, which correlates appropriately with a man of about 6'- 6' 3" tall. Also, the Bible clearly states the all things were made by the Word and Jesus Christ was/is the Word of the Living God. Is He not? This same idea also proves true concerning Jerry Savelle's description of "God." Jesus was and still is God in *flesh*. He still has a body today! To assume any other interpretation of this statement is an insult to the intelligence of every Bible believing Christian!

Robert W. Tozier comments appropriately concerning the idea of "God" having dimensions of some sort:

> **"THE DIMENSIONS OF GOD**—It's just as ridiculous to suppose that anyone believes that God has height and weight. Many times people use figurative language to illustrate various concepts. This is one example that Hanegraaff uses to prove that the God of the Faith movement is not the God of the Bible. This claim is utterly preposterous and hardly worthy of comment. I'm really astonished that Hanegraaff would suppose that either Roberts, Copeland or Savelle would actually believe that God had dimensions as man has, or that he was some sort of human shaped giant. In his description of God Hanegraaff says that 'Savelle seems oblivious to the fact that Isaiah is using figurative language.' I would respond that Hanegraaff seems oblivious to the fact that Savelle is using figurative language."[3]

Morris Cerullo also gets in on the *action* when Hanegraaff opposes him by implying that he had some occult-like "out-of-body" experience,[4] in which he saw God, Who appeared to him in the form of a man. First of all, I would like to ask Hanegraaff: "Were you present with Cerullo during this experience? How in the Name of Jesus could you possibly know whether or not this experience really happened?" The Bible is clear that God appeared to many as a Cloud, Fire, a burning Bush, etc. Hanegraaff believes these experiences are contrary to the Word of God, but are they really?

Therefore, why couldn't the Glory of God appear to someone in the form of a human being? Jesus, Who exists in a body even today, can and many times does appear to people. Therefore, it is not erroneous for someone to say that *God* appeared to him in a human form, despite their wording. All things are possible with God!

Benny Hinn was charged by Hanegraaff for believing and teaching "tritheism"[5] because he quoted something that Fines Dake had written. But, Hanegraaff even acknowledged that Hinn admitted to *Christianity Today* that he had made a mistake by quoting Dake's book.[6] Therefore, if Hinn admitted to making a mistake, why would Hanegraaff continue to publicize his blunder, implying that he actually believed in tritheism? Even Hanegraaff's own research proves that Hinn in no way believes the erroneous teaching of tritheism. Thus, I ask myself, "So what is the point of even discussing Hinn's mistake?" In reality, there is absolutely no point!

During my research I found something that Hinn wrote in his book, *Good Morning Holy Spirit*, which will better clarify his belief concerning the Godhead.

> "It is so easy to **limit** the Godhead or to *divide* the Godhead unscripturally. Young Christians often ask, 'How can God be one and three at the same time?' **God is one**. But God is three: Father, Son and Holy Spirit. And while this book dwells on the Holy Spirit, *I am distinguishing them on purpose to show you the triune being*. God is *like* the sun in the sky. If you look at its brightness you see one sun. In reality, however, it is a triune sun that keeps our planet alive. There are three distinct **elements**: the sun, light, and heat. And so it is with the Trinity. The Father *is like* the whole sun, **Jesus is the light, and the Holy Ghost is the heat you feel**."[7]

Hinn is simply saying that God is One God *manifested* in three person Trinity. In other words, God is manifested in three different ways, but He is still One.

Furthermore, the Godhead would have to be able to be separated, *to some degree*; otherwise, Jesus the Man would have to have ceased to be God while on earth. I say this because He was *separated*, not in heaven, from His Father for the period of 33 years.

Moreover, I also found another interesting quotation from Hinn concerning the dimensions of God.

> "What does God look like? *There's not one place in the Word of God where the Father is described in detail*...God the Father has a form but no man knows what it looks like (Phil. 2:6)...Next, you need to understand that **the Trinity** is the glory of God. God the Father is the glory of God; God the Son is the glory of God; and God the Holy Spirit is the glory of God...When the Holy Ghost talks to you, all three are talking, but the Holy Ghost is the one you hear [*because they are One*]."[8]

Having a spiritual form does not necessarily mean that one is attempting to reduce God to the likes of man. Jesus did say that "no man has seen God the Father's shape or form." If Jesus and the Father have some sort of spiritual form, then why couldn't the Holy Spirit as well? I don't understand how this could be possible, but He is God, isn't He, and the spirit realm is so much higher than this natural earthly realm.

A perfect example of how God can have three distinct parts, but at the same time still be One is found in the three part being called man. Man was made in God's likeness. *What is the likeness of God?* It is in our being a three in one being (spirit, soul & body—1 Thess. 5:23) like God. Man has three distinct parts, but the only One Who can divide them is the Word of the Living God.

> **Hebrews 4:12 (NKJV):** "For the word of God *is* living and powerful, and sharper than any two-edged sword, piercing even to the division of soul and spirit, and of joints and marrow...."

Hence, such trivial nonsense is not actually worth acknowledging. God is able to do anything that He needs to do in order to accomplish His plan in the affairs of men. How could we try to limit a *limitless* God with a bunch of so-called "theological" rules and regulations for studying Him, like one would study a bug?

Who's Next?

Hanegraaff never ceases to charge Kenneth Copeland with the most bizarre things. He claims that Copeland *literally* believes that God is the biggest failure in the universe. He supports his assumption with the following quotation from Copeland.

> "I was shocked when I found out who the biggest failure in the Bible actually is...The biggest one in the whole Bible is God...Now, the reason you don't think of God as a failure is He never said He's a failure. And you're not a failure till you say you're one."[9]

At first glance, it appears that Copeland believes that God really is the biggest failure in the Bible. Without Super-natural insight, one could assume that God did indeed fail. To Satan and natural man, God is a failure because He lost His creation.

Still, in reality, this is not the truth. I've heard Copeland make statements on this subject before and when he made them he was referring to our natural understanding of what took place in the Garden of Eden. *To the natural mind*, God failed miserably. Nevertheless, this is not the truth!

Copeland also made another statement that runs headlong against any such notion which Hanegraaff has attempted to propose.

"There's no such thing as a God made failure. **God *doesn't* fail.** Failure came into human life and man's existence when he [man] hooked up with the devil. The devil is the author of Sin, sickness, demons; fear. All that steals, kills and destroys; he is the author of it. He [Satan] is the one that brought that on the human family. Now let's remember that! Jesus suffered everything that could possibly ever cause you or I any failure large or small…He was our Substitute and our Sacrifice"[10]

Tell me something. *"How can God be a failure and not fail all at the same time?"* It's simple—He can't! Therefore, the quotation that Hanegraaff used was actually an illustration of how natural man views what took place in the Garden, **not** that God is really a failure. Dear Lord, when will this brother think before taking pen in hand? If he would have done so, *he* would saved the Church a lot of debate!

Hanegraaff continues in opposing Copeland by quoting him explaining what took place on earth in mans life at the "Fall of man."

"Adam committed high treason; and at that point, all the dominion and authority God had given him was handed over to Satan. Suddenly, God was on the outside looking in….After Adam's fall, God found Himself in a peculiar position…God needed an avenue back into the earth…God laid out His proposition and Abram accepted it. It gave God access to the earth and gave man access to God…."[11]

Copeland's statement is very simple to understand. I'm surprised that an intelligent man like Hanegraaff seems to fail to comprehend his meaning.

First of all, God gave Adam (man) authority and dominion over all the works of His hand on earth. When man committed "high treason" or Sinned, the earth that God created was immediately cursed. But you say, "It was not cursed until God proclaimed it after the fall." No, that is not true. God told Adam "in the day you eat, you'll die."

The **moment** they ate of that fruit, the curse came, and then God simply, *officially*, proclaimed man's fate because of his fall into Sin. Since the earth was cursed, God could not have anything to do with it or man because man, by Sin, had shut God out of his life and the earth. Satan had won over man from God along with man's *authority to govern* the earth. God's gifts are given **without** repentance.

Because of Sin, Satan ruled over man and hence, the earth which man was given by God to govern. Furthermore, Copeland better explains this idea during a teaching aired on the *Believer's Voice of Victory* broadcast.

"Under the influence of Adam's act God, Who had delegated that authority to Adam crowned him with His glory, gave him authority over all the works of His hands. Under the influence of what he [Adam] did, he had the right to do it. He had the right to commit high treason. But he didn't have the commission to do it. *That's like putting somebody in charge of your company, and giving them the right and authority and power of attorney; and they sell the company...*now see Adam's eyes were wide open. His wife the Bible says was deceived, He wasn't. When he did that **he put God in a position of having to honor that**. *Because, God have him the authority to do it. He didn't commission him to do it*. But He gave him the authority to do it. Therefore, He couldn't go back to *the dust of the earth* and make another man. The earth didn't belong to Him. He couldn't go in the Spirit and create another man...Why? Where was He going to get another man? **The process had already been laid down. The womb of a women was the authority of entrance into this earth.** *And without Adam and His wife God didn't have any entrance into this earth. He didn't belong here anymore*. So, under the influence of what he [Adam] had done God had to go back to His original method of creation. Which was what? *In the beginning was the Word*. So, He started speaking the Word. He started speaking the Word...How did speaking the Word cause something to come to pass when He didn't have the right to just say 'man be?' It had to come in the form of a promise. [God speaking] I'll do this and a man had to say 'All right I receive that and I hold You to it by covenant.' When that happened God would tell the devil, 'The man said I could.' See, that's the way God got it done."[12]

When man committed Sin, *he sold himself* over to Satan; hence, God no longer was his sole Lord or owner. Satan then became his "god." This act of disobedience shut God out of man's life and, in reality, out of *absolute* influence in the earthly realm. God no longer had *total* authority over man and the earth. Satan was now man's master (or god)!

God is sovereign, *but* He will **never** resist the free will of man. He desires that we love Him of our own will, not like a bunch of robots. God is a God of justice; therefore, He will not take back something that He has endowed, even after man turned his back upon Him. His gifts are given *without* repentance. Satan had authority over man, and therefore, authority over the works of God's hand, which was originally given to the man. One has authority to use anything that is delegated to him. Similarly, Satan had this sort of authority over *man* because he sold himself and his authority to Satan.

Moreover, Copeland comments again on how Satan obtained Adams authority.

"He [Adam] had given Satan authority over this earth as far as man-kind is concerned. He [Satan] didn't have authority over this earth as a planet, *but he had the use of it.* Because he had the *man* who had authority over it [the earth]."[13]

It is important to note that Copeland **never** states that Satan "owned" the earth, but rather that he *had the use of the earth*, because he was using man's authority from God.

Nevertheless, God *was not*, in any way, taken off-guard when man opened the human race to Satan's control by Sin, as Hanegraaff says the Faith teachers have taught. God knows the beginning from the end. Hence, nothing could possibly take Him by surprise. However, God has sovereignly chosen not to violate the will of man. Thus, when man chose to serve Satan, God *could not* stop him from choosing Sin.

Why couldn't He stop him? Because He had already chosen not to violate man's will. God is not like man that He should lie. He doesn't say something one day, and then turn around and do the exact opposite that He said the next day. That would be unjust and God isn't unjust! Since God is sovereign, He also has the ability to limit Himself whenever He chooses. God wasn't taken by surprise when man fell and the Faith teachers have *never* taught that He was.

Why Would One Deify A Loser?

"Now it is time to examine a new depth of doctrinal distortion as we examine the Faith teaching regarding the deification of Satan."[14]

The Faith teachers are attempting to deify Satan as a 'god,' according to Hanegraaff. But, is this another one of his odd misinterpretation? Without doubt, it is! Once again, such logic absolutely baffles me. In *Christianity in Crisis*, Hanegraaff *implies* that the Faith teachers actually believe and teach that God and Satan are two opposing forces of **equal** strength.

> "This Faith mythology features an implicit form of dualism: two forces fighting it out for control of the universe, and you never knew who is finally going to win...C.S. Lewis described this type of dualism as 'the belief that there are two equal and independent powers at the back of everything, one of them good and the other bad....'"[15]

How, in the Name of Jesus, did Hanegraaff conjure up this mythological fairy-tale? Perhaps he's been watching too much *Star Trek*. Perhaps he ate too much pizza the night before he wrote his chapter on the "deification of Satan!" I have never heard such religious nonsense in all my life. No doubt he thinks *they are* living in the land of Oz as well. Still, the Faith teachers have **never** taught any sort of farfetched idea as this.

For Hanegraaff or any other theologian to say that the Faith teachers believe that Satan is some sort of "god," equal in strength and authority with God Almighty, would be pure absurdity. This *bizarre* idea is similar to the Indian teaching of two brothers, one good and the other evil, fighting to the end for the control of both the natural and spiritual realms. Such teaching is pure **occultism** and is in no way embraced by any Faith teacher.

Kenneth Copeland clearly dispels Hanegraaff's misinterpretation by boldly stating that Satan is not a god, but a created being.

> "Satan **is not** a god. **He is a fallen angel.** He *is not* in the God class. Consequently, there is *no creative power in him*...Satan (or Lucifer) was forbidden to act by his own will; but he chose to exalt himself over God. He tried to use the power of words against God...**By choosing his own words**, *Satan broke a cardinal law in the spirit world*. He violated the limits of His authority and chose to stand against God."[16]

There should be no doubt as to whether or not Copeland is attempting to deify Satan. He plainly said that Satan *is not* a god, but rather a part of God's creation. To assume *anything* other than what Copeland has already plainly stated would be a complete lack of all rational logic and a blatant insult to all who embrace the Faith message. We know how to read, thank you very much!

82

These ideas are just **not** reality. And we're also discerning enough to know how to test the spirits for ourselves! Furthermore, Copeland elaborates upon the literal extent of Satan's power.

"Satan became the illegitimate stepfather of mankind through Adam's high treason. He received Adam's authority over the spiritual laws in the earth. **He did not put spiritual law into motion.** *He just perverted the laws that were already there.* **Sin was not a new law. It was righteousness perverted.** Death was life perverted. Hate was love perverted. Fear was faith perverted."[17]

Again, I'm sorry this does not sound like a man who believes that Satan has as much authority and power as God. Rather, it clearly shows the limited power that the enemy has. *Satan is not a god* and in no way can ever be one. That's what he desired to be, but he was put out of heaven. As I said, no Faith teacher believes such silliness.

The Supreme Court of the Universe

"The words 'God couldn't' alone should be enough to make us shudder. And just who in heaven's name sits on the so-called 'Supreme Court of the Universe?...If indeed God had to answer to Capps's cosmic committee, He by definition would not really be God. The God of Scripture is the ultimate Judge of the universe."[18]

As you have just read, Hanegraaff has no comprehension of what Capps means when he said "the Supreme Court of the Universe." When Capps said this, he was referring to God Almighty's own rules and regulations that He has put into effect. In other words, *God abides by His own rules.* He's not a hypocrite. **He practices what He preaches.** God has limited Himself, in certain areas, *by free will choice.* Thus, God is not like man that He should lie. He will do all that He has promised and even more. If we can't take Him at His Word on healing and prosperity, *then how could we ever believe Him when it comes to the area of salvation.* This is the same God Who promised them all. **It's simple!** We couldn't. Either He's the Truth *or He's not!* To make a promise, only to break it is called a lie— God isn't like man that He should lie!

To have *faith*, or to be a "believer," *means* one believes and acts upon God's Word without requiring **any** sense knowledge as proof. Carnality and carnal people require sense knowledge as proof before they will believe. The Bible says that the carnal mind is separated or Spiritually

Dead to God and all that He has promised! It grieves my heart, and the heart of God, to contemplate that there are so many supposed "believers" who refuse to believe God's Word without some form of physical evidence. This is carnality in its *truest* and *purest* sense!

It is truly amazing to me how Hanegraaff has no problem trusting God to save his eternal spirit from hell, but he has little or no faith in this same God to heal him and make him prosperous, so that he can live to give to all those in need. To me, this is a classic case of *spiritual Schizophrenia* (a double-minded man). Such psychotic logic is incomprehensible! He is able to believe God for salvation of his spirit, but is powerless to believe this same God for the salvation [*Soteria*—health, salvation, deliverance][19] of his *body* and *soul*. I have been very *diplomatic* thus far, but on a point such as the truth of the Word of God, I cannot keep from speaking out. For one to call one's self a "believer" but does not really believe all that God said…one is deceiving *himself!*

What an inconsolable relationship he must have with God. How can I assume this? Because the Bible says that a double-minded man is unstable in all his ways. When one is double-minded, one can not be happy in life, no matter what he does. The idea that God will save your spirit, *but doesn't care about your body & soul,* is evidence of a person with *spiritual Schizophrenia* (a man with two minds that are *diametrically* opposed). This is double-mindedness in its purest sense.

Nonetheless, God is not a double-minded liar Who cannot be trusted to stand behind the promises that He has already made in His Word. How can anyone have faith in someone if they can't even take him at his own word? The answer is plain—they can't! No one can have faith in God if they cannot trust what He has said to them in His Word.

8

WHO HAS *AUTHORITY* TO
DEMOTE CHRIST?

Who could possibly demote Jesus Christ? According to Hank Hanegraaff, the Faith teachers can! I guess they must *really* be powerful! In his own words he says, "Almost all cults and world religions compromise the deity of Christ, and the Faith movement is no exception."[1] In order for one to truly demote Jesus, one would have to have greater power and authority than Jesus Himself. As we have already seen, this notion is a perverted interpretation of the Faith message. Not one of these ministers would dare say that they are *exact* equals with the Almighty.

Hanegraaff contests Copeland's statement that Adam and Jesus were alike:

> "...If you stood Adam upside God, they look just exactly alike. If you stood Jesus and Adam side-by-side, they would look and sound exactly alike."[2]

Unfortunately, I must admit that this quotation appears to say that Adam and God Almighty (*the Father*) look exactly alike *in a physical sense*. However, despite the choice of words that Copeland used, it is extremely doubtful that he was literally referring, to **the Father**. *Jesus is God too—Is He not?* Therefore, it is easy to see how Copeland said "God", but he probably meant "Jesus." *As human beings*, Adam and Jesus were spiritually alike except that Jesus knew the difference between good and evil by observation and Adam did not until after he learned by experience. Copeland may have used the wrong choice of words, but that does not make his words *heretical*. Copeland addressed this issue briefly in a convention he held in 1995:

> "...He [Jesus] paid the penalty as if He had opened the door for the devil and gave Him this whole thing. That's the reason He's called **the last Adam**. That's the reason He preached 'I am the Son of Man'...in Hebrew, 'I am Ben Adam.' I am Adam come again. Not reincarnation, **but in the same role.** *Before* Adam sinned."[3]

Copeland is attempting to illustrate the fact that Jesus came to earth <u>in the same role as the first Adam,</u> and did what Adam foolishly did not do. I do not believe that he meant that they looked alike *physically*. Rather, they looked exactly alike *spiritually* **meaning** they both had God's glory, character, and way of being; not that they **both** were "God" or deity. Before Adam sinned, he had the character/nature of God working in him, just like Jesus. Some may not like his wording; nevertheless, Copeland's statement is still not heretical.

Hanegraaff continues by mocking a prophecy that Copeland gave, in which he claims Copeland said that Jesus *was not* God: "…But I didn't claim I was God; I just claimed I walked with Him and that He was in Me…."[4]

Is this word from the Lord so strange? Did Jesus run around announcing that He was *God Almighty*, as Hanegraaff would lead one to believe? Was Copeland attempting to deny the deity of Christ, as Hanegraaff has portrayed? Please continue reading and judge for yourself!

"**Q**: Brother Copeland, some time ago I read an article in your magazine in which you said Jesus didn't claim He *was* God, but rather claimed He walked with God and that God was in Him. I'm confused. Does that mean you question the deity of Jesus?

A: **ABSOLUTELY NOT!** The deity of the Lord Jesus Christ is something that can **never be questioned** by any born-again believer.—The phrasing of the statement you referred to is very important. I didn't say Jesus *wasn't* God, I said He didn't *claim* to be God when He lived on the earth. — During His earthly ministry, Jesus acknowledged that he was the Son of God, **the Messiah**. He referred to God as His Father, but He **never** said He *was* the most High God.— Because He didn't come to earth as God, He'd come as man. He'd set aside His divine power [attributes] and taken on the form of a human being—*with all it limitations.*—They [many people] don't realize that when Jesus came to earth, He voluntarily gave up that advantage [divine power, attributes], living His life here not as God **but as a man**. He had no innate supernatural powers. He had no ability to perform miracles until after He was anointed by the Holy Spirit (see Luke 3:22). He worked wonders, not by His own power, but by the power of the Father…."[5]

Because of Hanegraaff's traditional religious background, he seems to think that the term "Son of God" means that Jesus was *openly* acknowledging, "I am God!" I guess since the Church is called *the sons and daughters of God*, that makes us God *too*? Jesus *repeatedly* said, "My Father is greater than I." So, if Jesus walked this earth as "Almighty God", then how could His Father be greater? Was Jesus living on earth in complete equality with His Father, *as* He was before His incarnation? **No**, Jesus came in submission to the will of the Father, rather than in *almighty splendor* and *unlimited power*. *The Amplified Bible* makes this point **embarrassingly** clear.

> **Philippians 2:6, 7 (TAB)**: Who [Jesus], although being essentially one with God *and* in the form of God [*possessing the fullness of the attributes which make God God*], **did not** think this equality with God was a thing to be eagerly grasped *or* retained, But **stripped Himself** [of **all** privileges and rightful dignity], so as to assume the guise of a servant (slave), in that He became like men *and* was born a human being.

These verses show the actuality of what happened to Jesus when He was incarnated. It shows how He voluntarily stripped Himself of *all* privilege and dignity to become a human. He came here as the Last Adam with a mission to destroy the works of the enemy. Also, these verses completely support all that Copeland has said about Jesus— prophetically and otherwise. If Hanegraaff would have simply done more intensive research, he then could have come to the same conclusion as Copeland, the Lockman Foundation and the Zondervan Corporation. When Jesus said, "I am the Son of God," He was acknowledging His *Messianic* role—the Christ: "the Anointed One of God."[6] He wasn't confessing deity—consider John 10:30-35 in its context. God *literally* was His Father, spiritually **and** physically. It would be *a lie* to say He wasn't!

Copeland gives another insightful comment on Jesus' living as a man:

> "Why are they [believers] so offended when a man or woman of God says or behaves as though they're anointed? After all, Jesus did it and He's our pattern. 'Well, that's entirely different. Jesus is the divine Son of God!' Yes, He is. *But, He didn't* **operate** *as the Son of God when He ministered on the earth.* **He 'made himself of no reputation, and took upon him the form of a servant**, and was made in the likeness of men' (Philippians 2:7). That's why He called Himself the Son of man. He laid aside His divine privileges

and ministered as a prophet under the old covenant. *He was completely dependent upon the anointing.* His flesh and blood body couldn't heal anyone any more than your flesh and blood body can. He had to have the anointing of God!"[7]

Moreover, Kenneth Hagin makes a vitally important statement in terms of understanding how Jesus was still "God", but yet He lived on earth as a man.

"...Jesus was anointed by God to minister. He didn't minister as the Son of God; He ministered as a man anointed of God. In other words, Jesus needed to be *anointed* to minister...We can see certain truths from this passage of Scripture in Luke 4 (v.18). One thing we can see is that if Jesus was ministering just as the Son of God —**as God manifested in the flesh** — He wouldn't need to be anointed. If Jesus was ministering as God manifested in the flesh, would God need to be anointed? **I mean who's going to anoint God!**...Even though He was the Son of God, He became as a man. In other words, Jesus laid aside His mighty power and glory when He came to the earth. <u>How did He do it? I don't know.</u> The Bible plainly said He did it, so I just believe it."[8]

The point that Hagin is making in this quote *should be* clear. If Jesus walked this earth **in the fullness** of His glory, and Deity, as He had before He came to earth, then why would He need to be Anointed by God; since He would have been already walking in the fullness of God on this earth. No, He lived His life as a man Anointed of the Holy Spirit, the same way that every believer must also do. In addition, the term "*Son of God*" is used 47 times[9] in the New Covenant, but only about 27 times in the Gospels. On the other hand, Jesus referred to Himself as "*the Son of Man*" around 83 times out of the total 88 times[10] in which this term is used. Thus, it is obvious which term Jesus openly promoted. Furthermore, Jesus told His disciples not to tell anyone that He was the Christ—the Anointed One of God!

Matthew 16:20 (TAB): Then He **sternly** *and* **strictly** charged *and* **warned** the disciples to tell no one that He was *Jesus* the Christ.

So, if Jesus wanted to promote His Messianic role, why didn't He want His disciples to make Him known to the people? It was because in the minds of most Jews at the time thought the Christ was to be a Warrior King. However, Jesus' Kingdom was not of this earth, but in the hearts of men instead. The term "Christ" does not denote *deity*. If

"Christ" really meant "deity", then all believers would be little deities. I say this because all believers are Anointed or *Christ-ended* by God. God the Father promised to send a deliverer to free His people. But, nowhere in the Bible did God **ever** promise to send Himself as that deliverer of the nations from Sin. Jesus *never*, at any time, openly said, "*I Am Almighty God!*"

Hanegraaff *emphatically* opposes the notion that Jesus did not openly proclaim His preexistent deity while on earth:

"If Copeland's followers would follow his suggestion to search the Gospels, they would discover how wrong he really is. To begin, consider the Gospel of John. In John 10:30 Jesus says, 'I and the Father are one.' Modern readers might misunderstand the significance of His statement, but the ancient Jews most certainly did not."[11]

Despite Hanegraaff's education in *theology*, it is amazing how little he really comprehends. He claims the Jews certainly understood Jesus' words to be a confession of equality with God. **If this is so, then why did Jesus contradict both Hanegraaff and the ancient Jews?**

John 10:32-35 (TAB): "…For which of these [works] do you mean to stone Me? The Jews replied, We are not going to stone You for a good act, but for blasphemy, because You, a mere Man, make Yourself [out to be] God. Jesus answered, Is it not written in your Law, I said, You are gods? [Ps. 82:6] So men are called gods [by the Law], men to whom God's message came—and the Scripture cannot be set aside *or* cancelled *or* broken *or* annulled."

Jesus' words totally refuted the notion of Him proclaiming that He is Almighty God. He says, "**men** are called gods," in Psalm. 82:6, but that does not make them Deity. If these Jews were so "wise" in the Scriptures, why did Jesus call them the blind leading the blind, and fools? In reality, these Jews actually believed the same religious tradition that theologians attempt to promote today. That tradition did not "wash" in Jesus' day and they still will not today!

Jesus came to this earth as a man, although He truly was God. He limited Himself voluntarily to become a human. He came to do what Adam failed to do. If Jesus came as "God" and lived on earth sinless "*as God,*" then it would be **unjust** of Him to tell us to live like He lived. Why? I say this because we are not "God." If Jesus walked this earth as

God, then it would be impossible for us to "be holy even as He is holy." We could not possibly life holy as He did because we are human. God would **never** require us to do something that we **could not possibly do**. Jesus is our example of how a human, Anointed by the Holy Spirit, can live a totally victorious life on this earth.

Now look back at John 10:30. When Jesus said, "I and My Father are One," He was merely saying that they *were* One! *How were Jesus and God One?* They were One in mind, One in purpose, and One in nature. What is God's divine nature? **Righteousness**! Jesus was in complete unity with His Father. However, He still had to learn and grow. He did not come knowing all there was to know about everything. His knowledge was much higher than our knowledge because He never sinned, but that does not mean He came here as "Mr. Brain."

The Bible clearly says Jesus learned and grew in favor with God and man. The **only** advantage Jesus had over us, as a Man was that He was sinless (born without sin). However, Jesus took care of that disadvantage by re-creating the spirit man in us at conversion. So, in God's eyes He sees us as sinless because we are in Christ and He is in us.

Before Abraham Was Born—I AM

John 8:56-58 (NKJV): "'Your father Abraham rejoiced to see My day, and he saw *it* and was glad'...'before Abraham was, I AM.'"

When only reading this verse of Scripture it would appear that Jesus was speaking of Himself when He said, "I AM." However, one must examine this verse in its context. Notice verse 54 & 55 in John chapter eight:

(The Amplified Bible): Jesus answered, **If** I were to *glorify* Myself (magnify, praise, and honor Myself), *I would have no real glory*, for My glory would be nothing and worthless. [My honor must come to Me from My Father.] It is My Father Who glorifies Me [Who extols Me, magnifies, and praises Me], of Whom you say that He is your God. Yet **you do not know Him** or recognize Him and are not acquainted with Him, **but I know Him**...."

When the Jews asked Jesus how he could have seen Abraham, He responded "I AM." To the traditionally minded, this seems as if Jesus was referring to Himself. But, John 8:54, 55 proves this to be false. Jesus said, *"If I glorify Myself...My glory is* **nothing**." So who was Jesus glorifying when He said, "I AM?" He was glorifying His Father Who was in Him, **Whom He knew**. God Father knew Abraham and showed Him how Abraham was happy to see His day.

Plus, Jesus could read about Abraham's joy in the Scriptures (Genesis 12:1-3). Jesus said the Jews did not know His Father, but that He knew Him. Since He knew Him, He could also know how Abraham was excited to see the day of the Messiah, the Christ, the Anointed One. Jesus **never** glorified Himself. Therefore, He could not have been referring to Himself when He said, "I AM." This proclamation was an acknowledgment of His close, personal relationship with His Father—the Great I AM!

Again, as usual, the Jews only heard *what they wanted to hear*. They heard His words as *self-exaltation*—as arrogance. But, Jesus clearly said, "I *don't* glorify Myself. I glorify My Father Who sent Me." Now this is not to say that Jesus was not God, but that He did not come here to exalt *Himself*, but to **promote** His Father's work.

Furthermore, the **emphasis** of Jesus' words, in the before mentioned passage, were not focused upon Himself, but rather upon His Father, thereby giving Him *all* the glory! Likewise, the Holy Spirit *is God*, but He did not come to promote or glorify Himself. The Holy Spirit came to glorify Jesus. Jesus came here to glorify the Father, Who was within Him! Remember, we cannot isolate *one* verse of Scripture and build a doctrine. We must examine it in its proper context. Glorification of self is exactly what the Jews saw when Jesus said, "I AM." Sad to say, this too is what Hanegraaff seems only to see.

Hanegraaff further contends with Benny Hinn for saying that Jesus *would have* sinned without the Spirit's help.

> "And let me add this: Had the Holy Spirit not been with Jesus, He would have sinned...it was the Holy Spirit that was the power that kept Him pure."[12]

Hanegraaff also implies that Hinn is ignorant of the fact that Jesus said, he was the Son of Man; hence, claiming his deity—Divine Messiah.[13] On the contrary, when He called Himself *the Son of Man*, He was actually referring to His humanity, **not** His deity. He was actually referring to Himself as being the Last Adam the One Who would defeat Satan in Adam's (humanity's) place.

Now, was Hinn heretical when He said Jesus *would* have sinned? Doubtful! I, personally, would not go as far as to say that Jesus *would* have sinned, but rather that He **could** have sinned if He hadn't had the Holy Spirit's help to keep Him pure. Jesus was born without Sin. *He had no desire for Sin.* **But**, on the other hand, so was Adam, and yet he sinned. I believe that it is safe to say that Jesus was *dependent* upon the Holy Spirit to stay pure. However, it is *difficult* to speculate on whether or not He **would** have actually sinned apart from the Holy Spirit's help.

Hanegraaff might argue that Jesus *could not* have sinned because He was deity. Such reasoning is shear ignorance. If Jesus did not have the capacity to sin, then why did the Holy Spirit lead Him into the desert to be tempted by the devil (Luke 4:1, 2). If it were impossible for Jesus to be tempted, hence sin, then there would have been absolutely no reason for Him to be led into the wilderness in the first place. You cannot tempt someone to do something that they're *incapable* of doing! This is a perfect display of the ignorance of traditional religion at work. It does not add up, therefore, it must have been birthed in traditional religious ignorance (Hosea 4:6).

In The Image of Jesus

Hanegraaff criticizes Charles Capps for saying that God purposed to make millions and millions of people exactly like Jesus;[14] in what He calls "A billion incarnations of God."[15] However, what was Capps actually saying?

> "Jesus was called *the firstborn* **among many brethren**. In other words, there isn't going to be one born from spiritual death to life, but *many* born just as He was!…He became *the firstborn* **among many brethren!** In other words, there are going to be millions and millions of them exactly like **Jesus!**"[16]

Mr. Hanegraaff's objection to Capps' above statement is very absurd. Capps is not insinuating that we are little **exact** replications of God Almighty. He is merely pointing out that Jesus was the Firstborn among **many** brethren. Since Jesus was born out of Spiritual Death, so were we.

Therefore, we are to live our lives in the same Spirit and power that Jesus did. Jesus Himself said we are to do greater works that He. How are we to live and act exactly as Jesus did? We must live holy, as well as go into the world to preach the Gospel—with signs and wonders following the Word of God as we preach. It is obvious that Capps *isn't* claiming that God desired to create millions of *sovereign* beings. He was merely communicating that God's desire was to create a nation that lives by Jesus Christ's example!

The Word Became Flesh!

Hanegraaff continues with his illogical reasoning against Capps, by opposing the idea that Mary was impregnated by nothing more than the Word of God.[17] I'm not sure why Hanegraaff objects so much to Capps' statement on how Mary was impregnated. According to the concordance, Jesus is the Word of God (the Logos) made flesh.[18] The Word of God was the Seed deposited into Mary's heart, and when the time came for the miracle implantation, the Holy Spirit Super-naturally deposited the Word of God into her womb.

Had Mary not received, the Word of the Lord from the angel into her heart, she would not have been able to be God's chosen virgin. Why? This would be due to a lack of faith. But, of course, God knew *in advance* that she would receive His word and open herself to His work. Again, Hanegraaff is splitting spiritual hairs! It seems obvious that he does not have much important work to do. Consequently, he occupies his time by recording videos 24 hours a day from TBN so that he can find any small point to protest.

As usual, Hanegraaff's charges of heresy fall flat when one **simply** looks below the superficial exterior of his over exaggerated claim that the Faith teachers are purposely eroding the foundation of "orthodox" Christianity. In reality, the only thing being eroded is *Hanegraaff's* interpretation of "orthodox Christianity."

This is frightening him half to death I might add! Hence, this is the *primary reason* why he is so vehemently opposed to the Faith teachers and their message. Still, heresy exists purely in the mind of Hanegraaff and those who embrace his systematic theological interpretation of *supposed* "orthodox" Christianity.

Jesus: *The Christ*

Briefly, I would like to address the question: "Did Jesus *openly* promote Himself as **the Christ**"? Again, Hanegraaff would say, "Without a doubt, Yes!" However, we are not interested in the opinions of men. We are interested in what the Word of God actually says happened.

Mark 4:33, 34 (NKJV): "And with **many** such parables He spoke the word to them as they were able to hear it. But *without a parable* He **did not speak** to them...."

Matthew 16:16, 20: "And Simon Peter answered and said, *Thou art the Christ*, the Son of the living God...**Then charged he his disciples that they should tell *no* man that he was Jesus the Christ**."

Matthew 26:63, 64: "But Jesus held his peace. And the high priest answered and said unto him**, *I adjure thee by the living God, that thou tell us whether thou be the Christ, the Son of God*.** Jesus saith unto him, Thou has said...."

Luke 4:41: And devils also came out of many, crying out, and saying, **Thou art Christ the Son of God**. *And he rebuking them suffered them not to speak:* **for they knew that he was Christ.**

John 10:24: Then came the Jews round about him, and said unto him, *How long dost thou make us to doubt? If thou be the Christ, tell us plainly.*

We now need to examine the previous verses of Scripture. In the book of Mark chapter four verses 33, 34, we're plainly told that Jesus **never** taught **publicly** without using a parable (a metaphorical story). He did this so that the people could hear the message of the Kingdom of God without Him plainly and openly explaining it. Many did not understand—including Jesus' own staff. However, in many cases He would **privately** elaborate upon the parables so that His staff members would be able to grasp the message of the Kingdom. We who read the Bible can see *all* that Jesus said publicly and privately, but often times we forget that He only expounded on His parables to His disciples. Therefore, many times we mistakenly assume that the thronging crowds openly knew His private teachings. This was not the case.

In addition, we find Jesus warning His disciples *not* to tell anyone that He was the Christ, the Anointed One, in Matthew 16:16, and 20. Also, in Luke 4:41, Jesus rebuked a spirit for exposing Who He truly was—*the Christ!* If Jesus really sought open publicity of Himself as being *the Christ*, why did he warn his disciples and rebuke the spirit? Without question, Jesus **did not** *privately* deny that He was the Christ, the Anointed One of God, but He also did not want this knowledge published openly until after His resurrection from the dead. As I said earlier, this was because the Jews were seeking a Warrior King, and He did not want any part of their religious kingdom.

Please understand that the title, "the Christ", *literally* means "the Anointed One of God" or One sent, not Almighty God. Many Christians ignorantly over look this fact, and suppose that Jesus' title, "the Christ", actually implied His pre-incarnate state of being. However, according to a Greek concordance, this *is not* the case. Moreover, the Bible reveals in Matthew 26:63, and 64 and John 10:24 that up until that point Jesus hand *never* plainly told the multitudes that He, in fact, was their promised Messiah. This is why in John 10:24 they said, "If You are the Christ, tell us plainly." Obviously, prior to this encounter, Jesus had not told them plainly who He really was?

So did Jesus ever plainly reveal His true identity? In other words, did Jesus ever publicly admit to being *the Christ*—the Anointed One of God?

Mark 14:61, 62: "But he held his peace, and answered nothing. Again the high priest asked him, and said unto him, **Art thou the Christ, the Son of the Blessed?** And Jesus said, I am...."

Jesus finally let the cat out of the bag, so to speak. I believe the *only* reason that He did so was because He *knew* that they would not crucify Him otherwise. They considered His words blasphemous and worthy of death. Yes, Jesus did publicly admit to being the promised **Messiah** not *God*. But He did not do so until He was forced to give His accusers a "reason" to kill Him. Why? Because He was not a show-off, **lusting** to "prove" Who He really was. His miracles were *to destroy the works of the devil*, **not** to show off His mighty Anointing and Deity, as some have assumed.

Kenneth E. Hagin illustrates this fact with *unquestionable* evidence:

"Many of us have been taught that the only reason Jesus healed was to prove His deity. **If that be the case, He didn't prove His deity in the city of Nazareth**, for He never did the works there that He had done elsewhere [Mark 6:5]...The Amplified New Testament says, 'He laid His hands on a few sickly people.'...**W.E. Vine's Expository Dictionary of New Testament Words** also brings out the fact that the Greek reads, 'He laid His hands on a few folk with minor ailments and healed them.' Jesus

did not heal people merely to prove His deity. He was not ministering **as** the Son of God. He was ministering as a prophet of
God, anointed with the Spirit…Their unbelief hindered Him."[19]

Please note that Mark 6:5 does not say what most religious people attempt to make it say. It literally says, "And **He was *not able* to do**
even one work of power there, except that He laid His hands on a few
sickly people [and] cured them" (*The Amplified Bible*). If Jesus walked this
earth as Almighty God, possessing all the majestic qualities of His Father,
then their unbelief *should not* have stopped Him from doing many powerful works, seeing that God is sovereign. *Such a verse puts a wrench into the
doctrinal teachings of those that constantly harp upon the sovereignty of God.*

Many theologians have implied that Jesus simply *refused* to do any
mighty works, but that is *not* what the Word of God clearly states. Jesus
the Christ **was not able** to do any mighty works there because of their
unbelief. Unbelief ***always*** hinders the work of God in those who refuse
to believe. Faith always works *in the absence* of unbelief.

9
SPIRITUAL DEATH AND THE CROSS

For some time, I have been hearing the various *heresy hunters* complaining about the Word of Faith's teaching concerning Spiritual Death. I was unable to get my hands on much information regarding this subject. So being the curious person that I am, I resolved to do some research on Spiritual Death for my own knowledge. This extensive, detailed chapter is the result of my research. I suggest that the reader set aside time to *thoroughly* research it for one's self and ask God for His Wisdom and revelation.

Thou Shalt *Surely* Die

Genesis 2:15-17: And the LORD God took the man, and put him into the garden of Eden to dress it and to keep it. And the LORD God commanded the man, saying, Of every tree of the garden thou mayest freely eat: But of the tree of the knowledge of good and evil, thou shalt not eat of it: **for in the day** *that thou eatest thereof* **thou shalt surely die**.

Does God ever waste words or make *idle* threats? Of course the answer is without a doubt, no! God told man that **in the day** that he ate of the tree he would die; however, Adam lived a total of 930 years. If God truly meant what He said, then why didn't Adam die on the day that he ate of the tree of knowledge? Did God make an *idle threat*, or did Adam actually *die* just as God warned him that he would?

God's prophetic Word came to pass just as He said, and Adam **literally** died. However, the death that he experienced had little to do with the death of his physical body. At the *exact* moment of his disobedience, man partook of *Spiritual Death*. A death took place in man but it was in the realm of his spirit. Man had spiritually disconnected from God. He was, therefore, unable to receive revelation from God.

What Is Spiritual Death?

Romans 6:23: "For *the wages of sin* **is death**...."

The above verse explains Spiritual Death perfectly. The wages (price paid) for Sin is [Spiritual] Death. **Spiritual Death** is the wages, reward, or the result of a life of sinning, which is *ultimately* eternal separation from the Presence of the Living God. The very day that man ate of the fruit, he experienced spiritual separation from his Father.

> **Genesis 3:9, 10 (TAB)**: But the Lord God called to Adam and said to him, Where are you? He said, I heard the sound of You [walking] in the garden, and *I was afraid* because I was naked; and I hid myself.

Fear of God was the immediate result of Adam experiencing Spiritual Death. Those who are Spiritually Dead have a "built-in" *fear of God.* They do not have a respectful fear of God, but rather a frightful fear that He will punish them because their guilty (sinful) heart condemns them. Before sin entered the earth Adam & Eve had never experience fear.

Jesus Was Our *Substitute Sacrifice*

> **Matthew 27:46**: And about the ninth hour Jesus cried with a loud voice, saying, Eli, Eli, lama sabachthani? that is to say, My God, my God, **why hast thou forsaken me.**

Why did Jesus cry out to God concerning His being forsaken? According to the concordance, *forsake* denotes: "to leave behind in some place, **to abandon:--forsake,** *leave,* reserve; to leave down, behind, by impl. To abandon, forsake; leave...."[1] Why would God the Father abandon, forsake or leave His *faithful* Son? We will answer this question gradually as we continue through this chapter. We have lot of background information to address in order for the biblical perspective to come into light. We need whole Bible context.

> **Psalms 22:1-11**: *My God, my God, why hast thou forsaken me?* **why art thou so far from helping me, and from the words of my roaring?** O my God, I cry in the daytime, **but thou hearest not**; and in the night season, and am not silent. *But thou art holy,* O thou that inhabitest the praises of Israel. Our fathers trusted in thee: they trusted, and thou didst deliver them. They cried unto thee, and were delivered: they trusted in thee, and were not confounded. *But I am a worm, and no man; a reproach of men, and despised of the people.* All they that see me laugh me to scorn: they shoot out the lip, they shake the head, saying, He trusted on the LORD that he

would deliver him: let him deliver him, seeing he delighted in him. *But thou art he that took me out of the womb: thou didst make me hope when I was upon my mother's breasts.* I was cast upon thee from the womb: thou art my God from my mother's belly. *Be not far from me;* **for trouble is near;** *for there is* **none to help.**

According to *The Amplified Bible Expanded Edition*, Psalm 22 is called "The Psalm of the cross."[2] It is *theoretically possible* that Jesus quoted this very Psalm while He was nailed to the cross.[3] Also, this Psalm is prophetic of the many things that Jesus suffered (sacrificially) in our place, from before the cross to His resurrection.

Hank Hanegraaff has troubled the Word of Faith preachers, especially Kenneth Copeland, for saying that Jesus was a "worm." However, Jesus plainly stated this in Psalm 22:6. Nonetheless, again note that this Psalm is a prophetic picture of the many things that Jesus would have to suffer in our place. Thus, Jesus confessed, "I am a *worm* and no man...."

The word *worm* denotes "a crimson color,"[4] or a blood red color. Seeing that Jesus shed His *precious* blood on our behalf, it is easy to understand why He said He was a "worm." And if Jesus said it was so, then it was so. It is impossible for God to ever lie.

What Trouble Is Near?

Psalm 22:11: Be not far from me; **for trouble is near;** *there is none to help.*

Could there possibly be anything more troubling than the cross of Calvary? Was Jesus speaking of something far more shameful and terrible than even the cross?

I believe that Jesus was referring to the three days and nights that He would spend *captive by man's Spiritual Death* in the belly of the earth.

K. R. "Dick" Iverson has also given us an insightful commentary on Psalm 22 in *The Spirit Filled Life Bible*:

"My God, My God: while on the cross, the tortured Jesus cried out those words (Matt. 27:46; Mk. 15:34). Hell is **total separation** from God as a **punishment** *for unrepented sin,* **a state of being** *forsaken*. Jesus went through this hell experience *in our place* for our sins, so we will not have to."[5]

Iverson believes Psalm 22 as a proclamation of Jesus' experiencing *total separation* from His Father, **on the behalf** of His creation. He also notes that this separation did not only take place while He was on the cross, but rather *also* while He endured our punishment in hell itself. He paid the *complete* price, not just half of it!

Chastisement & *Substitute* Suffering

Isaiah 53:5-9: But he *was* wounded for our transgressions, *he was* bruised for our iniquities: **the chastisement** of our peace *was* upon him; and with his stripes we are healed. All we like sheep have gone astray; we have turned every one to his own way; and the LORD hath laid **on him** *the iniquity of us all*. He was *oppressed*, and he was *afflicted*, yet he opened not his mouth: he is brought as a lamb to the slaughter, and as a sheep before her shearers is dumb, so he openeth not his mouth. He was *taken from prison and from judgment*: and who shall declare his generation? for **he** *was cut off out of* **the land of the living**: *for the transgression of my people was he stricken*. And he made his grave with the wicked, and with the rich *in his death*; because he had done no violence, neither *was any* deceit in his mouth.

The time has come for us to examine Isaiah 53 in the light of what the Bible actually says *instead of* by the doctrines of our traditional Sunday school lessons. It's time for the Body of Christ to stop fooling around with the *Substitute Sacrifice* of Jesus Christ. He paid an **awesome** price to redeem us from Sin, and we need to acknowledge the price He paid.

The later portion of Isaiah 53:5 tells us, "*the chastisement* of **our** peace was upon him....*" The concordance defines *chastisement* as: "to chastise, lit. (*with blows*) or fig. (**with words**); hence to instruct: **bind**, chasten, **correct**, **punish**, reform, **reprove**....*"[6] Jesus, therefore, received *our* punishment, correction, and reprisal for Sin. Still, how does the Bible define the punishment for Sin?

Ezekiel 18:4b: "...the soul that sinneth, it shall **die**." [Also: Gen. 2:17]

Romans 6:23a: "For the wages of sin is **death...**"

The Bible does not teach that the *complete price* for Sin is physical death, although that's part of it, rather it teaches that Spiritual Death (*separation from God's Presence*) **is** the **ultimate** price that one will have to pay for rejecting the Substitute Sacrifice of Jesus. Furthermore, Ezekiel 18:4 (in my Bible) gives a cross-reference to Romans 6:23 tying them both directly together. Jesus Christ paid this *complete* price of Sin—spirit, soul, as well as body.

Jesus took our chastisement [punishment] upon Himself so that we could have peace with God. That kind of peace can only come through a renewed relationship with our God. He was punished with our separation (Spiritual Death) so that we would never have to be punished/separated from God for Sin. This is why Romans 8:35 can *legally* say: "Who shall *separate us* from the love of Christ...?"

Imprisonment—Judgment & *Substitute* Suffering

Isaiah 53:8—emphasis added: "He was taken *from prison and from judgment*: and **who** shall declare his generation? [**Why?**] for he was cut off **out of** the land *of the living*: for [*because of*] my people was he stricken."

Most traditionally-minded Christians would argue that this verse of Scripture is merely talking of Jesus' imprisonment prior to His crucifixion. I can understand why they would say this, and I believe that this sort of reasoning is partially true. However, in order to receive the *full* revelation of what this is saying, we must read the whole verse.

Isaiah asks "Who shall declare his generation?" The question we must now ask ourselves is: "Why did Isaiah ask who will declare his generation—(with the implied) *for Him?*" If we were to read the next sentence, then we'd find out the answer. He asked this question **because** Jesus was "cut off **out of** the land of the living." In other words, He was in the land of the Dead (departed spirits), otherwise known as Hades.

Furthermore, I believe that Jesus "began" to be *cut off out of* [from] the land of the living while He hung on that cross (spiritually speaking). He was made to be Sin **after** He had made Atonement for man's Sin.

Moreover, why was Jesus cut off out of the land of the living? The next sentence tells us, "for [or because of] my people was he stricken." Jesus was cut off out of the land of the living (Spiritual Death) because He became Sin, and our Sin **caused** Him to be separated from His father (**after** *He made Atonement*). Believers understand that Sin **always** causes separation from God's Presence. *It's Spiritual Law!*

Seeing that Sin puts into motion *the Law of Spiritual Separation*, and God's Laws work the same way **no matter who** is affected by them, then why would our Sin affect Jesus any differently than it does us? Some would say, "*Jesus was God; therefore, Sin couldn't possibly affect Him like it does us.*" **Correction**—Jesus was **fully** man *as well as* God, but He voluntarily *limited* Himself so that He could be a man. Jesus (the Man) had the same limitations that we had. The only advantage that He had over us was the fact that He had never sinned, but He took care of *our disadvantage* by paying the complete price for Sin.

As we have seen, Jesus was taken from prison and from judgment. But, what does the Bible mean by prison and judgment? The concordance defines prison and judgment as:

"[Prison] to inclose; by anal. to hold back; also to maintain, rule, *close up*, **detain**, *fast, keep* (*self close*, still), **prevail**, *refrain*, **reign**, **restrain**, *retain*, shut (up), slack, stay, stop, *withhold* (self)."[7]

"[Judgment] *a sentence or* **formal** *decree* (human or [partic.] **divine law**, individual or collect.), the act the place, the suit, *the crime*, **and the penalty,** to be judged."[8]

Jesus was imprisoned [in closed, detained, kept; restrained by the devil] in hell because of our Sin, the same as we would have been *had we gone* to hell for our Sin. Jesus received the divine sentence and penalty of Death (separation without God) in our place, because we could never possibly pay the *complete price* for our rebellion. Jesus paid our debt in His spirit, soul and His body.

Perhaps you're thinking "Fine, but show me some more Scripture to prove that Jesus was imprisoned for me!"

Acts 2:27, 31; 24 emphasis added: Because thou wilt not leave *my* [Jesus'] *soul in hell*, neither wilt thou suffer thine Holy One to see corruption. He [David] seeing this before *spake of the resurrection of Christ*, that *his soul was not left in hell*, neither his flesh did see corruption. Whom God hath *raised up*, having **loosed the pains of death**: because it *was not possible* that he should be holden of it.

David the Psalmist spoke prophetically of Jesus' resurrection, stating that God would not leave His soul in hell [Sheol or Hades].[9] We could get into a lengthy debate concerning the terminology used here to describe hell, but *perhaps* we can take this up at a later date. David *could not* have been referring to Abraham's bosom, **because** there was *no pain or punishment* where Abraham dwelt. **No!** Whether we want to face the truth or not, David *was* talking about **the pit** itself.

The Bible goes on to say that Jesus was loosed from the pains [*birth throws, sorrow, travail*] of Death.[10] It is impossible for me to have a baby, but from my own limited experience with birth, I can *see* that the throws of birth are not very pleasant. Why?

It's because they are extremely painful. Jesus (at His resurrection) was released from the spiritual birth throws that are beyond man's ability to communicate or understand. And He voluntarily did all of this for us! A majority of traditionally-minded believers would aggressively argue against this point; nevertheless, they have nothing scripturally to prove their disagreement to the contrary.

God Was Pleased—*Substitute* Suffering

Isaiah 53:10-12: Yet *it pleased the LORD* to bruise him; he hath put him to grief: when thou shalt **make his soul an offering for sin**, he shall **see his seed**, he shall *prolong his days*, and the pleasure of the LORD shall prosper in his hand. He shall *see of the* **travail of his soul**, *and shall be satisfied*: by his knowledge *shall my righteous servant* **justify** *many*; for he shall **bear their iniquities**. Therefore will I divide him a portion with the great, and he shall divide the spoil with the strong; *because he hath* **poured out his soul unto death**: and he was *numbered* **with** *the transgressors*; and *he bare the sin of many*, and made intercession for the transgressors.

Was Jesus offered by God *only* in a physical sense? Isn't man a three part being—*spirit, soul & body* (1 Thess. 5:23)? Therefore, the real man *is not* what we see (the body), but the spirit which is merely housed by that body of flesh. Thus, for Jesus to be *completely* offered by God, wouldn't He have had to be offered in spirit **and** soul *and* body? In order for Jesus to redeem the *complete* man from Sin's control, He would have had to been offered up completely—spirit, soul, as well as body. We must remember that Sin is not a physical aliment. Sin is an aliment of the spirit and soul.

The Bible says that God made Jesus' *soul* an offering for Sin. Did God mean His soul (mind, will & emotions) *only*, or did this offering go even further? In the Old Testament *soul* is defined as:

"[*Nepes*] soul; self; person; heart…The inner person is *nepes*, while the outer person, or reputation, is *sem*…."[11]

Consequently, the Bible dictionary denotes *Nepes* as both soul **and** spirit. It's because the center (heart) of every human being is the spirit. And the Word of God many times refers to the inner person (man) as *the spirit of man*.

In addition, the **only** "thing" that is capable of dividing (separating) the difference between soul and spirit is the Word of God because they are an **inseparable unit**. Only God and His Word can separate them. The prophet Isaiah goes on to tell us that once God had made an offering of Jesus' soul (and spirit) God the Father saw the *travail* [labour, pain, sorrow, trouble][12] of His soul and then He was *satisfied* [to have enough, fill, be weary of].[13]

Moreover, the Scripture clearly teaches that God *made* Jesus to be Sin, that we might be *made* the Righteousness of God in Christ. He *took* our Sin, and we *received* His Righteousness: "For he hath **made** *him to be* **sin** *for us*, who knew no sin; that we might be *made the righteousness of God in him*" (2 Corinthians 5:21).

The Bible dictionary defines *made* as "to become."[14] Thus, God caused Jesus to become Sin with our Sin so that we could become righteous with His Righteousness. You might be thinking, *"How could a sinless man become Sin?"* A sinless man could become Sin if he voluntarily accepted the Sin of the whole human race [*and its punishment*] upon Himself. In like manner, this was precisely what Jesus Christ agreed to do with the Father.

His Sorrow Was Unto *Death*

Matthew 26:38: Then saith he unto them, My soul is exceeding sorrowful, *even unto* **death**: tarry ye here, and watch with me.

Jesus, when He was in the Garden, said that He was under the pressure of such sorrow that it was about to kill Him. Jesus was experiencing extreme heaviness (oppression) or pressure by an attack of sorrow. Why was Jesus attacked with so much pressure from sorrow? It was because His heart was despising the very **thought** of being separated from His Father, especially for a group of people like us.

> **Hebrews 12:2:** "…who for the joy that was set before him **endured** [*stayed under a curse*] the cross [*exposure to death*], **despising** [*to think against*] the shame…."

> **Matthew 26:39:** And he went a little farther, and fell on his face, and prayed, saying, O my Father, *if it be possible*, let **this cup** *pass* from me: *nevertheless not as I will, but as thou wilt.*

Jesus put Himself under the cruse or allowed Himself to be exposed to Death—physical & Spiritual. He was resistant to the *thought* of going through this separation, yet He did it so that we could be joined once again to His Father.

As a result, the pressure of that sorrow was **literally** about to kill Him because He was struggling with His own will. It's obvious that if there had been another way to accomplish the Father's plan, Jesus would have taken it. But once He surrendered His (human) will, He received a peace that empowered Him to go through with God's *master plan of the ages*. When He surrendered His will to the Father, the pressure of sorrow was broken and peace ruled.

Jesus desired that the **cup** might pass from Him. What did He mean by this "cup?" *Cup* [poterion] is defined by the concordance as "a drinking vessel, the contents thereof; fig. a lot or fate."[15] If God's will for Jesus was **only** that He go into the protected place in hell (Abraham's bosom), then why was Jesus abhorring thought of drinking it? Was He *afraid* of the cross? *No way*! Jesus detested drinking that cup because He knew exactly what it represented—Spiritual Separation!

The very fact that Jesus would be nailed to a cross (tree) meant that He would be brought under a curse (the curse of the Law), because the people that He was to redeem were under the same curse. In order to redeem a cursed people He had to be cursed in our place.

> **Galatians 3:13-14:** Christ hath redeemed **us** *from the curse of the law*, being **made a curse for us**: for it is written, *Cursed is **every one** that hangeth on a tree*: That the blessing of Abraham might come on the Gentiles through Jesus Christ; that we might receive the promise of the Spirit through faith.

I can hear someone, even now, saying *"How could Jesus Christ, God's only Son, ever be cursed by Him?"* First of all, the Word of God states that every one who is hung on a tree is cursed. I didn't write Galatians chapter three verse fourteen; however, the One Who holds Supreme Authority did! Hence, **if God said it then it is so!**

It is time for the Body of Christ to stop believing what *they think* happened and believe what God Himself *actually said* happened.

Next, Jesus was brought under the dominion of a curse because God's creation was in bondage under a curse. He received our curse (*and its punishment*), so that we could be released from the curse of the Law, and be dominated by a New Law—*the Law of the Spirit of Life*. Moreover, in John. 19:30, *"received"* denotes the act of taking something,[16] and the sour wine (mixed with gall) represented **a curse**.

Was There *Virtue* In The Cross?

Many in the Body of Christ today speak of *the cross* of Christ as if *it* were almost some kind of "god." They sing songs about *it* nearly every Sunday. They speak concerning *it* as if *it* were **sacred**. However, is *the form* of death which our Lord experienced really worthy of all the religious hype that the crucifixion has received? They cling to the **"old rugged cross,"** more than they cling to *the Christ* of that cross. The cross represents a curse. We are to cling to Jesus!

Before you contemplate that I'm belittling what happened to Jesus at the cross of Calvary, please let me explain myself. Jesus paid an awesome price to reconcile us to God. *Nevertheless*, was there any virtue (purity, uprightness) in **the act of the crucifixion** *itself?* The best way that I know to answer this is by referring to a servant of God whom I love and respect deeply—Dr. Morris Cerullo:

> "There is no virtue in the cross. When Jesus Christ died on the cross, there was nothing virtuous *in that cross*. It was a piece of wood. The fact that He died on a cross was not virtuous; *there were thousands of people who died on crosses* in their day. Today, Jesus might have been hanged, put in a gas chamber, or electrocuted in the electric chair. Would we then **venerate** *the electric chair* by having it reproduced in gold charms to wear about our necks? The virtue was not in the cross, but **the virtue was in Jesus Christ** *Who died on the cross*. That was the thing *that was different* from the other deaths on crosses…the person!"[17]

This shocking thought was included in order to cause us to wake up and stop deifying the cross of Calvary. The *only* real significance that "the cross" (the *literal* form of dying) actually had is that God the Father prophetically spoke of it as being the way the Messiah would be Sacrificed. He could have said Jesus would be Sacrificed by having His throat slit so that He would shed His blood. Crucifixion merely happened to be the chief form of execution in Jesus' day. This is why God said He would be crucified.

Another thought simulating question. "Did Jesus *literally* offer the **physical** blood that He shed on Calvary *in heaven*?" When I ask this question, I mean, "Was the actual *physical* blood that poured out of His veins, and dried on His body as well as on the wood, offered in heaven?"

Jesus **did** indeed offer His blood to the Father while on the cross. However, His blood was also preserved and contained *in the realm of the Spirit*, so that He could offer it to His Father in heaven **after** He died, went into hell and was resurrected.

In other words, this took place *after* He was released (resurrected) from Hell. Jesus did not ascend to the throne of God until **after** He'd been resurrected (released) from hell.

Jesus Paid The Price To Redeem— The *Complete* Man!

"Death is always, in Scripture, viewed as *the penal consequences of sin*—it was as *the Bearer of sin* that the Lord Jesus submitted thereto on the Cross. And while the physical death of the Lord Jesus was of the essence of His sacrifice, *it was not the whole*—He was left alone in the Universe, **He was forsaken**...."[18]

The price for Sin's penalty *must always* be paid—which is Death (physical & Spiritual). Jesus paid *our complete penalty*, which was Death—in body, in soul & in spirit. Because, man is more than merely a physical body. He is a complete unit (*spirit, soul & body*). Therefore, Jesus was ordained by God to redeem man *in his totality*, with His own (human) spirit, soul & body.

Jesus received the penalty of *our* Sin (**Spiritual separation from God**), because He was the only Way to God. He was the **only** One qualified to pay the price (make compensation for), our complete penalty since He lived a **sinless life** here on earth, hereby, fulfilling the Law as a human being. He fulfilled the Law (as a man) *on our behalf.*

The *Precious* Blood Jesus

1 John 1:7: But if we walk in the light, as he is in the light, we have fellowship one with another, and *the blood of Jesus Christ* his Son *cleanseth us* from **all** sin.

Romans 3:25: "Whom God hath set forth to be a propitiation through faith *in his blood*, to declare *his* righteousness for the remission of sins that are past...."

Romans 5:9: Much more then, being now justified *by his blood*, we shall be saved from wrath through him.

Revelation 12:11: And they overcame him by **the blood of the Lamb**, and *by the word* of their testimony; and they loved not their lives unto the death.

Having read this chapter thus far, you may be wondering, *"Does he even believe in the saving power of the blood of Jesus?"* Absolutely, I would be a complete fool not too, especially when the Bible clearly states that our Redemption is through faith in the blood of Jesus. I personally "plead" the blood of Jesus over the life of my family and many others on a daily basis.

However, a part of what Jesus' blood has redeemed us from was the bondage and penalty of Sin (the curse of Sin). We were not *just* redeemed from a sinful lifestyle. We were redeemed from the bondage (control) and penalty of Adamic Sin *which was* eternal bondage, punishment and separation for Him in hell. That is what Sin's wages truly are! Jesus' shed blood made the way for Him to redeem us back to God by His (spirit, soul & body) sacrifice from bondage, punishment and separation. He did this by taking the curse, our curse, upon Himself. He submitted Himself to Death—*not just the death of His physical body*, otherwise He would never have died physically.

Why? Because the Scripture says that the soul *that sins* shall die. Jesus never sinned; thus, He *could not* have possibly died, *apart from* taking upon Himself the Adamic Sin and its penalty. His blood is the key factor in our Redemption, but without Him receiving *the wages* of our Sin, we could never be made the Righteousness of God. It is because our Righteousness is in and through His *Substitute Sacrifice*. If He did not receive our wages (separation), then the Father could in no way see us as righteous. The curse of Sin was much more than just our living a ungodly lifestyle—*we were* **Dead!**

What Happened At His Resurrection

Hebrews 1:1-9: God, who at sundry times and in divers manners spake in time past unto the fathers by the prophets, Hath in these last days spoken unto us by *his* Son, whom he hath appointed *heir of all things*, by whom also he made the worlds; Who being the brightness of *his* glory, and the express image of his person, and *upholding all things by the word of his power*, when he had **by himself** purged our sins, **sat down** on the right hand of the Majesty on high; Being made so much better than the angels, as he hath by inheritance obtained a more excellent name than they. For unto which of the angels said he at any time, Thou art my Son, **this day** *have I begotten thee*? **And again**, *I will be to him a Father*, and he shall be to me a Son? **And again**, when he bringeth in **the first begotten** *into the world*, he saith, And let *all the angels of God worship him*. And of the angels he saith, Who maketh his angels spirits, and his ministers a flame of fire. But unto the Son *he saith*, Thy throne, O God, *is* for ever and ever: a sceptre of righteousness *is* the sceptre of thy kingdom. *Thou hast loved righteousness, and hated iniquity*; **therefore** God, *even* thy God, hath anointed thee with the oil of gladness *above thy fellows*.

Please note the latter part of verse three where we read, "*...when he had* **by himself** *purged our sins....*" Here the writer of the book of Hebrews is saying that once Jesus had purged us (or the temple) *by His Substitute Sacrifice*, He sat down at God's right hand. *The Amplified Bible* says it this way: "*When He had by offering Himself accomplished our cleansing of sins* **and** *riddance of guilt....*" Exactly how did our Lord Jesus purge us "by Himself," or by "offering Himself" for our cleansing and riddance of guilt? He did it—**spirit, soul and body.** Jesus **unreservedly** said:

John 10:15b, 18a Emphasis Added: "*...I lay down my *life* [spirit] for the sheep...No man taketh *it* [My spirit] from me, but *I lay it* [My spirit] **down**...*"

Moreover, the Word of God also states in the book of James that without the spirit, the body will cease to live.

James 2:26 Emphasis Added: "For as the body without the *spirit* [life] is dead, so faith without works [*corresponding action*] is dead also...."

Thus, as a result, there is *no doubt* that when Jesus said, "*I lay down My life for My sheep*," He was referring to the surrendering of Himself (spirit, soul and body) for the Redemption of His sheep (the Church). Jesus did not just lay down His physical body—He laid down the life (spirit) of that physical body which was His human spirit. He gave Himself completely!

He's No Longer Called The *Only* Begotten

Hebrews 1:5, 6: "For unto which of the angels said he at any time, Thou art my son, **this day** have I *begotten thee*? **And again**, I will be to Him a Father, and he shall be to me a Son? **And again**, when he bringeth in **the first begotten** *into the world*...."

Romans 8:29: For whom he did foreknow, he also did predestinate to be conformed to the image of his Son, *that he might be the firstborn* **among** *many brethren.*

Colossians 1:15, 18: "Who is the image of the invisible God, *the firstborn of every creature*...And he is the **head** of the body, the church: *who is* **the beginning, the firstborn** *from the dead*; **that in all things** *he might have the preeminence.*"

Since the resurrection, Jesus Christ ceased to be referred to as the *only* begotten Son of God. T*he Amplified Bible* calls Him "the Firstbegotten or the Firstborn from [among] the dead." What does the Bible mean when it calls Him the Firstbegotten or Firstborn?

[Firstbegotten—Firstborn: a composite definition] "firstborn, first (of all) former...to produce seed, as a mother, a plant, *be born*, *bring forth*, **be delivered**, be in travail."[19]

Colossians chapter one verse eighteen states that Jesus is the firstborn **from** the dead, that *in all things* he might have preeminence. Again, *the Amplified Bible* says, "the Firstborn from **among** the dead." In what way is He the firstborn "from among" the dead? Jesus was the first man to ever be born permanently **out of** death physically, and *especially* Spiritually. He has preeminence in all things—does He not? The Word of God clearly tells us this in the passage above.

110

Therefore, He received what we received, *except* He received it all **first**. *What does all this mean?* It means that Jesus Christ was the first **man** to ever receive Spiritual Reconciliation with God the Father.

In other words, He was the first to be reborn Spiritually *from Death to Life*, or more commonly known as *the new birth*. Jesus had to be Spiritually reborn (**spiritually brought back into *fellowship* with God**) because He had voluntarily received the Sin of the human race—which separated Him.

When I say Jesus experienced *the new birth*, I mean He experienced a rebirth, a resurrection, or a **reconnection** with His Father in a spiritual sense. Jesus' human spirit experienced a rebirth from the bondage of our Sin to God's righteousness. His human spirit was **protected** by God from being *corrupted* (He never saw corruption) by the Sin of the human race while He was in hell.

Our Sin was wrapped around Jesus like paper wraps a present. His human spirit was protected inside that sin wrapping by the Father, so Sin could not control His nature—Righteousness. But He wasn't protected from the penalty (punishment) of Sin. The spirit of man had to be recreated because *it was* corrupted by Sin, but Jesus' spirit was not recreated because it *was* protected.

The New Birth Is *Spiritual Law*

John 3:3-6: "…Verily, verily, I say unto thee, *Except* **a man** *be born again*, he cannot see the kingdom of God…Verily, verily, I say unto thee, *Except a man be born of water and of the Spirit*, he cannot enter into the kingdom of God. That which is born of the flesh is flesh; and *that which is born of the Spirit* **is spirit.**"

Jesus told Nicodemus **every man** (indicating that this is Spiritual Law) must be born-again in order to see the Kingdom of God. Nicodemus could not comprehend this so he asked, "How can a man be born again when he is old…?"

I believe that when Jesus replied with "Except a man be *born of water* and of the Spirit," He was actually saying that a man must be first born of water (his mother), and then he must be born also of the Spirit. Some believe "of water" is referring to baptism, but that could not possibly be the case. Why? It would mean that no one could go to heaven *unless* they were baptized in water, but the Bible in no way supports this unreasonable notion.

Jesus clearly informed Nicodemus that **ALL** men, (including Jesus, Himself) had to receive the new birth, *from Death to Life* [from Sin to Righteousness]. How can I be so sure that He was including Himself? First, He said *every* man had to be born-again to see God's Kingdom. Next, He was as much man *as He was* God. Therefore, Jesus (*the Man*) was included in this statement. Jesus submitted Himself to every ordinance [Natural & Spiritual Law] of God and man. Our Sin caused Him to Die Spiritually.

Reconciliation Meant—The Suffering *of Death*

Hebrews 2:9-17: But we see Jesus, who was *made a little lower* than the angels *for the suffering of death*, crowned with glory and honour; that he *by the grace of God should* **taste death** *for every man.* For it became him, for whom *are* all things, and by whom *are* all things, in bringing many sons unto glory, to *make the captain of their salvation perfect through sufferings.* For both **he that sanctifieth** *and they who are sanctified* **are all of one**: for which cause **he** is not ashamed to call them brethren, **Saying,** *I will declare* **thy** *name unto my brethren, in the midst of the church will I sing praise unto thee.* **And again**, *I will put my trust in him.* **And again,** *Behold I and the children which God hath given me.* Forasmuch then as the children are partakers of flesh and blood, *he also himself likewise took part of the same*; that **through death** he might *destroy him that had the power of death*, that is, **the devil**; *And deliver them* who through fear of death were all their lifetime subject to bondage. For verily he took not on *him the nature* of angels; but *he took on him the seed of Abraham.* Wherefore in all things it behoved him to be **made like unto his brethren**, that he might be a merciful and faithful high priest in things *pertaining* to God, *to make* **reconciliation** *for the sins of the people.*

Jesus was made lower than the angels, because *Adam* had bowed his knee to a fallen angle—therefore placing himself under (in submission to) that fallen angel. Jesus took on this same position of authority, in order to elevate man back to his *original* position of authority as God's under-lord of this planet. Jesus has caused us to sit in heavenly places (positions of authority), with Himself. Jesus has not only given us back our original dominion, but He has also given us the ability to walk, live and act in the same authority that **He** had over Satan. I'm *in no way*, saying that man is "an equal" with Jesus Christ in His *present day* position of authority.

However, man is now able to live and walk in the image of Jesus Christ *as He lived* here on this earth. We **are not** God! We will **never** become God or a god (Supreme Creator). We are the creation; *He is the Supreme Creator.* He simply lives in us and empowers us for victory by faith in the Name and by the blood of Jesus Christ!

The Word of God continues by telling us that Jesus was made a little lower than the angels [that includes Lucifer—*he's an angel*], for the suffering of *death* (spiritual). Why? That He should **taste death** *for* **every** *man.* If the form of death that is addressed here was physical death, then why do people still die physically?

The Scripture says that Jesus tasted of death for **every** man. Anyone over the age of *ten* knows that physical death is inevitable...apart from the rapture. If this passage was referring to physical death, no other human being would ever have to die physically. However, physical death **is not** the subject of this passage of Scripture.

Hence, verse nine *could not possibly* be addressing physical death. If that were the case, *then* the Word of God wouldn't be *the Truth*, because men still die physically. *On the other hand*, born-again believers die once *to Sin* and never have to taste of *Spiritual Death* again **forever**. Spiritual Death would be the only form of death that Jesus could taste for every man. The people who do not accept His *Substitute Sacrifice* will end up "paying" their share of the wages of Sin themselves but it will be for eternity.

> **Hebrews 2:11-13**: "...for which cause *he* is not ashamed to call them [us] brethren, [He is] Saying, I will declare thy [God's] name unto my brethren, in the midst of the church will I sing praise unto thee. **And again**, I [Jesus] *will* **put my trust** *in him* [God]...."

Please understand that Jesus Himself was the One Who said, "**And again**, *I will put my trust in Him*." Why would Jesus need to put His trust in God the Father "again." if there was not a separation between them? *But* if He [Jesus the Man] had been **disconnected** from the life of God by our Sin, then He would need to be spiritually reconnected *born-again* [or put His faith/trust back in Him]. God the Father and Jesus make the following statement in Hebrews chapter 1:

Hebrews 1:5, 6: "For unto which of the angels said he at any time, Thou art my Son, **this day** *have I begotten thee?* **And again**, I will be to Him a Father, and he shall be to me a Son? **And again**, when he bringeth in *the first begotten into the world....*"

Consequently, the Father was saying that Jesus had ceased to be connected to Him as His Son for a period of time, because we were the cause of His disconnection. God would not have said, "And *again* I will be to Him a Father and he shall be to me a Son," **if** there had not been a period of Spiritual separation between them. According the concordance, the word *again* in this verse means "once more."[20] Moreover, the Bible dictionary defines *shall* as "are to, must." Thus, this would be better understood if it were read like this:

Hebrews 1:5b, 6a: "*And again* [once more], I will be to Him a Father and he shall [are to, must] be to me a Son? *And again* [once more], when he bringeth in *the first begotten into the world....*"

God the Father [*once again*] became a Father to Jesus and Jesus, because He had never sinned, had to [are to, must] become reconnected to Him as His Son and there was nothing all of hell could do to stop it. Jesus had fulfilled the Law of God, walking and living **as a man**. Therefore, hell could not possibly hold Him past the Father's prescribed three days and nights. God gave Jesus so that we would never be separated from Him again throughout all eternity. This can legally take place in our lives because Jesus Christ took our punishment (separation) for us.

John 3:16: For God so loved the world, that he gave [delivered up, offer][21] his only begotten Son, that whosoever believeth in him should not perish, but have everlasting [eternal, non-ending] life.

God gave [delivered up] His Son [spirit, soul, and body] for us, that we would never have to be spiritually separated from Him again. The Father loves us with **the exact same love** as He loves Jesus. God gave Jesus up to Spiritual Death so that we would never have to be separated from Him *again* for all eternity. That's the loving God we serve!

He Took Part of *The Same*

Hebrews 2:14b, 15: "*...he also himself likewise took part of the same; that* **through** ***death*** *he might destroy him that had the power of death,*

114

that is, **the devil**; *And deliver them* who through fear of death were all their lifetime subject to bondage."

Jesus likewise took part of the same. What "same" did He take part of? He took part of everything that we human beings had. He took part of our humanity, part of our physical limitations, and also took part in our Sin. This began when He was on the cross, while He made Atonement for Sin, and ended when He was resurrected. Why did Jesus go through all this horrible torment? "…that **through** *death* he might *destroy him that had the power of death*, that is, **the devil**; *And deliver them.*" Jesus' main objective from the Father was for Him to partake of all that we **had**, so that He could go into hell as our substitute. And while He was there, He was to completely destroy him who **had** been given the power of Death (Spiritual), who *was* the devil.

Moreover, He accomplished His mission with one hundred percent success. The church of Jesus Christ (the Firstborn), is completely free from **all** of Satan's control. The only problem now is that most of us can't seem to comprehend that we really are free from Sin and **all** its demands. Many Christians see themselves as just saved sinners—how sad! Especially when the Word of God says He made a great exchange with us.

Hebrews 2:17: Wherefore *in all things* it behoved him to be *made like unto his* brethren, that he might be a merciful and faithful high priest in things *pertaining* to God, to make **reconciliation** for the sins of the people.

Our Lord and Savior, Jesus Christ, made reconciliation [to exchange mutually, to take for oneself][22] for us. He took upon Himself our sin, made a mutual exchange. What was that exchange? He took our Sin from us and then He gave us His Righteousness. This idea is disputed by *The Vines Expository Dictionary*. It says that *propitiation* is actually a more proper term than "reconciliation."

"[*Propitiation*]*…in Heb. 2:17 'to expiate, to make propitiation for'…'to make propitiation' is an important correction of the KJV, 'to make reconciliation.'…Never is God said to be reconciled, a fact itself indicative that the enmity exists on man's part alone, and that it is man who needs to reconciled to God, and not God to man. God is always the same and, since He is Himself immutable, His relative attitude does not change towards those who change…[Propitiation] 'an expiation, a means whereby sin is *covered and remitted.*"[23]

I can agree with the use of the word *propitiation* in the sense that Jesus made Atonement, indemnity, or payment for our Sin. We were the ones who needed to be reconciled. On the other hand, *Vine's* says that the Sin of man was *covered and remitted*; this is only partly true. Our Sin was not merely covered and remitted [forgiven].[24] The Old Covenant saints' sins were merely covered, but Jesus' Substitute Sacrifice **literally** removed the Sin nature from within us who believe—as far as the east is from the west.

He took our Sin upon Himself and in exchange for our Sin, He gave us His Righteousness. We have been made the Righteousness of God in Christ Jesus. Reconciliation means "to change or exchange hence, of persons, 'to change from enmity to friendship, to reconcile," according to the Bible dictionary. In order to see this more clearly, let us examine how *reconcile* (in reference to Christ's sacrifice) is used in other portions of God's Word.

Colossians 1:18-20: And he is the head of the body, the church: who is the beginning, the firstborn from [among] the dead; that in all *things* he might have the preeminence. For it pleased *the Father* that in him should all fullness dwell; And, having made peace through the blood of his cross, by him to reconcile [to reconcile fully and *to change mutually*], all things unto himself; by him, *I say*, whether *they be* things in earth, or things in heaven.

Ephesians 2:16: And that he might reconcile [same as above], both unto God in one body by the cross, having slain the enmity thereby:

Both of the passages of Scripture above are referring to *the same event* that Hebrews chapter two verse seventeen refers to. Again, a mutual exchange took place. He took our Sin upon Himself and we received His Righteousness in exchange. Thus as a result, the word *reconciliation* is in reality a better rendering than *propitiation*. Jesus paid the **full** price for our reconciliation—*spirit, soul and body.*

Spiritual Justification—And Jesus

1 Timothy 3:16: And **without controversy** great is the mystery of godliness: God was *manifest in the flesh*, **justified in the Spirit**,

116

seen of angels, preached unto the Gentiles, believed on in the world, received up into glory.

1 Peter 3:18 (NKJV): For Christ also *suffered* once for sins, the just for the unjust, that He might *bring us to God*, being put to death in the flesh but **made alive** *by the Spirit.*

Romans 1:3, 4 (NKJV): Concerning His Son Jesus Christ our Lord, who was born of the seed of David according to the flesh, *and* **declared** *to be* the Son of God with power according to the Spirit of holiness, **by** *the resurrection from the dead.*

In 1 Tim. 3:16 it tells us that Jesus Christ was *justified* in the Spirit. The word *justified* as defined by the concordance means "to *render* just or innocent, [to render] to be righteous."[25] In addition, the word *render* from the Bible dictionary is "to give up or back, furnish, provide and supply,"[26] whatever is needed. **Consequently**, it could be said the Jesus was *justified* with [rendered—given, furnished with, provided and supplied], Righteousness by the Holy Spirit. The word *Spirit* in this verse of Scripture denotes "a spirit, **Christ's spirit**, as well as the Holy Spirit."[27]

I believe this verse is speaking of a binary (twofold) combination. The Holy Spirit had to declare, and furnish Him with Righteousness because He was under the curse of our Sin. I am in no way saying that He was "unrighteous," as if He had sinned. I am saying that *our Sin* caused Him to be *a substitute* for the unrighteous human race, for a period of time, until God's time period was fulfilled by Him in hell. Then hell, Satan, and all his demons could not hold Him, because He truly was righteous. Sin's complete bondage was destroyed by the Holy Spirit *after* God's set time period was fulfilled. Furthermore, in 1 Pet. 3:18 the Bible says that Jesus was made alive by the Spirit. In *the King James Version* Bible, the phrase *made alive* is rendered "quickened." *Quickened* denotes "made alive, *to revitalize*, make alive, **give life**,"[28] so says the concordance. Hence, Jesus was made alive by, revitalized by, or given **life** by the Holy Spirit.

If Jesus Christ never Died Spiritually, then why did He need to be **given life?** Zoe is the God-kind of life—perpetual, *never* beginning/ending life. Zoe is the *real* part of God that "makes" God—God (never beginning, never ending life). If Jesus was living here on this earth **as God**, then He would never have needed to have life *given back* to Him. But the Word states that the Holy Spirit made Him **alive** again. He had to because Jesus was **dead in our sin** and cursed.

Moreover, the Word of God says in Romans 1:3, 4, that Jesus was declared to be the Son of God, according to the Spirit of holiness, by His resurrection from the Dead (physical/Spiritual). The term *resurrection* in the concordance means "raised to life again, rising again."

Again I ask—if Jesus was living on this earth "as God," then why would He need to be raised back to *life*? God's life is never beginning, never ending. It's because the word *life* denotes both physical and Spiritual Life. Jesus laid aside a portion of Himself (godly attributes) so that He could be a man. Jesus did not walk on this earth with all power, all knowledge, and the ability to be present in all places at all times. He was just as much man as He was God, but <u>never</u> acted on His own accord.

No He came to this earth as a man Anointed by the Holy Spirit specifically to walk the line of the Mosaic Law and bring *it* to completion on our behalf. This is why He was able to take our curse upon Himself and become spiritually separated from the Father. You might ask *"How could God 'lay aside' a certain portion of Himself?"*

I don't know, <u>but I</u> <u>do know</u> that's what He did according to the Word of God. After all, He is God, isn't He, and He is capable of doing millions of things that we can't even comprehend. That's a part of the sovereignty of God. I do not understand how God could pull off such a mighty work, but He did it!

Spiritual Justification—*By Identification*

Romans 3:24; 28: Being *justified freely* by his grace through the *redemption* that **is in Christ Jesus**: Therefore we conclude that a man is justified by faith without the deeds of the law.

1 Corinthians 6:16, 17 (NKJV): Or do you not know that he who is *joined* to a harlot is one body *with her*? For "the two," He says, "shall become *one flesh*." But he who is **joined** *to the Lord is* **one spirit** *with Him*.

Romans 6:6 (NKJV): "...knowing this, that *our old man was crucified* **with Him**, *that the body of sin might be done away with*, that we should no longer be slaves of sin."

2 Timothy 2:11 (NKJV): *This* is a faithful saying: For if we died *with Him*, We shall also *live* **with Him**.

We obtained our justification by *the Spiritual Law of identification* with Christ Jesus. Jesus identified with our SIN and we identified with His Righteousness. *Identification* denotes "an act of identifying: a state of being identified..."[29] and *identify* means "to cause to be or become **identical**...to be or become *the same*."[30] We became united in the realm of the Spirit with Christ, or became one with Him [*identical*—identified], so that the body of Sin might be destroyed by Christ Jesus. We died with Christ as He died—spirit, soul, and body and, therefore, we've also been raised again to new life *much like* He was. The apostle Paul said in Galatians 2:20 "I've been crucified with Christ...."

This event could only take place by identification. Jesus established our identity in Him as righteous, our Sin established His identity with us *as* unrighteous. Again, Jesus was righteous—*He* never sinned one time, but our Sin that He took upon Himself caused Him to identify with our unrighteousness. He became one with us in our Spiritual Death, in that we might become one with His never ending [Zoe] life. This **is not** to say, *in any way*, that we are now "God," but simply that we are *one with Him*, in the sense of possessing the promises of the Father which include **never ending** life.

Why Did Jesus Submit To The Baptism of John?

One Tuesday afternoon in September 1997, I was driving home from work in my car listening to a preaching tape when the preacher mentioned that Jesus went into the wilderness after he received *the baptism of John*. Normally a statement like that would not have shaken me to my shoes, but this day it did!

After the preacher made that statement, the Lord asked me, *"Why did I submit to the baptism of John?"* I said, "I don't know!" He then said, "What was the baptism of John?" I said, "It was a baptism **unto repentance**—the *precursor* to receiving the New Birth." Then He said, *"Why would I need to submit to a baptism that was unto repentance—Seeing that I never committed Sin?"* I said, "I *really* don't know that one!"

He then reminded me of Philippians 2:6, 7 in *the Amplified Bible*: which basically says that Jesus laid aside His glory [*Omnipresence, Omnipotence, Omniscience*] to become a human being. He said, *"I was submissive to the same Laws that you are. I wasn't submissive to the Law of Sin and Death until I was made to be Sin for you, but I was submissive to every other ordinance of man— the same way that you are.* **It was because, I was submissive to the New**

Birth as I was submissive to the baptism of John—I did all of these things for you!"

Jesus had to submit to these ordinances of God because He lived on this earth *as a man* Anointed by the Holy Spirit, instead of as "Superman." He had to rely upon the Anointing in the same way as we also must. Jesus didn't *call the shots* while on earth, but He rather followed His Father's leading. This is why He never performed a miracle until *after* He had been baptized.

Then the Holy Spirit descended upon Him! Jesus was our example to follow. He received everything that we have received...only He received it all first.

Committed—Finished & Fulfilled

Luke 23:46 (NKJV): And when Jesus had cried out with a loud voice, He said, "Father, into Your hands *I* **commit** [commend—KJV] *My spirit.*" Having said this, He breathed His last.

John 19:30 (NKJV): So when Jesus had received the sour wine, He said, "It *is finished!*" And bowing His head, He **gave up** *His spirit.*

Matthew 5:17 (NKJV): *Do not think* that I came to destroy the Law or the Prophets. *I did not come to destroy* **but to fulfill.**

The Bible states in Luke 23:46 that Jesus commended His (human) spirit to the Father. *Commend* is defined as "to deposit (as a trust or for **protection**),"[31] according to the concordance. Why would Jesus say to His Father, "I entrust my spirit to You for protection," if He was only going to the place called Paradise? *He would not have needed any protection there.* Abraham's bosom was already a protected place. Jesus entrusted His spirit to the Father so that it would be protected while He was wrapped by our Sin, and as He entered into the lower parts of the earth or the pit of hell itself (Ephesians 4:9). Jesus needed His Father's protection because He had to go into hell and face the punishment, plus separation caused by our Sin.

Similarly, Jesus, while on the cross, said, **"It is finished."** Most theologians would say, "*Now see there—that meant that the sacrifice was complete.*" According to the Strong's Concordance, *finished* means "complete, conclude, *discharge,* accomplish, *fill up,* expire."[32] However, Jesus made this statement in Matthew 5:17: "I did not come to destroy **but to fulfill.**" What did Jesus come to fulfill? He came to fulfill the words of the prophets of old, and to fulfill the Law of God.

When Jesus said, *"It is finished,"* He was proclaiming that **He had fulfilled the Law of God as a human being,** and He was also proclaiming that because of *that,* Satan's control over man was finished. He wasn't saying that His Substitute Sacrifice was finished. If this were the case, why did He commit His spirit to His Father for Him to protect it? Jesus knew where He had to go, and that's why He asked for protection—not **from** punishment but through the punishment. **His human spirit was protected from the *corruption* of our Sin.** He *did not* become some demonic creature. Sin's punishment (torment & separation) had to be paid (or inflicted) and Jesus was the only One qualified to receive it. He was the only One Who could experience the punishment of Sin *and still be able to rise* from the pit—**victorious!**

Moreover, in that same verse of Scripture, it says that Jesus *"gave up His Spirit."* The Spirit of God worded is, this way for a reason. G*ave* denotes "to surrender, intrust, cast, commit, deliver (up); put in prison, *bestow, grant."*[33] Jesus asked His Father for protection through the punishment of hell, then He gave up or delivered up His (human) spirit to be put in prison for man's Sin. He surrendered to **Death!**

When Was Eternal Redemption *Officially* Finished?

As I have noted, when Jesus said, "It is finished," He wasn't referring to the completion of His work for our Redemption. This notion couldn't possibly be true because ever since the beginning of the Law, *Atonement* (plus Eternal Redemption) was to be obtained by *more* than the shedding of the blood of the Sin offering. Kenneth E. Hagin sheds notable light upon understanding the meaning of Jesus' statement: "It is finished."

"Many have thought that when Jesus said on the Cross, 'It is finished.' He was talking about our salvation. No! No! No! Our salvation wasn't finished when Jesus died. **Salvation wasn't complete until He ascended into the heavenly Holy of Holies to obtain eternal redemption for us.** (See Hebrews chapter 9)S When Jesus said "It is finished' on the cross, He was talking about the Old Covenant being finished. And when He said those words, the curtain that sealed off the Holy of Holies in the Temple was rent in twain — or torn in half — from top to bottom (Mark 15:38)." [34]

Based on Hagin's quotation, I believe that it is important that we further examine the passages of Scripture that he referred us to, in order to see the whole picture of what Jesus did to obtain *Eternal Redemption* for us.

> **Hebrews 9:6-8 (NKJV)**: Now when these things had been thus prepared, the priests always went into the first part of the tabernacle, performing *the services*. But into the second part the high priest *went alone once a year, not without blood, which he offered* for himself and *for* the people's sins *committed* in ignorance; the Holy Spirit indicating **this**, that the way into the Holiest of All was not yet made manifest **while the first tabernacle was still standing**.

Old Covenant *Atonement* came *after* the blood was offered in the Holy of Holies—*not before*. Jesus wasn't able to offer His blood in the REAL Holy of Holies until **after** He had resurrected from death and ascended. Furthermore, the earthly Holy of Holies in Solomon's temple had to be first abolished—FINISHED, before Jesus was able to enter into heaven three days and nights later.

> **Hebrews 9:11, 12 (NKJV): But** Christ came *as* High Priest of the good things to come, with the greater and more perfect tabernacle not made with hands, that is, not of this creation. Not with the blood of goats and calves, but with His own blood *He entered the Most Holy Place once for all,* **having obtained** *eternal redemption*.

> **Hebrews 9:12 (TAB)**: He went once for all into the [Holy of] Holies [of heaven], not by virtue of the blood of goats and calves [by which to make reconciliation between God and man], but His own blood, **having found *and* secured** *a complete redemption* (an everlasting release for us).

Jesus entered into the Holy of Holies having obtained **Eternal Redemption—*not*** just an Atonement (*or covering*). At the cross, Jesus atoned (made a covering) for our Sin. However, Atonement was the *precursor* to **Eternal Redemption**, which was "officially" declared **after** Jesus presented Himself to the Father and had poured out His blood in heaven. Eternal Redemption wasn't possible without the full penalty being paid. *Separation and punishment* were an important part of how Adam's Sin was **blotted out!**

Hebrews 9:13-23 (NKJV): For *if* the blood of bulls and goats and the ashes of a heifer, sprinkling the unclean, sanctifies for the purifying of the flesh, how much more shall the blood of Christ, *who through the eternal Spirit offered Himself without spot to God,* cleanse your conscience from dead works to serve the living God? And for this reason He is the *Mediator* of the new covenant, **by means of death** [separation], for the redemption of the transgressions under the first covenant, that those who are called may receive the promise of the eternal inheritance. For where there *is* a testament, there must also of necessity be the death of the testator. For a testament *is* in force after men are dead, since it has no power at all while the testator lives. Therefore not even the first *covenant* was dedicated without blood. For when Moses had spoken every precept to all the people according to the law, he took the blood of calves and goats, with water, scarlet wool, and hyssop, and sprinkled both the book itself and all the people, saying, *"This is the blood of the covenant* which *God has commanded you."* Then likewise he *sprinkled with blood both the tabernacle and all the vessels of the ministry.* And according to the law almost all things are purified with blood, and without shedding of blood there is no remission. Therefore, *it was* necessary that the copies of the things in the heavens should be purified with these, **but the heavenly things themselves with better sacrifices than these**.

This is what Jesus did! Jesus' blood has needed to cleanse the heavenly temple, *the same as the earthly temple was cleansed* before the "official" declaration of Eternal Redemption could be proclaimed and made available to us. Note that the cleansing of the temple was an important part of Old Covenant Atonement, the same as it was in our receiving Eternal Redemption. It was not complete without it!

Hebrews 9:24-28 (NKJV): For Christ has not entered the holy places made with hands, *which are* copies of the true, *but into heaven itself,* now to appear in the presence of God for us; not that He should offer Himself often, as the high priest enters the Most Holy Place every year with blood of another; He then would have had to suffer often since the foundation of the world; but now, once at the end of the ages, He has appeared to put away sin by the sacrifice of Himself. And as it is *appointed for men to die once,* but **after this the judgment,** so Christ was offered once *to bear the sins of many.* To those who eagerly wait for Him He will appear a second time, apart from sin, for salvation.

Jesus experienced Death and judgment on the behalf of the human race. He became Sin and bore our sicknesses and diseases in our place. Sin was not *officially* (for eternity) put away **until after** Jesus presented Himself before the Father, and poured His blood in the Holy of Holies. *Jesus experienced judgment—Spiritual Separation for all men*!

John 19:30 (NKJV): So when Jesus had received the sour wine, He said, *"**It is finished**!"* And *bowing His head, He gave up His spirit.*

Mark 15:37, 38 (NKJV): And *Jesus cried out with a loud voice, and breathed His last.* **Then** the veil of the temple was torn in two from top to bottom.

No one would argue that the above portions of Scripture are referring to the same historical event—Jesus' last words in human flesh. Mark fifteen verse 37 tells us that He cried out with a loud voice. What do you think He cried out? **"IT IS FINISHED!"** Immediately after He cried out those words, what happened?

The Bible says the veil separating the Holy of Holies was torn from top to bottom, *denoting the meaning of Jesus' last words*. The earthly man-made temple, God's dwelling place, **was finished**! However, man did not become His temple until the day of Pentecost, after Jesus went to heaven.

Moreover, in John 20:17, Jesus said to Mary Magdalene: *"Touch Me not; for I am not ascended to My Father...."* **Why was Mary not to touch Jesus?**

Still, *after* Jesus had ascended to His Father and offered His blood in the Holy of Holies He returned to earth and told His disciples to touch [handle] Him (Luke 24:39): *"Behold my hands and my feet, that is I myself:* **handle me**, *and see; for a spirit hath not flesh and bones as ye see me have."* So, why was Mary told not to touch Him, but His disciples were told to do so **after** He had presented Himself and His blood to the Father?

The reason for this was because if she (an unsaved person) had touched Him, she would have made Him unclean by her sinfulness **before** He had ascended to His Father.

This openly shows that Eternal Redemption was not fully completed until *after* He presented Himself and His blood to the Father in heaven. Any other notion is illogical and a stretch at best. Eternal Redemption was *officially* proclaimed **after** Jesus died, went to hell, resurrected from *among* the dead, and appeared in heaven!

Jesus gave His life (*His spirit*) for the sheep. Jesus obtained our forgiveness He obtained our freedom from Sin's bondage, obtained Eternal Life and Righteousness for us, **but He also** obtained our freedom from punishment—He was our *Scape-goat* (our Substitute Sacrifice). The word Substitute means *our exchange*, alternate, in our place, and replacement for what we deserved.

The Day of Atonement:
God's Established Pattern—Eternal Redemption

The Bible plainly declares that God is the same yesterday, today, and forever; His plans, purposes, and ways **never** change (Heb. 13:8). Hence, it should be easy to see how God's Old Covenant pattern of *Atonement* was the *exact* picture of New Covenant *Eternal Redemption*, which Jesus made for the world. In order for us to gain tremendous understanding of all that we have discussed thus far, I believe it is very important that we examine God's *established* pattern of Atonement from its original Old Covenant foundation.

As we embark upon this almost overwhelming task of studying the Old Covenant pattern of Atonement, I need to remind the reader that in Jesus' day the Laws of the Sacrifice were very much in force. Therefore, all sacrifices for Sin would be conducted according to the Old Covenant pattern written in the Law of Moses. New Covenant Eternal Redemption was *no* exception! It was accomplished according to God's pattern!

Leviticus 6:24-26; 28, 30: And the LORD spake unto Moses, saying, Speak unto Aaron and to his sons, saying, This *is the law of the sin offering*: In the place where the burnt offering is killed shall the sin offering be killed before the LORD: **it *is* most holy**. The priest that offereth it for sin shall eat it: in the holy place shall it be eaten, in the court of the tabernacle of the congregation. But *the earthen vessel* wherein it is sodden *shall be broken*: and if it be sodden in a brasen pot, it shall be *both scoured*, and rinsed in water. And no sin offering, whereof *any* of the blood is brought into the tabernacle of the congregation **to reconcile** *withal* in *the holy place*, shall be eaten: it shall be **burnt in the fire.**

In this passage of Scripture, God is instructing Moses concerning the Law of the Sin offering. Please notice the various details and consider how they apply to the crucifixion of our Lord Jesus. God tells Moses that the Sin offering is *most holy*.

The precious blood of Jesus was a Most Holy Sacrifice, which covered our Sin **and** blotted it out for eternity. In verse 28 of this passage, it tells us that the "earthen vessel...shall be broken." Jesus, Himself, is quoted in 1 Corinthians chapter 11 verse 24 saying that His body was to be broken for us.

Finally in verse 30 of Leviticus 6, we are told that the Sin offering was to be burned with fire. How does this apply to the sacrifice of Jesus, you might ask? To answer this, consider the following verses of Scripture.

Psalm 86:13: For great *is* thy mercy toward me: and thou hast delivered my soul *from the lowest hell* [the pit].

Matthew 12:39, 40: But he answered and said unto them, An evil and adulterous generation *seeketh after a sign*; and there shall no sign be given to it, *but the sign of the prophet Jonas*: For as Jonas was three days and three nights in the whale's belly; so shall the Son of man be *three days and three nights* **in the heart** of the earth.

John 12:24-26: Verily, verily, I say unto you, Except a corn of wheat fall into the ground **and die**, it abideth alone: but *if it die*, it bringeth forth much fruit. He that loveth his life shall lose it; and he that hateth his life in this world shall keep it unto life eternal. If any man serve me, *let him follow me*; and where I am, there shall also my servant be: if any man serve me, him will *my* Father honour.

All three of the previous passages of Scripture are referring to the three days and nights that Jesus spent in the center of the earth (hell itself). I dare say that no one would question my saying that hell is a place of fire, heat, and burning. And seeing that Jesus took upon Himself *our punishment* for Sin, (eternal punishment in hell fire) He had to have experienced it.

Therefore, I believe one could say that Jesus experienced these things and worse during His three-day stay in hell. The price that Jesus paid for our freedom is *far greater* than anything the human mind can conceive.

Two Goats—*One* Sacrifice!

Leviticus 16:5-11: And he shall take of the congregation of the children of Israel **two** *kids of the goats for a sin offering*, and *one ram for a burnt offering*. And Aaron shall offer his bullock of the sin offering, which is for himself, and make an atonement for himself, and for his house. And he shall *take the two goats*, and present them before the LORD *at* the door of the tabernacle of the congregation. And Aaron shall cast lots upon *the two goats*; one lot for the LORD, and the other lot for **the scapegoat**. And Aaron shall bring the goat upon which the LORD'S lot fell, and offer him *for* a sin offering. *But the goat, on which the lot fell to be the scapegoat, shall be presented alive before the LORD,* **to make an atonement with him,** *and to let him go for a scapegoat into the wilderness.* And Aaron shall bring the bullock of the sin offering, which *is* for himself, and shall make an atonement for himself, and for his house, and shall kill the bullock of the sin offering which *is* for himself:

Carefully notice that God said Aaron was to take **two** goats to make **one** complete sacrifice for the sins of the people. One of those goats was used in the actual Sin offering itself, and the other was used as a "scapegoat." Now we know where the term "scapegoat" (one taking the place of another) came from. Jesus Christ was not only our Sin Offering, but He was also our **Scapegoat** from Sin, hell and Eternal Punishment.

Notice further that the priest made Atonement for himself as well. Through the three fold Substitute Sacrifice of Jesus, He also made Atonement for Himself (because He was to become Sin for us), so that He wouldn't have to remain under the bondage of *our* Sin for eternity. Again, that is in no way to say that Jesus ever committed any Sin; however, He did take our Sin upon Himself. Through His sinless life, plus His precious blood, He also made the way for Himself to be released from the punishment for the Sin of the world. In verse 9 of Leviticus 16, we are told that the scapegoat was to be offered *with* the goat for the Sin offering to make Atonement. It took *two* goats to make **one** Sin offering, and Jesus Christ was *the embodiment* of those two Old Covenant symbols. Most know what the goat for the actual blood offering symbolizes, but what does the *scapegoat* represent? Verse 10 of this same chapter answers this question. The scapegoat was to be released into the wilderness, or the *inhabitable parts* of the earth. The Bible declares that our Sin is separated from us, as far as the east is from the west. This is the purpose of the scapegoat. It was literally released into an uninhabitable part of the wilderness.

However, in spiritual terms, this is a parallel of our being separated from our Sin as far as the east is from the west. Moreover, the terms "wilderness" and "inhabitable parts of the earth" are used metaphorically to describe the pit of hell—the place of ultimate uninhabitability.

Hell is the place of confinement where Jesus was held for three days and nights on our behalf. Jesus was our Scapegoat! We escaped the torment of hell *because* He went into it for us. Had Jesus not gone to hell and received our punishment for our Sin, *we would still have to experience it.* Now, let us continue in our study of the Old Covenant pattern of Atonement by examining Leviticus 16: 15-18:

> **Leviticus 16:15-18**: Then shall he kill the goat of the sin offering, that *is* for the people, and bring his blood within the veil, and do with that blood as he did with the blood of the bullock, and sprinkle it upon the mercy seat, and before the mercy seat: And he shall *make an atonement for the holy place,* **because of** *the uncleanness of the children of Israel,* and because of their transgressions in all their sins: and so shall he do for the tabernacle of the congregation, that remaineth among them in the midst of their uncleanness. And there shall be no man in the tabernacle of the congregation when he goeth in to make an atonement in the holy *place,* until he come out, and have made an atonement for himself, and for his household, and for all the congregation of Israel. And he shall go out unto the altar that *is* before the LORD, and make an atonement for it; and shall take of the blood of the bullock, and of the blood of the goat, and put *it* upon the horns of the altar round about.

Just as the blood of the Sin offering made Atonement (a covering) for the Sin of Israel, so Jesus' blood made a covering for Sin. However, His blood not only covered Adamic Sin, it also *completely removed* it—an **eternal** removal of Sin and its wages or punishment. The sacrifice for Sin found in the Old Covenant had to be repeated once a year. However, the *complete* Sacrifice that Jesus made purchased *Eternal Redemption* for all those who will believe upon Him and His precious, priceless blood. As a child, I would cringe whenever I heard someone talk about "the blood of Jesus." Not because I was possessed or something like that, but rather because I did not understand the important significance of the blood of Jesus.

It is because He shed His blood that we can be reunited to God the Father and spend eternity with Him! The blood of Jesus was the key to our Redemption, but there was more to the price of Eternal Redemption. *There was also an eternal sentence of Death* (separation from God) that went right along with the Offering for Sin. The price of Sin was *a multifaceted tariff* that the human race could not possibly pay. This is why Jesus had to make **full** restitution for us. Wait, there's more!

> **Leviticus 16:20-22**: And when he hath made an end of *reconciling the holy place, and the tabernacle* of the congregation, and the altar, he shall bring the live goat [scapegoat]: And Aaron *shall lay both his hands upon* **the head** *of the live goat, and* **confess over him all the iniquities** *of the children of Israel,* **and all their transgressions** *in all their sins, putting them upon the head of the goat, and shall send him away by the hand of a fit man into the wilderness*: **And the goat shall bear upon him all their iniquities unto a land not inhabited**: and he shall let go the goat in the wilderness.

In like manner, Jesus (our High Priest) made an end of reconciling the holy place and tabernacle, which is His Body, while upon the cross of Calvary. **After** this process was accomplished, the next phase of the multi-faceted tariff of Sin came into focus. God instructed Aaron (the priest) to lay his hands upon the scapegoat, *which was alive*, and confess all the iniquities and transgressions of the people over it. The scapegoat would *bear* the Sin into the inhabitable wilderness. The Bible states that our Lord Jesus bore (was covered with) the Sin of us all. Now, please consider **Isaiah 53: 5-9**:

> But he *was* wounded for our transgressions, *he was* bruised for our iniquities: **the chastisement** of our peace *was* upon him; and with his stripes we are healed. All we like sheep have gone astray; we have turned every one to his own way; and the LORD hath laid **on him** *the iniquity of us all*. He was *oppressed*, and he was *afflicted*, yet he opened not his mouth: he is brought as a lamb to the slaughter, and as a sheep before her shearers is dumb, so he openeth not his mouth. He was *taken from prison and from judgment*: and who shall declare his generation? for **he** *was cut off out of* **the land of the living**: *for the transgression of my people was he stricken*. And he made his grave with the wicked, and with the rich *in his*

death; because he had done no violence, neither *was any* deceit in his mouth.

Somewhere between life and death, **after** the Atonement (covering) for Sin had been accomplished, God the Father (the Chief High Priest) laid His hands upon the head of our "Head" and He confessed the Sin of the world over Jesus. Because of this *transference* of Sin, Jesus was killed spiritually, separated *temporarily* from His Father, to pay the full price of our Spiritual Death and all its punishment.

At this point, Jesus turned His human spirit over to Death (Spiritual separation), and He entered into the heart of the earth, where He was held captive *in our place* for three days and nights. Remember what the Word of God says, "We died with him (spiritually)," as well as resurrected. He went through all of this unspeakable horror in our place, on our behalf, because we could not have possibly been able to succeed in doing so on our own. He entered the wilderness of hell, the place where we deserved to dwell for eternity. He endured separation so that we would never have to experience it. Remember, He did all of this *in our place*...He never sinned!

That proves how much He really loves us. We have already addressed the fact that Jesus *"burned in hell"* for you and I—what an extreme display of love. Hence, if Jesus went through all of this on our behalf, we are, therefore, extremely precious and highly prized by God! Contrary to what Hanegraaff and others like him think about this, what I am writing is *far from heretical*. It is the story of **the most-extreme** gift of love this world has ever known. If more people understood this story of Love, maybe they would treasure their salvation as the *most precious* prize known to men.

> **Leviticus 16:26-27; 30**: And he that let go the goat for the scapegoat shall wash his clothes, and bathe his flesh in water, and afterward come *into the camp*. And the bullock *for* the sin offering, and the goat *for* the sin offering, whose blood was brought in to make atonement in the holy *place*, shall *one* carry forth without the camp; and **they shall burn in the fire** their skins, and their flesh, and their dung. For on that day shall *the priest* make an atonement for you, to cleanse you, *that* ye may be clean from all your sins before the LORD.

In the New Covenant, our Lord Jesus was crucified outside of the city, the same way that the Sin offering was made outside the camp (city). Notice again the fate of the Sin offering. The Bible says that it was to be *burned with fire*. Without a doubt, Jesus, *our Sin Offering*, also had to be burned with fire *in our place*. I realize that the very thought of such things makes one cringe in pain. One thinks, "How could a righteous Man be tortured and burned in hell?" Nonetheless, He was our **Scapegoat!**

Some *Prophetic* Words?

Job 29:12-18: Because I delivered the poor that cried, and the fatherless, and *him that had* none to help him. The blessing of him that was ready to perish came upon me: and I caused the widow's heart to sing for joy. I put on righteousness, and it clothed me: my judgment *was* as a robe and a diadem. I was eyes to the blind, and feet *was* I to the lame. I *was* a father to the poor: and the cause *which* I knew not I searched out. And *I brake the jaws of the wicked*, and plucked the spoil out of his teeth. Then I said, **I shall die in my nest**, and I shall **multiply *my* days as the sand**.

Job had to be prophesying about the torment that our Lord Jesus was to experience. Job *did not* brake the jaws of the wicked, however, Jesus came to destroy the works of the devil (1 John 3:8). Job *did not* multiply his days as the sand, but the Bible says of Jesus in Isaiah 53:10 that because of His Sacrifice, God prolonged His days forever! Job could not possibly have been literally referring to himself. Because he did not go through the sort of things that he was addressing. However, Jesus Christ did!

I would like to address one last long portion of prophetic Scripture from the book of Job:

Job 30:10, 15-30: They abhor me, they flee far from me, and *spare not to spit in my face*. Terrors are turned upon me: they pursue my soul as the wind: and my welfare passeth away as a cloud. And now *my soul is poured out upon me; the days of affliction have taken hold upon me*. **My bones are pierced in me** in the night season: and my sinews take no rest. *By the great force of* **my disease** *is* my garment changed: **it bindeth me** about as the collar of my coat. *He hath cast me into the mire, and I am become like dust and ashes*. I cry unto thee, and *thou dost not hear me*: I stand up, and thou regardest me *not. Thou art become cruel to me*: with thy strong hand thou opposest thyself against me. Thou liftest me up to the wind; thou causest me to ride *upon it*, and dissolvest my substance. *For I know that thou* *wilt bring me to death,* **and** *to the house appointed for all living.* Howbeit he will not stretch out *his* hand **to the grave**, though they cry in his destruction. Did not I weep for him that was in trouble? was *not* my soul grieved for the poor? When I looked for good, then evil came *unto me*: and when I waited for light, there came darkness. My bowels boiled, and rested not: *the of affliction prevented me.* I went mourning without the sun: I stood up, *and I cried in the congregation.* I am a brother to dragons, and a companion to owls. **My skin is black upon me, and my bones are burned with heat.**

No man living on earth past or present has ever experienced the torments that Job was speaking of, *including himself.* Job's trial period was rough, but it was nowhere near the description given in Job chapter 30. Again, the words of Job here were prophetic in nature, in the same way that King David wrote prophetically of Jesus so many times in the Book of Psalms.

Job mentioned spitting. Jesus had a whole legion of soldiers who spit on and in His face shortly before He was crucified. The Bible also says in Isaiah that Jesus poured out His soul unto Death.

While Jesus hung on the cross, His bones were all out of joint and piercing through Him. Again, the book of Isaiah says that Jesus bore our sickness, disease, and carried our pains, and the weight (pressure) of all of this caused His visage (garment/body) to be horribly disfigured. Job says, "I cry unto thee, and thou doest not hear me."

Jesus is the only individual Who God was completely forsaken. God is aware of all our cries, but if they *are not* cries of faith, God simply *ignores them,* but not in the case of Jesus. God the Father **could not** look upon Him, because His human spirit was covered with the Sin of the world. Jesus is the only One, *this side of the grave,* Who has been truly forsaken by the Father. Job says, "Thou art become cruel to me...." Isaiah speaks clearly of this taking place to Jesus, saying, "Yet it pleased the Lord to bruise him; he hath put him to grief." He is truly the only One that God the Father has ever given Sin, sickness, disease, and pain. But He did so, with the purpose of Jesus defeating it for us.

<u>Pay close attention to verse 23</u>: "For I know *that* thou wilt bring me *to* death, and *to* the house appointed for all living." Jesus knew before He started His journey into the Reconciliation of man that He would be going into hell itself, but He also knew that He would be resurrected and once again enter the house appointed for all living (heaven).

Job, on the other hand, probably had no idea of what he was actually referring to. Job continues by saying, "Howbeit he will not stretch out his hand to the grave...." Was he in the grave? Not at all! However, the Lord Jesus was in the grave three days and nights without relief. Job continues with another shocking statement that also appears to be prophetic of Jesus' Substitute Sacrifice.

Job 30:30 (TAB): My skin falls from me in blackened flakes, and my bones are burned with heat.

Some may say, "This doesn't say that Jesus burned in hell." "But, did Job's bones literally burn with heat?" Without a doubt no. However, Jesus our Lord was detained in the place of eternal flames and heat by the Sin of the world covering His spirit. Job could not have possibly experienced the torment that was illustrated here.

He Was God—But He Lived *As A Man*

Philippians 2:5-7 (NKJV): Let this mind be in you which was also in Christ Jesus, who, being in the form of God, **did not** *consider it robbery to be* **equal with God**, but made Himself of no reputation, taking the form of a bondservant, *and* coming in the likeness of men.

Many Christians read the above verse of Scripture and think "See, He lived here 'as' God. I never could live the same way He did." This verse reads that Jesus **did not** consider (think) it was robbery to be **equal** with God. That, basically, is saying that He had a *Super-natural advantage* over us. Therefore, we could not possibly live how He lived. However, does the above verse really interpret Jesus the way He really was, while here on the earth? I suggest that we look at another translation to make a comparison.

Philippians 2:6, 7 (TAB): Who, although *being essentially on with God and* in the form of God [possessing *the fullness of* **the attributes** which make God God], **did not think** this equality with God was a thing *to be eagerly grasped or retained*, But *stripped Himself* **[of all privileges and rightful dignity]**, so as *to assume* the guise of a servant (slave), in that *He* became like men *and was born a human being.*

The Amplified Bible translates Philippians 2:6, 7, in a tremendously freeing way. It tells the life of Jesus the way He told it. He said things such as, "It's not Me—It's My Father in Me, *He does the works...*" In this version, it says that Jesus did not think equality was something to be retained while He was in human form. Therefore, **He** stripped Himself of all those privileges that most traditionalists attempt to ascribe to Him, during His earthly ministry. Notice that Jesus was the One Who did the "stripping" of Himself of all the advantages He had *before* He came to earth. Most traditional religious people probably hate *the Amplified Bible* just for these two verses alone, because it blows their theological, and philosophical doctrines apart. Jesus is and was God, but He walked this earth with the same limitations as other men only He never sinned one time.

However, He stripped Himself **of all privileges and rightful dignity** for the purpose of becoming a human being. Had He not done this, He would have defeated Satan as God and not as a human being (the Last Adam). Hank Hanegraaff has claimed that Jesus did not give up or give away His attributes and privileges, but that He simply covered them (or veiled them).[35] On the contrary, *The Amplified Bible* **totally** contradicts such thinking. The Bible does not teach that Jesus *hid* His glory while on earth; it says He ***stripped Himself,*** in order that He could come to earth as a man. Remember what God said to Moses, "You can not see my face and live." So, how could the people of Jesus' day see "the face of God" and not die, if He did not temporarily strip off His glory (attributes & privileges) while here on earth? How did He do it? *I have no idea*, but He was and is God, so I *know* that He was more than capable of handling the situation without a problem. Hanegraaff attributes so much of his theological perspective to the sovereignty of God, and this is one of the theological areas where one definitely needs to think of it in terms of God's sovereignty.

Finally, there is a lost and dying world who needs to know that God loves them every bit as much as He loves Jesus. If this were not true, then He would not have given Jesus up to Spiritual Death and torment, so that we would never have to experience it.

This is the message that will bring the lost people in by the millions. God loves them *in their sins*, just as much as He loves us in His Righteousness. Consider this before you go out "witnessing" the next time to your unbelieving family and friends! Salvation is a tremendously precious and high priced gift from God!

10

HE WHO KNEW NO SIN *BECAME* SIN

In this chapter, I intend to examine what *Christianity in Crisis* calls the re-creation on the cross and redemption in hell. First of all, let's start by dealing with what happened to Jesus on the cross. I realize that we've already dealt with this subject in detail, but here we need to address this topic according to the teachings of the Word of Faith. Is the Word of Faith teaching heretical doctrine about the cross, hell, and Jesus' Resurrection? Hanegraaff insinuates that the Faith teachers literally believe that Jesus was transformed from a divine being into a demoniac.[1] However, is this interpretation of their teaching accurate? He starts out his accusations by questioning a statement from Pastor Benny Hinn:

> "...Jesus Christ knew the only way He would stop Satan is by becoming one in nature with him...He did not take my sin; He *became* my sin. **Sin** is the nature of hell. Sin is what made Satan...He became one with the nature of Satan...."[2]

Today, *perhaps* Hinn would no longer agree with the above statement? Nonetheless, what was Hinn attempting to convey? I in no way believe that Hinn was *literally* implying that Jesus, Who is holy in nature, suddenly became demonic. He said that He became Sin, which is confirmed by 2 Corinthians 5:21. He also clarified what the nature of hell was—*Sin!* Jesus became Sin and experienced the punishment and abandonment that our Sin created.

However, Hinn *never* said that Jesus became some sort of demon possessed being. I believe that Hinn was actually saying that in the eyes of God, Jesus was literally Sin itself, even though He had never sinned. Hence, He was the object of the entire wrath of God—in our place. He experienced the punishment of Sin that we should have experienced. But, I do not believe that Hinn is insinuating that Jesus became unholy! For Hanegraaff to imply anything further would be for him to put words into Hinn's mouth.

Kenneth Copeland explains this in adequate detail:

135

"We were crucified with Him. God didn't crucify Him in order just to kill Him. See no man, no other man or women could qualify to pay the price for sin, not just sinful conduct. Sinful conduct is the result **of** SIN. Sin came into the world and death by sin, the Word says...SIN came into this world when Adam made an independent decision violated the Word of God, bowed his knee to Satan, and gave Satan lordship over the entire human race...he [Adam] gave authority over all this world to...God gave it to Adam, he gave it to Satan. Satan became then the step-father of man-kind. That's SIN, *the entire nature of the devil, everything in darkness, every sickness, every disease, every sin act; everything of destruction and death that exists* came into this earth that moment. That was the curse that came on this whole thing. Now when Jesus went to the cross He did not just bare your commission of a certain number of things against God, called sin. That's included. But, He didn't just bare that. He bore SIN itself. He paid the price for doing that. He paid the penalty **as if** He had open the door for the devil and gave him this whole thing."[3]

As Copeland points out, Jesus paid the price **as if** He had opened the door to Satan by committing Sin. When God looked upon Jesus (after He became our Sin), He saw Him *as if* He were us and He expended His wrath upon Him, Who was our Substitute. In God's eyes **He was us**, because He was representing us and taking our punishment upon Himself.

As usual, Hanegraaff is sure to not to leave out Kenneth Hagin as one of his so-called blasphemers. He too is accused of saying Jesus became demonic in nature.[4] Here again, Hagin was simply pointing out that Jesus became Sin in God's eyes! Jesus took the place of every man when He became Sin, but despite all that He went through, He, *in reality*, remained holy and righteous.

Moreover, Hanegraaff sees to it that Kenneth Copeland makes his list of blasphemers, too. He quotes Copeland and includes his own twist upon Copeland's words.

"The righteousness of God was made to be sin. He accepted the sin nature of Satan in His own spirit. And at the moment that He did so, He cried, 'My God, My God, why hast thou forsaken Me?'...Why do you think Moses, upon instruction of God, raised the serpent upon that pole instead of a lamb?...a snake up there—the sign of Satan?…it was a sign of Satan that was hanging on the cross…."[5]

Was Copeland's statement erroneous or is he making a valid point? Let me ask a question: "What does the serpent represent?" Satan! Since Sin is the *nature* of the devil, why would it seem so strange to picture Jesus *representing* the serpent on the cross, especially seeing that the serpent (Satan) is the originator of Sin? That is not say that Jesus became *unholy* while He became Sin. Notice I said He **represented** the serpent, **not** He *literally* became unholy like the serpent. The serpent on the pole represented how Jesus would defeat Satan by taking *our* Sin, sickness, and punishment.

I want to share another comment from Copeland that I believe will help explain the previous quote in question.

"I've had people go into long discussions with me about this. All based on religious ideas instead of what the Word says actually happened. Jesus said, 'Father into Your hands I *entrust* My spirit.' He did not plan on God **taking** His spirit, He planned on Him **protecting** it, because He knew where He had to go. He had to go in **among** the damned. He had to go into Satan's Citadel. He had to go into the depths of the earth. He had to go into the *bowels* of this earth. He had to go where nobody else had ever gotten out of—nobody ever knew that anybody could get out of it. That's where He had to go…That's what was settled in the Garden of Gethsemane. Into Your hands I entrust My spirit—not My will but Yours be done…."[6]

Copeland echoes what I said in the previous chapter. Jesus did not expect God to take His human spirit, but rather to **protect** it from contamination by Sin, while He was made to be Sin. Therefore, one can clearly see that while Jesus was made to be Sin, His spirit was protected holy and righteous as He truly was! Neither Copeland nor any of the other Faith teachers mentioned thus far is attempting to ascribe an evil, demonic nature to our priceless and sinless Substitute!

2 Corinthians 5:21

Hanegraaff goes to great length to "prove" that the word *made* in 2 Corinthians 5:21 should be better translated *to impute*.[7] However, upon deeper research, one finds that this is not actually the case. In 2 Corinthians 5:21 the word *made* is addressed two separate times. When it is used to address Jesus' becoming Sin (Poieo), it denotes: "abide, appoint, bear, bring, cause, give, make, observe, provide, put, ordain."[8] And when it refers to our being made righteous in Christ (Ginomai), it denotes "to cause to be ('gen'-erate), to become, come into being, be made, be married, be ordained, partake, be wrought."[9]

There is no doubt that Jesus had to be given *Sin* because He never sinned, and it is also obvious that we had to be given *Righteousness* because we did not have it in ourselves. Nevertheless, was Jesus' being *made* sin and our being *made* righteous merely imputed (reckoned, accounted)[10] in a metaphorical sense?

If this were the case, then all Christians are only **metaphorically** born-again. However, the Bible clearly teaches that the believer in Christ is not merely accounted as born-again, but rather has become *a new creation* all together. Consider what the apostle Paul said about this before you make your decision.

> **Romans 6:6, 7 (TAB):** We know that our old (unrenewed) self was nailed to the cross with Him in order that [our] body [which is the instrument] of sin might be made ineffective *and* inactive for evil, that we might no longer be the slaves of sin. For when a man dies, he is freed (**loosed, delivered**) from [*the power of*] sin [among men].

> **2 Corinthians 5:17 (TAB):** "Therefore if any person is [*ingrafted*] in Christ (*the Messiah*) he is a new creation (**a new creature altogether**); the old [previous moral and spiritual condition] *has passed away....*"

As a result, one can clearly see that we have been completely **recreated** by the Substitute Sacrifice of Jesus Christ. Therefore, our Righteousness in Christ could not possibly be *imputed* to us. Abraham's righteousness *had* to be imputed to him because Christ hadn't gone to the cross, but once He had, we began living in His redemption.

In regards to Jesus becoming Sin, I actually agree with Hanegraaff that Jesus **did not** become some evil demonic being. Jesus remained holy and pure despite our Sin. Nevertheless, I still believe that Jesus temporarily became Sin (*in a spiritual sense*) and bore all of its punishment. *How did this happen?* To be *our* Substitute, He would have had to been made like unto us, spiritually speaking.

How can a person have a sinful past in one sense and in another have no past sin at all? To the human mind that seems totally impossible, but God's Word still says its reality. Why is this so?

It is because there was an exchange that took place in the realm of the Spirit. Jesus took our Sin as His own, and gave us His Righteousness in exchange. I must admit that I do not understand how this could *literally* take place, but scripture is clearly states it did! As I wrote in the previous chapter, Jesus was wrapped like a package by our Sin so all that could be seen was our Sin. But the package, *the human spirit of Jesus*, was protected by His Father. In a crude way, one could say that Jesus was like a caramel coated apple, in which the caramel represented our Sin. Our Sin separated Him from His Father, but this *did not* affect the fact that He really was holy.

Jesus & Spiritual Death?

Hanegraaff further contends that it would be impossible for Jesus to have experienced Spiritual Death. "Finite individuals cannot fully comprehend the sense in which Jesus was momentarily 'forsaken' by the Father (Matthew 27:46)."[11] However, the one thing that he seems to have forgotten is how Sin affects one's relationship with God. Sin **always** causes a separation between God and man. Jesus never experienced a separation from His Father, until He was made to be Sin and placed under our curse. In *The New Inquisition*, Robert W. Tozier commented on how Jesus literally experienced Spiritual Death (separation) from His Father.

"**SEPARATION**—Hanegraaff says that because of 1 Peter 3:18 'Jesus' sacrifice was *physical* in character. He asks '...why is there no explicit mention of Christ's alleged 'spiritual' death, while the Bible is replete with details on the fact and significance of His physical death—especially if it was His spiritual death that did away with the curse. Hanegraaff quotes Kenneth Hagin regarding spiritual death saying that: 'Spiritual death also means having Satan's nature...Jesus tasted death—spiritual death—for every man.'...In the full context Hagin is merely stating what Stott so eloquently writes: 'He was not only '**made** flesh'...he was '***made sin***' on the cross...**in desolate spiritual abandonment...Our sins sent Christ to hell. He tasted the torment of a soul estranged from God**'...In proper context, Satan's nature means sin. Christ was made sin on the cross for us. Does Hanegraaff fail to grasp the fact that sin causes a spiritual separation and that 'desolate spiritual abandonment' is referring to spiritual separation?...Christ was and remains sinless, but He was 'made sin' in our place. If 'made sin,' **He then suffered for us the consequences of those sins**. He paid our '**wages**' so that we wouldn't have to. According to Stott, 'sin is transgression.' He goes on to say that the consequences of sin are 'alienation from God.'...Again Stott says: '**Sin brings inevitable separation, and this separation is 'death,' spiritual death**, the severance of a person from God."[12]

Kenneth Copeland, as well, explains how Jesus actually experienced Spiritual Death as our Scapegoat:

"I've had people ever since I've been in the ministry try to tell me that Jesus just went into the paradise area of hell, and not down into that pit. If that's truth then He didn't suffer and if He didn't suffer then you're going to have to. Now let's just settle that right now. Amen! Quit Mickey mousing around with the cross of Calvary...No human being has ever experienced **all** Sin and *all of its suffering* and **all** sickness and **all** disease. Nobody but Him!...what everybody gets so upset about is when you go to talking about Jesus experiencing Spiritual Death. *Which is separation from God!*...If He wasn't separated from God there's no way for you to ever be join to God. See! Whatever He did was for you and for me. He didn't do anything for Himself."[13]

Copeland's point makes complete sense. Jesus experienced all **Sin** and all its suffering, and all sickness and all disease, not to mention the suffering that accompanies them as well. He paid the price for Adam's fall from grace as if He was the One Who originally committed it. This is why He had to be *completely* abandoned by His Father for the three days and nights. This is what would have happened to us, except **we** would have been completely abandoned *for all* eternity.

Charles Capps wrote several comments in his book, *Authority in Three Worlds*, which I believe are important to add to our discussion, in order to help clarify the idea of Jesus experiencing Spiritual Death.

"In the Garden, Jesus said, *My soul is exceeding sorrowful* **unto death** (Mark 14:34). Here you realize there's something in Jesus' mind other than physical death. He certainly was not afraid to die physically. He was suffering the thoughts of the separation from His Father that He knew was soon to come. He was about to take

what should have been coming to mankind, and this would separate Him from His Father. This was the part that was so horrible:
the separation from God. He was to become sin. He wrestled
with it until blood came through His pores and dropped to the
ground."[14]

"There was **no way** Satan could get a hold of Jesus. There was **no
sin** in Him. Satan could not lay any kind of claim to Him. The
blood of God flowed in His veins. Jesus was a union of the *Word
of God* and *human flesh*. Jesus knew He was on His way to the cross
as He said, 'Satan cometh but he hath nothing in Me,' and 'No
man takes My life; I lay it down of Myself.'"[15]

"Jesus had to be without spot. **There could be no sacrifice offered that was blemished or had any cause of death in Him.**
The satanic forces were rejoicing that Jesus had been delivered
up...the Son of God was sentenced *illegally* and crucified. Jesus
had given Himself up to the Father's plan. He was nailed to the
cross. As He hung there, suspended between heaven and earth,
darkness covered the land for three hours...The Hebrew word for
death is plural—not *one* death, but *two*. 'He made his grave with the
wicked in his *deaths.*' *For he hath made him to be sin for us, who know no
sin; that we might be made the righteousness of God in him* (2 Cor. 5:21).
No! Jesus did not become a sinner! **He became sin!** He took
our sin upon *Himself* and bore those sins away...Jesus became sin
that we might be righteous...that we might have eternal redemption...**After** *the atonement* for sin (sin offering) was made, *Jesus was
made to be sin* and went to the place of the wicked dead. He made
His grave in hell with the wicked...."[16]

We have covered a great deal of information here, so let's examine this information that Capps has given and see if his doctrine is really
heretical as Hanegraaff would lead one to believe.

First of all, Capps illustrates why he believes Jesus was experiencing such terrible sorrow in the Garden of Gethsemane. He notes that
Jesus was being attacked in His mind concerning the fact that He would
be separated from the Presence of His Father. I agree with Capps' belief.
Without a doubt, Jesus was not afraid of going to the cross to be crucified, but He did fear something even greater—separation from His
Father. When I say "fear," I do not mean *fear* as in *fright*, but rather as in
an awesome respect for His Father's Presence, which He did not want to

lose. The *thought* of losing His Father's Presence was totally detestable to Him.

Contrary to what Hanegraaff has written, Capps makes one point completely clear. Satan had no hold on Jesus, because there *was no* sin in Him. This is why He had to become Sin, so He could bare our Sin away (as far as the east is from the west) and pay the **full** penalty for it, *as if* He had committed it. He further comments that Jesus **had to be** without spot. There could be no sacrifice offered that was blemished and **after** the Atonement for Sin was made, **then** Jesus was made to be Sin. Jesus *remained* holy and He also wasn't brought under the curse of our Sin until *after* He had made an Atonement (covering) for the Sin of the world.

The Father then laid His hands on Jesus' human spirit and confessed the Sin of the world over Him and He became separated from the Father. This took place shortly before He released His spirit from His body. Jesus couldn't possibly have been made Sin until He made Atonement. It was at this point that He became the Scapegoat the Sin bearer. The book of Leviticus records the Sin offering as: two animals—one sacrifice for Sin. Jesus was the Substitute for both of these animals.

If you recall in the book of Leviticus, the Sin offering was made with two young goats—Two goats, **one** sacrifice. One of these goats was killed and the blood was sprinkled upon and before the mercy seat for Atonement (Lev. 16:5-9, 15-18). The second goat was the *scapegoat* which was to be presented before the Lord **alive**. Then the priest would lay his hands upon it, confess the sin of the people over it and it would be sent away into the *uninhabitable parts* of the earth (Lev. 16:10,21;22), which was the Old Covenant type of what happened to Jesus at Calvary. His blood was shed for an Atonement (covering).

Then the Father laid His "hands" upon Jesus while He was alive *physically*, and confessed the Sin of the world over Him, He died Spiritually and went to hell (the most uninhabitable part of the earth). When Leviticus says, "a land not inhabited or wilderness," it was actually referring to hell itself. *The Amplified Bible* says it this way: "a land cut off (a land of forgetfulness *and* separation, not inhabited)!" This is where Jesus had to go for three days and nights as *our* Scapegoat.

Finally, Capps states that Jesus became Sin, not a sinner! He in no way is saying that Jesus' holy, precious character was turned into some evil, demonic character: "Jesus **did not** sin. *He was holy*. He went before us and received that which we should have suffered…No! Jesus **never** sinned at any time!"[17]

I would like to stress an important point concerning why Jesus *had* to go to hell. Why did Israel have to perform the Sin offering once a year? It was because the sins of the people could not be *blotted out* before the cross. In their day, Sin was only Atoned or *covered over* by the blood that was placed upon the mercy seat. But Sin still remained—it was covered, but **not** blotted out. On the cross, Jesus shed His blood and made the final blood Atonement. However, there was still a problem that needed to be dealt with. *Yes* Jesus' blood covered our Sin, but it was still not removed, as far as the east is from the west. Punishment was **every bit** a part of the price of Sin, as was His physical death. This is where His three day stay in hell comes into play.

In order for the blotting out of our Sin to be for all eternity, someone would have to pay the penalty for Sin, which *was not merely* physical death. **If** physical death was the complete penalty for Sin, **then** every person could pay their own penalty and go to heaven based on their works. No! The true penalty for Sin was Eternal Separation from God (*Spiritual Death*), plus punishment by fire in hell. We would have paid that punishment if Jesus had not done so. Once the full penalty (price & punishment) for Sin was paid for by Jesus, He **had to be** resurrected (spiritual then physically), and reunited with His Father, because He truly was righteous. Sin's *sentence* had been paid, and Sin could now be blotted out of our lives for eternity. If Jesus had not gone into hell and suffered under our sentence of Death, then resurrected, His crucifixion would only have made a temporary covering much like the yearly sacrifice of the Old Covenant. The appeasement of God's wrath upon Sin was the key factor in our Sin being *Eternally blotted out*—removed. And Jesus endured the wrath of His Father in our place!

It was payment of the penalty of Sin that caused God to blot out (never remember again) our Sin against us. And the resurrection of Jesus made the new birth available to all who would believe on His Name. Had He not resurrected, we would not have been able to be recreated in Him. **Eternal Redemption** was officially declared in heaven. After Jesus rose from the dead (Spiritual and physically), He presented Himself with His blood and poured it out upon the mercy seat in heaven.

This concluded *Eternal Redemption*, and the throne of God became open to all who would believe upon the Name & Blood of Jesus. Jesus paid the ultimate price/penalty to purchase us back from Satan's control. Thus, dedicating ourselves to Him is the least that we can do to say **Thank You**! The Day of Atonement was **never** finished *until* the blood had been poured out on the mercy seat and the scapegoat was released.

According to Hanegraaff, when Jesus said, "It is finished," He meant that the Atonement was completely finished.[18] However, according to Old Covenant Law, the Day of Atonement was not complete until after the blood was placed on the mercy seat and the scapegoat was sent away into the uninhabitable parts of the earth. Jesus accomplished all of these and then poured out His blood in heaven. Again, Kenneth Hagin shared some insightful comments concerning Jesus' last words.

"Many have thought that when Jesus said on the Cross, 'It is finished.' He was talking about our salvation. No! No! No! Our salvation wasn't finished when Jesus died. Salvation wasn't complete **until** He ascended into the heavenly Holy of Holies to obtain eternal redemption for us. (See Hebrews chapter 9). When Jesus said 'It is finished' on the cross, He was talking about the Old Covenant being finished. And when He said those words, *the curtain that sealed off the Holy of Holies in the Temple was* **rent in twain** — or torn in half — from top to bottom (Mark 15:38)."[19]

Seeing that we have already examined chapter nine of the book of Hebrews, we will not take the time to do it again. However, I would like to restate that after Jesus said, "It is finished" and gave up His spirit to Death (Spiritual) the veil in the temple was immediately torn in two pieces—from top to bottom. Hence, this is a confirmation that the Old Covenant had been fulfilled by a Man. Jesus lived on this earth as a man, and completed the Mosaic Law.

Moreover, if salvation was complete, why did Jesus have to spend three days and nights in the heart of the earth? If everything that was required to pay for salvation was done at the cross itself, then Jesus should have been able to go to paradise, preach the Gospel, and then resurrect immediately thereafter.

Nonetheless, most believers know that God set a three day time frame that Jesus needed to complete **before** He could be resurrected by His Father. There had to be a reason why the Father predetermined that Jesus would spend three days and nights in the heart of the earth. That reason was that He had to pay the full penalty of Sin, which was Spiritual Death and all its punishment.

The Resurrection: A Chronology

According to Hanegraaff, after Jesus died, He went **directly** into the place called Paradise. As proof, he sites Luke 23:43, "...I tell you the truth, today you will be with me in paradise."[20] But, is this the actual chronology that took place, starting when Jesus released His human spirit to Death and ending when He ascended (*arose to life*)? I dare say that Luke 23:43 is not the complete timetable of events involving Jesus' Death and resurrection.

> **Matthew 16:21 (TAB)**: From that time forth Jesus began [clearly] to show His disciples that He must go to Jerusalem and suffer many things at the hands of the elders and the high priests and scribes, and be killed, *and* **on** *the third day* be raised from death.

> **Ephesians 4:8-11**: Wherefore he saith, **When** *he* **ascended up** *on high*, **he led** *captivity captive*, and gave gifts unto men. (Now that he ascended, what is it but that *he also descended* **first** into the lower parts of the earth? He that descended is the same also that ascended up far above all heavens, that he might fill all things.) And he gave some, apostles; and some, prophets; and some, evangelists; and some, pastors and teachers.

First, the Word of God tells us that from the time Peter received the revelation that Jesus was the Christ, Jesus had begun to tell His disciples that He would be tortured by the nations, killed, and He would rise again to life (resurrect) sometime on the third day after His Death. Thus, we know that Jesus didn't resurrect (ascend back to life—spiritually or physically) until *sometime* during the third day after His crucifixion.

Next, consider for a moment the words of Paul in Ephesians 4: 8-10. Paul clearly points out that Jesus *did not* lead captivity captive, **until** He came back to life (resurrected) and ascended from the lower parts of the earth. The word *ascended* as defined by the concordance means "**to go up** (lit. or fig.):--**arise**, ascend (**up**), *climb* (go, grow, rise, spring) up, come (up)."[21] Hence, He became alive again, then ascend (climbed) **up** and led captivity captive. Jesus did not come back to life or ascend up into Paradise until **after** the third day, as prescribed by the heavenly Father! Note Paul's wording in this next verse of Scripture.

> **Ephesians 4:9 (TAB)**: [But He ascended?] Now what can this, He ascended, mean but that He had **previously descended** from

145

[the heights of] heaven **into** [the depths], the ***lower parts*** of the earth?

Paul is clearly saying that Jesus did ascend (rise up, climb), but **before** that event took place, He had to descend into the place called Hades where He had to remain until the day of His resurrection (the third day). Jesus had to come back to life *before* He was able to go into Paradise **with** the keys of death, hell, and the grave in His hand. How can I be so sure? It is because Paul clearly states that Jesus descended into hell *before* He rose from the Dead and climbed up into Paradise to lead captivity captive. Moreover, note that the Scripture said in Matthew 16: 21 that Jesus told the disciples that He must be killed and then rise to life **on the third day**, *not before.*

Furthermore, Ephesians 4: 8-10 shows us that Jesus **did not** ascend into Paradise and lead captivity captive, ***until after*** He had resurrected *on the third day.* That could **only** mean that He spent three days and nights in Hades (hell itself).

Then, He resurrected (arose, climbed up) to Paradise *after* He had taken away the keys of death, hell, and the grave from Satan. If this were not the case, those captive in captivity ***could not*** have been legally released from Death, because Death still would have reigned over them by Sin. Jesus had to defeat Death, hell, and the grave **before** He could reign over them. His victory over these enemies took place *on the third day*, when He resurrected victorious over Death, hell, and the grave.

Acts 2:24, 26, 27: Whom God hath raised up, *having* **loosed** *the pains of* **death**: *because it* **was not** *possible that he should be holden of it*...Therefore did my heart rejoice, and my tongue was glad; moreover also my flesh shall rest in hope: Because thou wilt not leave my soul **in hell**, neither wilt thou suffer thine Holy One to **see corruption.**

God, the Father, loosed the pains of Death from Jesus, and resurrected Him victorious over Death, hell, and the grave. At His resurrection, Jesus rose up the Conqueror over these enemies, and He ascended up into Paradise to lead captivity captive. Those captive in Paradise could not have been set free from death, until after Jesus was loosed from Death, because He was the Substitute Sacrifice. He did all of this in our place, on our behalf. Victory was His and ours on the third day at His resurrection.

It makes no difference what we like or don't like. What matters most are the facts that have been clearly noted in the Scriptures. Jesus had to defeat death, *before* those in Paradise could be pardoned. Without Jesus possessing the final victory over these enemies, no one else could have benefited from His Substitute Sacrifice. Jesus defeated them by Spiritually and physically resurrecting from among the Spiritually Dead. In other words, He was among those who were eternally sperated from the Presense of God.

Colossians 2:12-15 (TAB): "[Thus you were circumcised when] you were buried with Him in [your] baptism, in which you were also raised with Him [**to anew life**] through [your] faith in the working of God [*as displayed*] **when He raised Him up from the dead**. And you who were dead in trespasses and in the uncircumcision of your flesh (your sensuality, your sinful carnal nature), [God] *brought to life* **together with** [Christ], having [freely] **forgiven us all our transgressions**, Having **cancelled** *and* **blotted out** *and* **wiped away** the handwriting of the note (bond) *with its legal decrees and* demands which was in force *and* stood against us (hostile to us)…by nailing it to [His] cross. [God] disarmed the principalities and powers that were ranged against us and made a bold display *and* public example of them, in triumphing over them *in Him* **and** in it [*the cross*]."

Romans 1:4 (TAB): And [as to His divine nature] according to the Spirit of holiness was openly designated the Son of God in power [in a striking, triumphant and miraculous manner] by His resurrection from the dead, even Jesus Christ our Lord (the Messiah, the Anointed One).

Finally, I would like to make a few brief points from the above verses of Scripture. Colossians 2 tells us clearly that we were raised to new life along side of Jesus. This means we were also raised to new or renewed spiritual life. Also, when this passage says Christ forgave us our transgressions, the implication is that He has also cancelled, blotted out, and wiped away our Sin.

He had to become our Scapegoat and go to hell in order to do this? Furthermore, God disarmed all principalities and powers through Jesus' Death on the cross **and** by taking our punishment on Himself.

In addition, Romans chapter one verse four clearly shows how Jesus triumphed over all principalities and powers. However, He did so in a striking, triumphant, and miraculous manner, **because of** or by His resurrection. So again we see that Jesus **did not** officially triumph over Death, hell, and the grave, *until* He was resurrected in a miraculous display of God's power. And as Ephesians 4:8 states, "...**When He ascended** on high, [resurrected] He led captivity captive [*He led a train of vanquished foes*] and He bestowed gifts on men" (the Amplified Bible – Emphasis Added).

Jesus not only led the saints out of Paradise, He also led a train of conquered enemies behind Him and made an open show of His Victory. This is the point where Jesus "showed off," so to speak, to all of heaven, earth, and hell. How can I say that the vanquished foes were not the people in Paradise? This is simple because those who were temporarily captive in Paradise were not Jesus' foes (enemies). That is the reason why they were allowed to remain in Paradise until God sent the Deliverer. They were there because they were Friends of God. Ultimately, God's Word says without a doubt that Jesus triumphed over principalities and powers, which meant demonic forces.

Even A Ph.D. Can Comprehend It

I believe that the Holy Spirit has finally been able to get through to me on how I can explain the multifaceted Substitute Sacrifice of Christ, in such way that even a Ph.D. can comprehend it. It takes Him awhile to get through to me sometimes. Nevertheless, let us embark on this new endeavor in the briefest manner possible.

What happens to believers when they sin? They cause themselves to become separated from God. This does not mean there ceased to be some sort of relationship, i.e. "sonship" it simply means that they have *broken fellowship* with the Father. The ultimate punishment for Sin is eternity without God's Presence. When Jesus agreed to take our Sin it caused Him to be separated from His Father. Sin *always* causes a separation between the person who sinned and God, that is *Spiritual Law*, or **the Law** of Sin and Death. Jesus was our *Covenant Representative* or Substitute. This is not to say that Jesus was a sinner. **No!** He was the Bearer of Sin. He bore our Sins away as the Scapegoat into hell and received *our* punishment.

What is the punishment for Sin? Sins punishment is Eternal separation from God, and eternal torment in hell. But when Jesus bore our Sin He also bore our punishment (separation and torment). God required that He go through all of this, because He was our stand-in (Substitute).

He went to the cross and into hell in our place. He became identified with our Sin and all of its consequences. Again, this **in no way** insinuates that Jesus' nature was corrupted by our Sin.

Moreover, our punishment **was not merely** separation from God for eternity (that is punishment enough), but our punishment was also *eternal torment in hell by fire and every other terrible thing one can imagine*. Jesus also bore this part of our punishment, *in our place*, so that we would **never** have to experience this terrible horror. He did all this because God so loved the world that He *gave Jesus up*—for **you** & **me**!

11

THE FIRST BORN
FROM *AMONG* THE DEAD!

In *Christianity in Crisis*, Hank Hanegraaff, plainly and openly disputes any sort of idea that Jesus was (or could have been) born from Spiritual Death. He contends that it is *impossible* for the Son of God (God/Man) to ever experience Spiritual Death.[1] Nevertheless, was Jesus *born* out from among the Spiritually Dead souls that were imprisoned in hell?

Hanegraaff questions a statement made by Kenneth Copeland concerning Satan being trapped into his own defeat by Jesus' three day stay in hell.

"[i]n hell He [Jesus] suffered for you and for me. The Bible says hell was made for Satan and his angels (Matthew 25:41). It was not made for men. Satan was holding the Son of God there illegally...The trap was set for Satan and Jesus was the bait."[2]

Let us take a few moments to examine what Copeland was saying. Copeland said that Jesus suffered for the whole human race, I believe this idea is without question. Jesus, in fact, did suffer for us, but the present controversy asks, *"In what way did He suffer?"* Was Jesus' suffering **merely** physical in nature or was there a **deeper** dimension to His suffering? Is a human being simply a physical body of flesh and blood? Did Jesus give Himself totally for the human race or are we only partly redeemed? Virtually every believer, who has been in Christ for very long, realizes that we were in complete identification with Christ on the Cross. Everything that He did from the cross to the throne of God was for us and in our place. He did not go to the cross for Himself—He was *obedient unto Death* in our place. Now, what was man's condition prior to conversion? He was lost in our Sin and Spiritually separated from the Father—Spiritual Death.

While Jesus hung on the cross, *just prior to releasing His human spirit,* Jesus became *identified* with us in our Spiritual separation from the Father. Why? Sin **always** causes separation between God and man. The

Lamb of God had also become the Scapegoat. God the Father laid His *hands* upon the head of the Lamb and confessed the Sin of the human race over Him, and at that point, He bore *our* separation and was destined to endure *our* punishment for three days and nights. As I said earlier, Jesus was like a package that had been wrapped with our Sin and He bore its punishment in our place.

This is the whole meaning behind Paul's illustration of our Death, burial, and resurrection with Christ. As He died, we died with Him—He experienced our death. However, our problem was not physical—it was spiritual. This is because man was a Dead (separated) spiritually, and banished from the Presence of God.

> **Romans 6:4-6 (NKJV):**Therefore we were buried with Him through baptism into death, that just as Christ was raised **from the dead** by the glory of the Father, even so we also should walk in newness of life. For if we have been united together *in the likeness* of His death, certainly we also shall be *in the likeness* of *His* resurrection, knowing this, that *our old man was crucified* with *Him*, that the body of sin might be done away with, that we should **no longer be slaves of sin.**

Here, Paul exposes the source of man's bondage to Sin. It *was not* the fact that man had a physical body. We were in bondage to Sin because our old man (Dead human spirit) was keeping us in bondage to Sin. When Adam sinned there was a Spiritual transference that took place between him and Satan. Satan received Adam's authority to rule the earth and Adam received the nature of Satan (Sin), which caused Him to be Spiritually separated from the Father. Man's spirit was disconnected from its Source of life—God and was married up (united, one) with Sin and Satan. In Romans chapter 7, Paul clearly illustrates the fact that we were once married to Sin (hence Satan), but because of Christ, we died to Sin so that we could be married to another—Jesus Christ!

> **Romans 7:4 (NKJV):** Therefore, my brethren, you also have become dead to the law through *the body* of Christ, that you may be married to another—to Him who was raised from the dead, that we should bear fruit to God.

Furthermore, Kenneth Copeland brings home another point that is impossible to ignore:

"[Acts 2:21-24; 27; 31]…Whom God hath raised up having loosed the **pains** of death. So Jesus wasn't in that protected area of Paradise for three days and nights—**there wasn't any pain there**. And he's not talking about the pain of the dying of His physical body. I mean that was a horrible thing. But that's not what He suffered in the Garden of Gethsemane concerning. What He suffered in the Garden of Gethsemane was this cup, this agreement, this covenant with God that I will go pay the price for all they've done…**If** Jesus physical body and His physical dying could've paid the price for your Sin—**Then our Sin was only in the flesh**. No, No, not enough—*spirit* and *soul* and *body*. The Bible said His **soul** was *made* an offering for Sin, and God looked and saw His Seed and was satisfied."[3]

Here Copeland brings up a very important point. If the price for Sin was *merely* the physical death of Jesus' body, then there would be no redemption for the spirit and soul of man. Our bodies are redeemed, but this will not be manifested fully in us until the Rapture of the Church. Man is a three-fold being: spirit, soul, and body (1 Thess. 5:23). In the eyes of God, the "most" important part of man is the spirit—the real man. The spirit is the part of man that becomes born-again.

If the price for Sin was literally the physical death of *the body*, then each person could die physically for himself, however, that was not man's problem. Man could do nothing about the Dead spirit that was within his physical body. He needed Jesus to redeem him—spirit, soul and body! His [Jesus'] soul (spirit & soul) was a Sacrifice for Sin, then God saw His Seed and was satisfied. The **punishment** for Sin had finally been inflicted. Sin had a price (the precious blood of Jesus), but it also had a punishment (Eternal separation & torment in hell). Jesus took the responsibility of paying the price and receiving the punishment for Sin. I realize that we are restating many of the points that have already been made in previous chapters; nevertheless, I feel that it is important that we have reemphasized the various points thus far.

Returning again to Copeland's first statement, Satan was in fact trapped by his own doing. The Bible says in 1 Corinthians 2:8 that, "none of the princes of **this** world knew: for had they known *it*, they would not have crucified the Lord of glory." The previous verse of Scripture is not only speaking of *natural* rulers, but it is also referring primarily to the rulers of darkness and, most particular, Satan himself. Satan had no idea that Jesus would be able to make a prison break out of hell. Jesus was the "bait" (so to speak) that would seal-up Satan's case against the human race for all eternity. Satan's fatal mistake was in forgetting that Jesus had never sinned; therefore, it was not possible that Death (Spiritual or physical) could *retain* a hold on Him (Acts 2:24).

The Problem With Old Covenant Atonement

There's an important point that Hanegraaff has seemed to miss. The Old Covenant sacrifices were temporary. What is the difference between Old Covenant Atonement and Eternal Redemption? Also, why did the sacrifices of the Old Covenant need to be redone every year? Finally, what was the missing *ingredient* that made up the difference?

> **Hebrews 9:12-15, 18-28**: Neither by the blood of goats and calves, but by his own blood **he entered in once into the holy place, having obtained eternal redemption *for us.*** For if the blood of bulls and of goats, and the ashes of an heifer sprinkling the unclean, sanctifieth to the purifying of the flesh: How much more shall the blood of Christ, *who through the eternal Spirit offered himself without spot to God*, purge your conscience from dead works to serve the living God? And for this cause he is the mediator of the new testament; that **by means of death**, for the redemption of the transgressions *that were* under the first testament, they which are called might receive the promise of eternal inheritance. Whereupon neither the first *testament* was dedicated without blood. For when Moses had spoken every precept to all the people according to the law, he took the blood of calves and of goats, with water, and scarlet wool, and hyssop, and sprinkled both the book, and all the people, Saying, This *is* the blood of the testament which God hath enjoined unto you. Moreover he sprinkled with blood both the tabernacle, and all the vessels of the ministry. *And almost all things are by the law purged with blood; and without shedding of blood is no remission* [forgiveness]. *It was* therefore necessary that the patterns of things in the heavens should be purified with these; but the heavenly things themselves with better sacrifices than these. For Christ is not entered into the holy places made with hands, *which are* the figures of the true; but into heaven itself, now to appear in the presence of God for us: *Nor yet that he should offer himself often, as the high priest entereth into the holy place every year with blood of others; For then must he often have suffered since the foundation of the world*: but now once in the end of the world hath he appeared to put away sin by the sacrifice

of himself. And as it is appointed unto men once to die, but after this the judgment: So Christ was once offered to bear the sins of many; and unto them that look for him shall he appear the second time without sin unto salvation.

The difference between Old Covenant Atonement and Eternal Redemption was, first of all, the fact that these sacrifices were made in the earthly temple with blood that was *affected* by the curse of Sin. The animals *did not* commit Sin; therefore, their blood could be used to cover (atone) for Sin, but they were still affected by the curse that came upon the earth because of Sin. The next, most important reason was that the Scapegoat which God used prior to Christ's coming was merely a physical type of the spiritual being that would finally take the punishment for Sin—Christ, our Substitute. The Scapegoat would be sent away yearly, but it would only die physically and, therefore, couldn't take the punishment of separation from God—it had no spirit, only a soul!

Jesus, on the other hand, was both the Substitute Sacrifice and the Scapegoat. His blood made the covering (Atonement), as well as blotted out Adamic Sin for eternity. As I noted in the previous two chapters, Eternal Redemption was not officially declared until Jesus poured out His priceless, sinless blood on the Mercy seat in heaven. This all took place **after** Jesus resurrected from among the *Spiritually* Dead. The missing ingredient that made up the difference between Old Covenant Atonement and Eternal Redemption is the blood of Jesus poured onto the Mercy Seat **in heaven**. Thus, a man had finally paid the punishment for Sin (separation & torment). That man was none other than Jesus Christ (the Man). A human representative **had** to shed his blood on behalf of the human race and receive Sin's punishment. Christ Jesus was that representative. If the representative did not have to be a human, then why wasn't our Sin removed from God's eyes until *after* a sinless Man gave Himself: spirit, soul, and body?

Hanegraaff Does Have A Point

At this moment, I would like to stress that Hanegraaff does have a point in some of his contention. He is correct in saying that Jesus **did not** become a demonic being and that He *was not* reborn in the exact same way as we were. His human spirit **was not** corrupted by Sin, because His Father protected it while He was made to be Sin. However, Hanegraaff has unfortunately misunderstood the point that the Faith teachers have been attempting to emphasize. Jesus, according to the Old Covenant pattern of Atonement, produced Eternal Redemption for His

Body by being the blood Sacrifice and the Scapegoat, all in One. That is the *greatest* love story **ever** told! This is true because Old Covenant Atonement and Eternal Redemption are two *different degrees* in God's Eternal plan.

Hanegraaff has, unfortunately, misinterpreted this teaching of the Word of Faith, as if to say they are teaching that Jesus became some demonic being. It is note worthy to say that, at times, the Faith teachers could better clarify their statements. Nevertheless, in the previous chapter, we already documented the fact that Hanegraaff's interpretation is not, nor ever was what the Faith teachers teach [See chapter 11]. *If* this were the case, then Hanegraaff would be completely in the right to contend with such teaching.

The First Born *From Among* The Dead

Ever since Jesus was raised from the dead, the Bible began to call Him the First born from the Dead or the Firstbegotten. Hanegraaff contends that the term "First born" does not literally mean *reborn*. Again, Hanegraaff does have a point, seeing that this term is not literally defined as "reborn." However, what does the Bible mean when it uses the terminology the First born from among the dead?

According to the concordance, the First born is simply the Firstborn or Firstbegotten.[4] Therefore, we will use Hanegraaff's definition of First begotten, which he said, "simply means 'born.'"[5] The word Firstbegotten literally denotes one being born. What was Jesus born from and how was He born? No doubt Jesus is our Head and has preeminence over His Body, but in what way was He *born* after His crucifixion?

This terminology does not denote the idea of being *reborn*, but it does give the notion of one being born *in some way*. So how was Jesus "born" after He was crucified? He was born *out of* the bondage of our Sin, which He took upon Himself. He was born *out of* the punishment of our Sin. Thus, He was born out of or from among those who were Spiritually Dead, what we (the Redeemed) commonly call the New Birth. Finally, the separation that our Sin caused between Him and His Father was abolished, and He was *reconnected* to His Father. This why Hebrews 1:5, 6 says:

> **Emphasis Added**: "For unto which of the angels said he at any time, Thou art my Son, **this day** *have I begotten* [born] *thee*? **And again**, I will be to him a Father, and [again] he shall be to me a

Son? **And again**, when he bringeth in the firstbegotten into the world...."

Please note that this passage of Scripture is the words of God the Father at Jesus' resurrection. He said that He would *again* be a Father to Jesus and He also denoted that Jesus would *again* be His Son. How could their Father-Son relationship have been tampered with? There must have been a period of separation between Jesus and God the Father. Sin *always* causes broken fellowship.

Kenneth Copeland makes a valid point concerning the meaning of the Firstborn:

"...He was raised from that depth of that pit, and He came and He came up into the region called Paradise and there He preached the Gospel and He lead captivity captive...**And again** when he bringeth in the Firstbegotten into the world—Now Jesus was the only begotten Son of God, until He was raised from the depth; raised from the dead. That means out from **among** the dead [spiritually]. And He was never and has never ever since been called the only begotten Son of God. He called the Firstbegotten, the Firstborn from the dead...Now I'm gonna say something here again and if your half listen' you'll write an ugly letter and I won't answer it. I'll just know you wasn't listening. Jesus is called the what? First, First—Firstborn, Firstbegotten. Well now God's not gonna call Him the Firstborn **if He wasn't actually never born first**. Well He was born brother Copeland of Mary. ***No His body was born of Mary***...He was the first Man to ever receive the New Birth...**from Sin to the Righteousness of God**...He was born-again! He was *born out of Sin, He was born out of death*...He was born out of it all just like you were; *only He didn't commit it*—He did it for you."[6]

As Copeland appropriately points out, God would not say that Jesus was the first to be born if He was not born first. How were *we* born of God? *We* have been born a new out of our Sin and Spiritual Death. However, both *our* birth and His was a birth that took place in the realm of the Spirit. The Spirit of God made Jesus alive (Spiritually), and so were we, except His human spirit **had not** been corrupted by Sin like as was ours. Jesus was born (made alive) first of all from Spiritual Death, which was caused by our Sin. Then He was resurrected physically. Moreover, since Jesus has preeminence to us in all things, He must have also experienced a Spiritual birth *similar* to ours. Since He was the first to partake in all of the things that we have, we can't have it both ways folks; either He has preeminence over us in **all** that we posses <u>or He doesn't</u>!

No Mention of Spiritual Death?

Hanegraaff contends that the Bible doesn't state that Jesus experienced Spiritual Death, but that it is replete concerning His physical death.[7] My question to Hanegraaff is this: *"Is the Bible a physical book or a spiritual book?"* Without a doubt, the Bible is a spiritual book that touches on physical themes. The Bible says that God is a Spirit and our worship must be in Spirit & Truth. Thus, many of the things that God said in the Word of God have a <u>double meaning</u>: a *natural* meaning and a *spiritual* meaning. For example, consider carefully what was said of Jesus by the writer of the book of Hebrews:

> **Hebrews 2:9**: But we see Jesus, who was made a little lower than the angels *for the suffering of death,* crowned with glory and honour; that he by the grace of God should **taste death for every man**.

How could Jesus possibly taste of physical death for every man? The answer is simple—He couldn't! However, when one considers this from a spiritual denotation, one can clearly see how Jesus could have tasted of Spiritual Death so that not one person should ever have to experience separation from the Father. If this were referring to physical death, *then* it would have to be saying that no man should ever have to face physical death again. But, we all know that this notion is totally ridiculous. On the other hand, the believer is born out of Spiritual Death through Christ and never has to experience separation from God again.

Moreover, the Bible clearly states in Isaiah 53:10 that God made Jesus' soul as an offering for Sin. After the Sacrifice of Jesus, God saw His Seed, and He was satisfied. The word *soul* in this verse of Scripture denotes, "soul, as well as spirit or breath."[8] Therefore, proving that Jesus' Sacrifice was every bit as much spirit & soul, as well as it was body. Hence, this plainly refutes Hanegraaff's notion that in the Word of God there is no mention of Spiritual Death.[9] Jesus was offered: spirit, soul and body—*the complete man.*

Based on the Biblical evidence presented in this chapter it is fair to say that Jesus experienced *some sort* of Spiritual birth and that He also experienced Spiritual Death on behalf of every man. Like it or not folks, as far as Jesus' Sacrifice is concerned, there was a Spiritual Death and birth that He partook in.

The Incarnation

Hanegraaff has been quite *vocal* concerning his difficulty in understanding how Jesus could exist on earth as a man and also be God while experiencing Spiritual Death.[10] *To him*, the Bible gives no references to this taking place. I must confess that his failure to comprehend this truth really baffled me. Until I realized that the root cause of his difficulty lay in his understanding of what took place at Jesus' incarnation. **Without a doubt herein lies the problem**!

Now, the Bible clearly states that Jesus was a man and at the same time was Emanuel (God with us). How could a man be "God" and still exist with the same limitations as other men? The answer can be found when we receive a revelation from God about the incarnation of Christ. *The Amplified Bible* tells us that Jesus put aside **all** right and privilege of dignity. In other words, He did not walk this earth as an all-knowing, all-powerful, all-present human being (God). This is argued by "scholars," based on the translation of other versions of the Bible. However, can the interpretation of *the Amplified Bible* be proven from a medical standpoint?

"Physiologists have proven beyond a question that the mother does not impart her blood to the babe that is formed. Let me quote from 'The Chemistry of the Blood' by M.R. De Haan, M.D., pages 31 and 32: 'It is now definitely known that the blood which flows in an unborn babe's arteries and veins is not derived from the mother but is produced within the body of the foetus [sic] itself **only after the introduction of the male sperm**. An unfertilized ovum can never develop blood *since the female egg does not by itself contain the elements essential for the production of the blood*. It is only after the male element has entered the ovum that blood can develop... The male element has added life to the egg...Since there is no life in the egg until the male sperm units [sic] with it, and the life is in the blood, **it follows that the male sperm is the source of the blood**'...If a fertile hen's egg is put in an incubator for several days, tiny veins of blood will form inside; *that is not true of an egg that is not fertile*...But He [Jesus] was conceived of the Holy Spirit, **the life that was imparted to Him was from God. The blood, which was the life of His body, came from the Most High** Who overshadowed Mary. The blood of that Babe *was not* the blood of a *comman* [sic] man. It did not have the taint of

159

Sin...There is a union in some way of spirit and blood, how we do not know"[11]

I bet I can tell you what you are thinking right now: "Kenyon wrote in the 1940's. Is there any medical evidence to 'prove' this theory *today*?" When I read Kenyon's book and found this quotation, I was so blown away that I asked myself that same question. Being a nursing student (at the time of this writing), I wondered if there may have been some more recent studies that could refute Dr. De Haan's research. I got out one of my nursing books and began to research his theory in order to either prove or disprove it. It took a while to find any information on this subject, but eventually I was successful!

I opened up my nursing book, *Maternal & Child Health Nursing* by Adele Pillitteri, Ph.D., RN, PNP, and much to my surprise this is what I found:

"For practical purposes, there is **no *direct* exchange of blood** between the embryo and the mother during pregnancy; the exchange is carried out *only by selective osmosis* through the chronic villi."[12]

I, as well as Hanegraaff, had a difficult time understanding how Jesus could have been one-hundred percent man and yet still be God. Nevertheless, when I saw this truth, God exploded a revelation within my spirit, and I could finally understand the process clearly.

Because as Dr. De Haan pointed out, it can now be medically proven that the "Sin Nature" in man is transferred on to future generations through the blood line of the father. This idea is also confirmed in Scripture from Leviticus 17:11 which says, "...the life of the flesh *is* in the blood." Therefore, there **must** be some sort of spiritual connection between fallen human blood and the nature of Sin. Consequently, one might even say that at conversion, the new believer receives a *spiritual* blood transfusion by the Spirit of God.

Again, as Dr. De Haan pointed out, the Lord Jesus' blood *was not* the blood of common (fallen) man. His blood was human blood, but it was **sinless** human blood, like Adam's blood *before* he fell. Mary's ovum (egg) was simply the part of Him that made Him human flesh, but His sinless blood line originated from His *real* Father—the heavenly Father. The sperm (Seed) of God that impregnated Mary when it united with her ovum caused Jesus' sinless human blood to generate. Hence, Jesus' nature was still the same as His Father's, except He was now in human form.

This can be proven by focusing upon Jesus' life before His baptism. Jesus is and always was the Son of God, but He never did one miracle until *after* His baptism. Why? Because He was God incarnate, God in a human body. **He was not the One doing the miracles!** Jesus said this Himself, "It's not Me. It is the Father in Me, *He does the work*." Jesus couldn't just "turn on" and "turn off" the Anointing, any more than we can.

The incident that took place in Nazareth proved this. The Bible *clearly* says, He came to Nazareth and could do **no** might works—because of their unbelief. That means He was unable to do the works, *not* He refused to do them. Therefore, the people's unbelief *hindered* the Anointing (the Holy Spirit) that was upon and in Him from operating. If Jesus (the Man) were living here *as God Almighty*, then He *should have* been able to override their unbelief and heal them.

But just like many healing evangelists today, the Anointing upon Jesus *could not* function in the midst of their unbelief. Why? It's because God the Holy Spirit will not manifest Himself in an event <u>where He is not welcomed</u>. The Bible also says that He did no miracles before He received the baptism of John when the Holy Spirit *Anointed* Him. Yet, He was God walking in human flesh!

Even though Jesus wanted to work miracles among the people, He *could not* because the Holy Spirit's manifested Presence for those people was absent—**He was grieved**. This also illustrates how our unbelief has the ability to hinder God's Presence and power in our lives. Unbelief <u>always</u> hinders faith's active abilities within one's own life.

Jesus our Lord was every bit as dependent upon the leading and working of the Holy Spirit as we are today. He did not live here as "Superman." Unbelief hindered His ministry the same way as it hinders many modern healing evangelists. Why? God will respect our choice to reject His touch. He only fellowships with those who open the door to Him and welcome Him in.

12

WHO'S CONFORMING TO CULTURE?

Having read "Cultural Conformity" in *Christianity in Crisis*, it amazes me how little Hank Hanegraaff actually knows about the financial activities of those he has accused. He has portrayed them as arrogant, self-indulging brats who are teaching the Word of God merely for profit.[1]

However, is Hanegraaff being fair in his depiction of the financial dealings of many of the Word of Faith? Are the majority of the Faith teachers only teaching for their own financial gain? Without a doubt, there have been a few teachers who have lusted after fame and fortune. But, does their failure mean that **all** "Faith" preachers are greedy for gain? Sounds to me like a case of "guilty by association." Why do so many always throw out the baby with the bath water? The irony surrounding all of Hanegraaff's accusations is that he himself lives in a luxurious home in an exclusive gated area of Southern California.[2] Not to mention that "he commands an *excessive* six figure yearly salary"[3] as well.

Moreover, his critics have said that "in 1993 CRI with-drew from the Evangelical Council for Financial Accountability so the ministry wouldn't have to comply with an ECFA conflict of interest clause, which states that ministry personnel cannot receive royalties from sales of books that are used for fund-raising purposes."[4]

Thus, the very thing he has accused the Word of Faith of committing he appears to be doing himself. This reminds me of what the apostle Paul said, "You that say don't steal—do you steal?" Psychologists would call this method of accusation, *projection*: attributing one's faults onto another. Again, only God knows if Hanegraaff is guilty of the charges waged against him, but the fact that they have been brought up in a legal action by a group of former colleagues should cause concern about his motivation.

Hanegraaff attacks John Avanzini for teaching that Jesus was not some poor beggar living on the street, as the traditional church world has attempted to portray.

"Avanzini actually attacks apologists and theologians for teaching that Jesus was poor. In utter disgust he snorts, 'I don't know where these goofy traditions creep in at, but one of the goofiest ones is that Jesus and His disciples were poor.'"[5]

Without a doubt the Bible does state that, "Jesus became poor that we might have abundance" (2 Cor. 8:9). But, what is this verse of Scripture saying? In what way did Jesus become poor? According to traditional theologians, Jesus came to this earth a poor little baby and lived in poverty all His life. Is this really the truth? Let's see!

The Birth of Jesus

Luke 2:6-11: And so it was, that, while they were there, the days were accomplished that she should be delivered. And she brought forth her firstborn son, and wrapped him in swaddling clothes, and laid him in a manger; **because there was no room for them in the inn**. And there were in the same country *shepherds abiding in the field*, keeping watch over their flock by night. And, lo, the angel of the Lord came upon them, and the glory of the Lord shone round about them: and they were sore afraid. And the angel said unto them, Fear not: for, behold, I bring you good tidings of great joy, which shall be to all people. For unto you is born this day in the city of David a Saviour, which is Christ the Lord.

Matthew 2:7-11: Then Herod, when he had privily called **the wise men**, inquired of them diligently what time the star appeared. And he sent them to Bethlehem, and said, Go and search diligently for the young child; and when ye have found *him*, bring me word again, that I may come and worship him also. When they had heard the king, they departed; and, lo, the star, which they saw in the east, went before them, till it came and stood over where the young child was. When they saw the star, they rejoiced with exceeding great joy. And *when they were come* **into the house**, they saw the young child with Mary his mother, and fell down, and worshipped him: and when they had opened their treasures, they presented unto him gifts; **gold, and frankincense, and myrrh**.

Notice these two passages of Scripture carefully. For some bizarre reason, whenever most churches teach on the birth of Christ, they always seem to over-emphasize Jesus' being born in a manger. Almost as if to say, "They were too poor to get a room at the Inn." However, the

164

Scripture clearly teaches that it wasn't their <u>lack of money</u> that kept them from staying at the Inn, but that it was full to capacity. If Joseph didn't have the money to stay at the Inn, he wouldn't have tried to rent a room.

Similarly, note that the first people to search for Jesus immediately after His birth were the shepherds who were working not far from the manger, *not* the three kings. The kings did not find Him until He was around two or three years old. And when they arrived, the Bible says, "They came into the house." Whose house? Jesus' family obviously had a house. Joseph was a carpenter; most likely he built his family a house in Bethlehem. Finally, when the Kings entered the house, they gave the baby Jesus: *rags, rocks and skunk oil? No*, they gave Him **gold, frankincense and myrrh!**

Well, if Jesus was poor when He was born He sure wasn't poor any more. See, this foolish doctrine of Jesus being some little *welfare stricken beggar* simply does not prove to be true in the light of what the Scripture actually says...**It just doesn't!** So what does the Scripture mean when it says that He became poor that we through His poverty might have abundance? How does heaven compare with earth, in terms of prosperity? The earth *in comparison* to heaven is object poverty. All this verse of Scripture is saying is that Jesus came into a place that was totally poverty stricken in comparison to the splendor of heaven. That's all that it was referring to! Hence, we can see from His birth that Jesus, in fact, was not poor, at least when measured by this world's standards.

Now let me make something perfectly clear. I *am not* saying that Jesus ran around wearing a new gold Presidential Rolex with a golden spoon in His mouth, not that there is anything *evil* about that. However, what I saying is that God blessed him financially from His birth. His earthly father had enough money and skill to build his family a suitable house. This is very different from them living on the streets without anything to eat.

No Place To Lay His Head

Hanegraaff contends with Avanzini's teaching of Luke 9:57, 58 saying that:

> "Avanzini's version of the biblical account finds Jesus on His way to conducting a 'seminar' in Samaria...His 'advance team' had not taken care of business properly and the 'Jesus seminar' got canceled."[6]

Hanegraaff's comment *gushes* with sarcasm; however, he **never** offers any viable explanation for why the apostle Luke worded this passage of Scripture the way he did. To find out the truth, let's examine the Gospel of Luke 9:51-58.

> And it came to pass, when the time was come that he should be received up, **he stedfastly set his face to go to Jerusalem**, And *sent messengers before his face*: and they went, and entered into a **village of the Samaritans**, *to make ready for him*. And **they did not receive him, because his face was as though he would go to Jerusalem**. And when his disciples James and John saw *this*, they said, Lord, wilt thou that we command fire to come down from heaven, and consume them, even as Elias did? But he turned, and rebuked them, and said, Ye know not what manner of spirit ye are of. For the Son of man is not come to destroy men's lives, but to save *them. And they went to another village*. And it came to pass, that, as they went in the way, a certain *man* said unto him, Lord, I will follow thee whithersoever thou goest. And Jesus said unto him, Foxes have holes, and birds of the air *have* nests; **but the Son of man hath not where to lay his head**.

According to the above passage of Scripture, Jesus set His face to go to Jerusalem, which was the reason why His meeting in Samaria was canceled. They would not receive Him; thus, He *was* without a place to stay that evening. Furthermore, Jesus did in fact have "field or advance men" who were sent before Him in order to prepare for His meetings. This has a striking resemblance to today's traveling ministries. In addition, could this be how modern ministries have acquired this practice? Hanegraaff and his peers do not like Avanzini's interpretation of this passage; nonetheless, Avanzini's explanation is viable, unlike Hanegraaff's rendition.

Schizophrenic Jesus?

According to Hanegraaff, Jesus would have to have been *mentally ill* (Schizophrenic) if He were to live a financially comfortable lifestyle while teaching His disciples not to labor for that which perishes.[7] However, was Jesus teaching us that it was evil to have financial abundance, or was He addressing something else? In John 6:27, Jesus said not to labor **for** money, but this was not to say that financial abundance was immoral. He was addressing those who have "*dollar signs in their eyes*," so to speak. Jesus told the rich young ruler to sell all that he had and give it to the poor for two reasons. First of all, his money was his god. Next,

Jesus made an incredible statement which proves His will for financial increase.

> **Mark 10:29, 30**: And Jesus answered and said, Verily I say unto you, There is no man that hath left house, or brethren, or sisters, or father, or mother, or wife, or children, or lands, for my sake, and the gospel's, **But he shall receive an hundredfold now** *in this time*, *houses, and brethren, and sisters, and mothers, and children, and lands, with persecutions*; and in the world to come eternal life.

Jesus literally said to the rich young ruler, "If you will give all that you have away, the Father will bless *you* with an **hundredfold** increase *in this life*." These are the words of the Lord Jesus, **not** some modern day Tele-evangelist. He wasn't telling him: "give all your money away because it is evil." No, He was saying *sow* all that you have as a seed and your seed will increase an hundredfold.

Further, Jesus wasn't telling every believer to give away all they have. He centered in on this man's problem—money was his god. Jesus told him to give his money away because he had allowed his money to take the place of God. Had this man kept his financial life in proper perspective, Jesus *most likely* wouldn't have told him to sow all his money. Anything in our lives that takes the place of God needs to be forsaken (at least for a period of time) until we are able to reestablish the proper priorities.

Jesus is not implying that money is inherently evil, but that *God must be worshipped* **with our money**. Still, Hanegraaff insinuates, "Christ did not come to bring financial prosperity; He came to focus our attention on *eternal* prosperity."[8] I must agree with him that Jesus did point us to eternal prosperity. Nevertheless, He also promoted financial prosperity, which totally contradicts Hanegraaff's assumption.

> **John 10:10**: **The thief** cometh not, but for to steal, and to kill, and to destroy: **I** am come that they might *have life*, **and that they might have it more abundantly**.

In John 10:10, Jesus clearly states that all thieves come to kill, steal, and destroy, but that He has come to give us life (spirit, soul, and body), and that our life should be more abundant (spirit, soul, and body). See, Jesus always thinks on these three realms of existence when He deals with man, and financial prosperity is covered in them. God cares about man in every aspect of human existence (Matthew 6:32, 33).

Amazingly, Hanegraaff concedes that some Faith teachers claim that they don't teach prosperity as merely a means to acquire things, but still he remains unconvinced.

"Our time, talent, and treasure should be used for God's glory…While some Faith teachers assert that they have the same concept in mind, the evidence shows otherwise…There can be no denying that primary prosperity proponents teach a lifestyle of self-indulgence and selfishness, as opposed to a lifestyle of self-denial and selflessness."[9]

As I said earlier, it amazes me how little Hanegraaff actually knows about the financial activities and teachings of those he has accused. As far as he is concerned, their teachings are simply promoting a lifestyle of excess and greed. However, does Hanegraaff **really** know what he's talking about, or is he just haphazardly barking up the wrong heretical tree?

Promoting A Lifestyle of Greed?

Understanding the magnitude of Hanegraaff's accusations, I believe it would be helpful if we were to take a brief look into the teachings and lifestyles of some of the well- known teachers of the Word of Faith, so as to observe their real motivation and lifestyle.

John Avanzini takes the brunt of most of Hanegraaff's allegations. So, we'll start our investigation with him.

"Friend, please begin to hear me on this. Deuteronomy 8:18 tells you that God has given you the *power to get wealth*. Read the verse *in context* and you will see *why* God is giving you that power!…God has given you power to get wealth so that His covenant can be established…God has given every one of His children the *power* to get wealth so **that they can be established financially to generously fund every need** that arises *for the operation of the covenant* He made with Abraham. That alone is the **primary reason** the saints have been given the power to get wealth!"[10]

"If enough Christians grasp the principles of biblical economics and apply them in their lives, every church, mission outreach, and Christian television ministry will have enough money to finance the gospel. Ask God how large your special financial gift should be **to your local church**...do not just give your money without thought or without prayer. Ask God where you should direct you gifts, and even ask Him how much you should give...If you will apply God's principles of biblical economics in your life...Ministers will be trained and sent forth, because there will be more than enough money to send them."[11]

According to Avanzini's writings, God's purpose for giving us the power (ability) to obtain wealth *is not* for us to squander it upon ourselves and live a greedy lifestyle, as Hanegraaff has supposed. No, he teaches that **the primary purpose** for God giving us this power is for the establishing of His covenant, for the preaching of the Gospel worldwide. This doesn't sound like a teaching of "self-indulgence" to me! He teaches that we should prosper—yes, but that we are also to give of our abundance to bless others.

Another candidate on Hanegraaff's anti-prosperity Gospel list is Dr. Frederick K.C. Price. Price is the Faith teacher whom Hanegraaff has openly criticized because he drives a Rolls Royce—*possibly a hint of jealousy?* Anyway, he too has been accused of teaching and living a lifestyle of excess and greed. Nevertheless, is this really the truth?

"Listen, if you are a Christian, you can have five Cadillacs if you can afford them. God doesn't care how many Cadillacs you have...God is not opposed to us having things, HE IS OPPOSED TO THINGS HAVING US. There is a vast difference, friends. **He doesn't want you seeking those things first**. He wants you to seek **Him** first, and He will give you those things...That is where many make the mistake. They want to get the things first..."[12]

"Prospered to Bless...This text [Deut. 8:18] tells us that wealth exist to establish and verify the covenant. **It should not be squandered selfishly.** Clearly God wants our needs to be met, and He wants us to have our heart's desires; but after our needs are met, what can be done with the surplus of His blessing? Can you live in more than one house at a time? *God desires that we use our abundance to bless others*...Wealth is more than money and possessions...God's covenanted prosperity is always a means to an end and **never** an end in itself."[13]

"Sharpening Our Priorities...Life consists of far more than just obtaining and possessing things. Rather, God wants us to enjoy a full, complete, and balanced life; and He has made provision through His Word for us to be fulfilled in that way...But He also wants us to keep our priorities clear: **'Seek first the kingdom of God.'**"[14]

Without a doubt, Price does believe and teach that God wants His children to be prosperous; however, he also teaches that one must have a *balanced* life in all areas—including prosperity. Price, like Avanzini, says that God's purpose for giving us wealth is not merely for squandering it upon ourselves selfishly, but so that we can help establish the covenant of God in this earth, and be a blessing to others. Again, Hanegraaff's interpretation of this message is proven false.

At this point, I want to redirect the focus of this chapter to some of the other well-known Faith teachers, whom Hanegraaff has not addressed in his chapter "Cultural Conformity," to see if they too agree with Avanzini and Price's interpretations of the prosperity message.

Jerry Savelle is a man who boldly teaches that we must *life to give*, we must bless other since we are blessed. He has been criticized by Hanegraaff (among others) for imitating Kenneth Copeland and various other Faith teachers.[15] Despite this criticism, Savelle has been used by God to be a blessing to millions, both in his preaching and in his living to give.

"The Lord hath been mindful of us, He will bless us. What's on the mind of God? How He can bless you...Not how He can harm you, but how He can bless you...Not only so that you will be blessed, but so that you can be a blessing. It's two-fold. **God wants you blessed, so you can be a blessing**...*It's not just so we can be blessed. It's so we can be a blessing*...Listen to what God says about prosperity. We all know the verse that says, 'The wealth of the sinner is laid up for the just.' But a lot times you don't hear the first part of that verse quoted. And the first part of the verse says, 'A good man leaveth an inheritance unto his children's, children, and the wealth of the sinner is laid up for the just.' God's idea of prosperity is not only that you have every need met **and much left over where you can support the work of the Gospel.** *And enough left over where you can get involved in the needs of others.* But enough in store for 3 generations—2 generation's after you...."[16]

"Now you know there are a lot of people today that have the idea that all we have to do is just kind of rush through the Bible. Find us some formula and confess it a few times and God will bring us prosperity. There's a whole lot more to this than just you finding a few Scriptures that kind of tickle your insides. And you confess them 3, 4 times and then God is going to jump on that and cause that to come to pass in your life. There's much more to it than that. *I realize that sometimes people have given that idea*...There's more to it than just finding Scriptures to confess...**I'm talking about a lifestyle here**. I'm talking about you determining, once and for all that you are going **to spend the rest of your life seeking God**...God blesses people who seek Him...We're not talking about some get rich quick scheme...We're talking about a lifestyle."[17]

In no way can I understand how Hanegraaff can come against men of God like Savelle because they teach and live a financially prosperous lifestyle. I wonder how much surplus income he's given away, or how many airplanes he's donated to others? *One would have the right to be critical if Savelle were to heap his prosperity only unto himself.*

Moreover, I can recall a story about God telling Savelle to give away an airplane that his ministry had bought and had only flown 2-3 times. Yet, when the Lord told him to sow his airplane as a seed for his dream airplane, which he called "Willie," he did as he was instructed.[18] Then, 20 years after God told him to believe Him for a Cessna Citation business jet, the manifestation of that Word from God came into being in 1995.[19] He sowed an airplane as a seed to another ministry and reaped the harvest of his dream airplane.

This leads me to another Faith teacher who is often brought to task for teaching and living a prosperous lifestyle—Kenneth Copeland.

Hanegraaff has made a fortune out of challenging Copeland because of his prosperous life and teaching. If he had refrained from writing about Copeland in *Christianity in Crisis*, it *probably* would have been a 60 page mini-book. Nonetheless, I believe we should continue by doing some research concerning Copeland's teaching and life of giving. Does Copeland live and teach a lifestyle of giving? He says:

"Financial prosperity. It's a subject that never fails to light a fire in people. In some that fire is one of faith. In others, it's a fire *of a less favorable kind*...in the minds of many people, money is dirty business...**God intends for us to use the wealth He gives us to help establish His covenant on the earth...Establishing**

171

God's covenant on the earth and giving to those in need!
Those are God's purposes for prosperity!...I've actually heard
people say, 'I don't need much prosperity. I'm a simple person
with a simple life. So I just ask God for enough to meet my
needs.' They think that's humility, but it's not. **It's selfishness!**
They could ask God for a million dollars, take out just enough to
meet their own needs, and give the rest...they've been brain-
washed by a world that says if you have it, you have to keep it!
Without realizing it, what these people are actually saying is, 'All I
care about is meeting my own needs. I have no ambition to help
meet anyone else's.'"[20]

"What are you willing to do where the devil and demons and
lusts of other things and the deceitfulness of riches and persecu-
tion and affliction—what are you willing to go through? Well just
how far are you willing to go when they go calling you crazy and
they go calling you nutty and bad mouthing your mother and
your daddy? **And calling you and extremist, and greedy and
all that because God started blessing you financially?**...We
[Gloria & Kenneth] were called Bible nuts, extremist! I am an extremist! Now there are people that go to the extreme *to the point of
getting out and off of the will of God*, but that's not for you to judge
where somebody else is concerned...Where you *really* become
an extremist **is when you get out beyond the Bible.** *You're
trying to believe for things or do things beyond what the
Word promises you.* Now when you get out beyond the Promises of
God you're out on real dangerous ground (i.e. believing that you'll own
every oil well in the world—that's not Promised in His Word)...I
[we] must get my [our] wants **in line** with the Word...You're going to have to find out what's promised, and stay in those
Promises."[21]

Consequently, Copeland's words graphically show that he agrees
with the rest of the Faith teachers who have been addressed thus far. He
in no way believes nor teaches people to live a greedy, self-centered lifestyle. In fact, he teaches and lives the **exact** opposite, despite the various
fantasies that Hanegraaff desires to create.

For example, Kenneth Copeland Ministries generously supports
a number of ministries who are doing the work of preaching the Gospel.

"Sowing into Kenneth Copeland Ministries stretches farther than
the millions of lives KCM touches...When you give to KCM, 10

percent of every gift is given **to other ministries who reach people we can't**. We actually re-sow a 10th of every gift and product purchase into lives all over the world."[22]

That's just the beginning. Jay Sekulow, of the American Center For Law and Justice, testified how KCM helped his ministry finance the reproduction of documents for three court cases which he needed to go to the Supreme Court.

"In 1990 and 1991, we were a small ministry…our caseload consisted of one case, which at the time was before the Supreme Court…All of a sudden—and of course I know the Lord was in control of this—I got calls from two other ministries which had cases before the Supreme Court. Now, I had three cases to argue, and a budget of only $105,000. We needed a lot of money and fast, because when you take a case to the Supreme Court of the United States, the printing alone costs $40,000. **That's just for getting the printed briefs**…That's when I got a call from Gloria Copeland. She said that their ministry had been praying for us, and they were going to plant a seed into our ministry. Well, that seed paid for the printing **of all three** Supreme Court cases.[23]

If my calculations are correct, and I know that they are, this means that KCM gave an offering (seed-gift) to Sekulow's ministry that totaled *no less than* $120,000. Not to mention the fruit that they helped produce by allowing Sekulow the opportunity to argue these cases before the Supreme Court for three ministries.

I've saved the best blessing for last. Remember the dream airplane of Jerry Savelle that I told you about earlier. Well, the Copeland's miraculously acquire **the very** airplane "Willie" that Savelle pointed at 20 yrs. earlier and called into his ministry. This was the very first Cessna Citation business jet ever built—001. Well, Savelle was planning to purchase "Willie" from KCM in cash, when Copeland announced to Savelle in a meeting, "[Jerry] that airplane is yours…No you don't understand, that airplane is yours…No, you don't understand son…*I'm giving it to you*."[24]

According to Savelle, that airplane (offering) was worth three quarters of a million dollars ($750,000).[25] Now you tell me who's teaching and living a lifestyle of greed and excess. If Copeland was a covetous man, he wouldn't be giving other ministries gifts totaling almost a million dollars. I dare say that Hanegraaff owes at least Savelle and Copeland an apology for judging them without finding out the facts. It is easy for one to sit back and judge a ministry such as theirs, until one finds out the raw truth about their financial generosity. Someone might say, *"Yeah, but they don't need an airplane that's just lusting to be a 'big-shot.'"* No, that sort of attitude is pure and simple **jealously**. No one has the right to judge whether or not they ***need*** an airplane—that's between them and God only!

Consequently, Hanegraaff has *absolutely no grounds* for criticizing those noted who preach and live a prosperous lifestyle. However, criticisms in cases like these all boil down to one thing: **pure and simple jealousy**. Because if giving away expensive equipment and large sums of money is considered by Hanegraaff to be *nominative* "cultural conformity," then, I must ask, *"What culture is **he** living in?"*

13

PTL: [P]ASS [T]HE [L]UTE?

While preparing to write this chapter in rebuttal to *Christianity in Crisis'* "Cons and Cover-Ups," I was at a loss for wording for its title. Suddenly, in my minds eye, I went back to when I was a young heathen at the age of about 9 or 10, when my brother and I used to tease my mother about her favorite Christian television show—The PTL Club. We used to tell her that the acronym PTL stood for *"Pass The Lute."* We were young and foolish at that time, and really didn't know any better than to talk that way. Perhaps you're thinking, *"Wow you and your brother were prophesying, because that's about what was happening."*

Yes, it's true that there were many unfortunate things taking place at Heritage U.S.A., but I have learned over the last 20 years that I can not *slander* someone else or their ministry without tearing down myself too. Despite all of the mistakes that Jim Bakker made, I still had **no right** *to judge* that man as if to say, "I was untouchable." I have learned to discern the Body of Christ, meaning I learned that we are all one in Christ, and if I attack another with *evil intent*, then I am also attacking myself and the God that both of us serve.

I've read in *Charisma Magazine* that Bakker has since denounced the "Prosperity Gospel" as the "source" of his downfall.[1] Without being disrespectful to Bakker, I wish to say that the "Prosperity Gospel" *was not* the cause of his downfall, but rather it was **his** *unbalanced version* of that *message* which caused him to fall. We must remember not throw the baby out with the bath water! [We'll address this again later]. My use of PTL in cynical terminology *is not* meant as a cruel incitement against Bakker or his former ministry.

Unfortunately, Hank Hanegraaff has called most of today's Faith teachers "Con-men" and has compared them and their ministerial activities to the likes of Johann Tetzel, a man who convinced the Roman Catholic Church to sell indulgences as payment to be released from sin.[2] Furthermore, in the process of his cynical remarks towards these ministers, he also *implied* that he himself is some sort of modern-day Martin Luther bringing a new reformation of traditional "Orthodox" Christianity.[3]

175

I find it *curious* that he has compared himself to Martin Luther, because there is a historical fact about Luther that not many people know. Martin Luther not only wrote the famous Ninety-Five Theses, but he also wrote aggressive *anti-Semitic material against the nation of Israel* (because he couldn't win them to Christ), which was a major source of inspiration to Hitler to exterminate every Jew from planet earth.[4] Could Hanegraaff's *methods* of writing be inspired by the same spirit that inspired Luther to write?

According to Hanegraaff, the Faith teachers, similar to Tetzel, are still capitalizing on the spiritual insecurity and Scriptural illiteracy of believers today.[5] It saddens me how he can compare anointed men and women of God to a con-artist, who was only fleecing the Catholic flock. Tetzel **was not** *twisting* the Scriptures; he was writing his *own* doctrinal version of "Scripture," which is a far cry from a *few* preachers who became overbalanced in an area and "fell from grace." I'm sorry; I see **absolutely no comparison** between the offenders of the prosperity message and the occult actions of Tetzel.

Please understand I am not attempting to justify the sins of those who have fallen due to their unbalanced teaching on prosperity. Nevertheless, most of those who have fallen started out on the right road, but ended up being deceived by Satan and fell. Just a reminder: "*Who are we, anyway to look down on those who have erred? We too could be attacked as they were and fall if we do not abide in the Word and the Word in us.*" Now let's look and see if the majority of the Faith teachers today are to be remotely compared with the likes of Tetzel?

In Need—Plant A Seed

In his attack against evangelist Oral Roberts, Hanegraaff relies rigidly upon the words of Richard Roberts' (son of Oral Roberts) former wife, Patti Roberts. For him to rely upon a source such as an ex-wife for the "truth" again shows he is resorting to the level of tabloid journalism. To me, her motivation for assisting Hanegraaff and writing her own book was obvious: self-indulgent retribution. Like Hanegraaff, she too attempts to compare Roberts (among others) to Tetzel's disreputable actions.[6] How can Hanegraaff seriously rely upon the affidavit of an ex-wife with a *clear* motive against the Robert's family?

Concerning Oral Roberts' controversial fund raising appeals, I say this, "If one can prove **beyond a reasonable doubt** that Roberts is lying about Jesus appearing to him (etc.), then one might have a case against him. But since one *can't*, it is best to just shut up and pray if one does not agree."

For me personally, I favor the fund raising methods of a few of today's TV preachers: Copeland, Hagin, Savelle, and Duplantis, just to name a few. Why do I favor their methods? It is because they **never** get on the television or write in their correspondence and make **emotional financial** appeals. *They practice what they preach. They believe God to speak to the hearts* of those He wants to give to their ministries.

As far as Roberts is concerned, his methods of raising money may not appeal to some, but I will *in no way* attempt to criticize him for doing what he says God told him to do. I look at it this way: one day he will have to stand before God and answer for those methods, and until then, I will "judge nothing that I can't prove before its time." It is one thing if someone is blatantly violating Scripture, like Tetzel, but unless that is the case, we have no business bringing them to task. And even if someone was in error, our purpose for confrontation must be restoration, not *excommunication* of the errant people involved. That's the Bible method of correction!

The 8 Million Dollar Man?

"On January 4, 1987, Roberts launched his most notorious campaign to date. Roberts told his followers that if he did not raise a total of 8 million dollars by March, God was going to take his life."[7]

I recall the so-called "notorious" plea from Roberts in 1987. What stands out most vividly in my mind is how the world (the church included) barbecued Roberts for trying to raise the money. In fact, there were even bookies making bets in Las Vegas on whether or not Roberts would be able to raise the money or lose his life. I, personally, am not the type to make such public statements, but as I said before, I wasn't there. I don't know beyond all doubt that God didn't speak to Roberts.

However, I remember being in shock listening to him because I could not believe how much of the Church world hated Oral Roberts when he said, "If I don't **begin** to raise the 8 million dollars to send out medical missionaries, God will take me home."

As best as I can recall, I do not remember Roberts saying that he must have 8 million dollars by March 1987 or God would kill him. He said that he had disobeyed God by not raising the money and sending out medical missionaries, which would commit for a period of time on the foreign field in exchange for their tuition cost being paid. If I was told to do something like that, then most likely I would have done it differently, but I am still very hesitant to judge his actions. I wasn't there when Jesus came to him. As Christians we should think long and hard before we speak in judgment!

Whether Roberts was right or wrong, Hanegraaff does not have the right to accuse him or his son of appealing to the sympathies of his partners as well as their greed.[8] Such language is unfair and uncalled for. With such language, he is attempting to say that Roberts knowingly and deceitfully plotted to defraud his partners of 8 million dollars. *Without plausible proof of Roberts' motivation*, Hanegraaff has no business raising this issue in the court of public opinion.

Mark my words: God knows the motive behind every man's work—including Hanegraaff's. And one day the hidden things will be revealed at the Judgment Seat of Christ. After all, what is so "sinful" about asking financial *partners* to help raise money to do what God has called us all to do—preach the Gospel to every creature?

The Hundredfold Principle Under Attack

"Today a new breed of prosperity teachers champion even bigger promises of financial reward—the so-called 'hundredfold' return. In a book titled *God's Will Is Prosperity*, Gloria Copeland springs the 'hundredfold' on her constituents. Expanding on the promise of Jesus to provide a 'hundredfold' return to those who leave everything...Gloria writes, 'Give $10 and receive $1,000; give $1,000 and receive $100,000...'"[9]

"John Avanzini has been used by Faith teachers from Crouch to Cerullo to raise money by using the 'hundredfold' tactic...If the hundredfold message were fact, prosperity teachers would never again have to ask for money. Instead, they would be in the streets giving it away as fast as they could so they could get more."[10]

In no uncertain terms, Hanegraaff displays a great disdain for the Biblical teaching of the hundredfold return. I wonder if he has ever tried it for himself. My wife and I have had answers to our prayers through the confessing of the hundredfold return principle over our offerings.

Not only that, but as I have preached the message of the hundredfold return in churches in Germany, I have had praise reports come back to me of people receiving a hundredfold return: spirit, soul, and body. Nevertheless, no one is implying that the hundredfold return is an instant "get rich quick scheme." The Bible does not support this and neither do any of the Faith teachers that we know. This is simply a promise given by our Lord Jesus Himself!

At this point in our investigation, I believe it would be helpful if we were to establish the Biblical perspective of the hundredfold financial return in the Bible.

Genesis 26: 12: Then Isaac **sowed** in that land, and *received* **in the same year** an *hundredfold*: and the LORD blessed him.

Matthew 19:29: And every one that hath forsaken houses, or brethren, or sisters, or father, or mother, **or wife**, or children, or lands, for my name's sake, *shall receive an* **hundredfold**, *and shall inherit everlasting life*.

Mark 10:30: But he shall receive an **hundredfold** *now in this time*, houses, and brethren, and sisters, and mothers, and children, and lands, with persecutions; and in the world to come eternal life.

All of the above verses of Scripture are associated with the act of sowing or planting *something*. When one sows, he forsakes the seed into the ground. In the sense of one's house or money, one would forsake or sow that item as a sacrifice to do God's unhampered will. Furthermore, Genesis 26:12 is specifically referring to the principle of one sowing something and then receiving back a hundredfold return in the same year—in this lifetime! No matter how we approach these verses, they are referring to one receiving a hundredfold increase of whatever they have been sowing (forsaken or given away). The Bible does in fact teach of a Super-natural system of giving away something (seed, money, a house), and receiving in return a hundredfold increase in proportion to that which was given. This teaching may not tantalize the palate of some traditional Christians, but nonetheless, it is supported by Scripture.

The Origin of Seed-Faith Giving

"Despite Roberts's claims that his seed-faith concept came directly from Jesus Christ, it does not fare well in the light of Scripture,"[11] so says Mr. Hanegraaff. However, Hanegraaff's assumption is simply one born out of his ignorance of the Word of God.

Commenting on Matthew 17:20, he says, "Matthew 17:20 is not a blanket promise that God is obliged to give us whatever we demand from Him."[12] *Yet*, according to the cross reference in *The Spirit-Filled Life Bible*, Matthew 17:20 is tied **directly** into Mark 11:23, which basically says, "We must believe that **whatsoever** things which **we say** will take place and they will." The word w*hatsoever* denotes **anything** we say **will** come to pass. For a detailed study on the power of our words please see my book *When the Holy Spirit Reveals*.

> "To make matters worse, this Jesus also claims that the New Testament, in its entirety, is based on seed-faith—even trying to use Galatians 6:7...But as is obvious from its context, the Galatians passage does not appeal to man's greed by formulating a give-to-get scheme...Rather, it appeals to people to crucify their selfishness and serve God...."[13]

Does Galatians 6:7-9 merely teach us to deny selfishness, or does it really teach a double meaning, in which both meanings are true and coincide? I know that it does because according to its **full** context, it isn't referring *primarily* to reaping the consequences of Sin (the negative side of the Law), but rather to sowing and reaping of the financial increase of our *well-doing*.

> **Gal. 6:6-7; 9 (TAB)**: "Let him who receives instruction in the Word [of God] share all good things with his teacher [**contributing to his support**]. Do not be deceived *and* deluded *and* misled; God will not allow Himself to be sneered at (scorned, disdained, or mocked by mere pretensions or professions, **or by His precepts being set aside**). [He inevitably deludes himself who attempts to delude God.] For whatever a man sows, **that *and* the only is what he will reap**...And let us not lose heart *and* grow weary *and* faint **in acting nobly *and* doing right**, for in due time *and* at the appointed season we shall reap, if we do not loosen *and* relax our courage *and* faint."

> **Gal. 6:6-9**: Let him that is taught in the word **communicate** unto him that teacheth in *all* good things. Be not deceived; God is not mocked: for whatsoever a man soweth, that shall he also reap...And let us not be weary **in well doing**: for in due season we shall reap, if we faint not.

For Hanegraaff's information, these verses of Scripture are focusing *primarily* upon our communicating [giving financially] to the one who teaches us in the Word. Hence, we will reap our increase in the form that we have sown it [love, peace, money, houses…]. Furthermore, Paul tells us not to grow weary in *well-doing*, **not** *wrong-doing*, therefore, we can expect to reap of our *well-doing*—if we faint not. The central point of Galatians 6:7-9 is clearly not "crucifying selfishness," but rather joyfulness because of our receiving the increase of the good (well-doing) that we have communicated (given). It is unfortunate that Hanegraaff seems to only be able to center upon the negative side of this Scripture and completely misses the "hidden" blessing within it.

At the beginning of this section I indicated that I wanted to deal with the true Biblical origin of the Seed-Faith principle. Contrary to Hanegraaff's theology, the Bible *plainly* states that the whole Kingdom of God **is** based on the principle of Seed-Faith giving (sowing & reaping).

> **Mark 4:2, 3, 8, 10, 13-14, 23-24; 26-32**: "And he taught them many things by parables, and said unto them *in his doctrine,* Hearken; Behold, there went out **a sower to sow**…And other fell on good ground, and did yield fruit that sprang up and increased; and brought forth, *some thirty, and some sixty, and some an hundred* …And when he was alone, they that were about him with the twelve *asked of him the parable*…And he said unto them, *Know ye not this parable?* **and how then will ye know all parables?** The sower soweth the word…If any man have ears to hear, let him hear. And he said unto them, *Take heed what ye hear:* **with what measure ye mete, it shall be measured to you**: and unto you that hear shall more be given…And he said, **So is the kingdom of God**, as if a man should *cast seed into the ground; And should sleep, and rise night and day, and* **the seed** *should spring and grow up, he knoweth not how.* For the earth bringeth forth fruit of herself; first the blade, then the ear, after that the full corn in the ear. But when the fruit is brought forth, immediately he putteth in the sickle, because the harvest is come. And he said, **Whereunto shall we liken the kingdom of God? or with what comparison shall we compare it?** *It is like a grain of mustard seed, which,* **when it is sown** *in the earth, is less than all the seeds that be in the earth: But when it is sown, it groweth up, and becometh greater than all herbs, and shooteth out great branches*; so that the fowls of the air may lodge under the shadow of it."

> **Isaiah 55:9-11**: For *as the heavens are higher than the earth, so are my ways higher than your ways, and my thoughts than your thoughts.*

For as the rain cometh down, and the snow from heaven, and re-turneth not thither, but wthe earth, **and maketh it bring forth and bud**, that it may give *seed to the sower, and bread to the eater.* **So shall my word be that goeth forth out of my mouth**: it shall not return unto me void, but it shall accomplish that which I please, and it shall prosper *in the thing* whereto I sent it.

The whole idea of Mark chapter 4 is a parable about how the Kingdom of God functions and operates, related to the people by use of its earthly *parallel* (farming). When Jesus taught them the parable of the sower, He *was not* merely referring to the production of the incorruptible Seed in the New Birth. He was *literally* referring to the production and increase of the incorruptible Seed (the Word of God which lives and abides forever), **whenever** and **wherever** it is sown in fertile (good) ground. This parable is the grandfather of all Kingdom principles.

Jesus asked them two vitally important questions: *"Know ye not this parable* **and how then will ye know** *all* **parables?"** In today's ver-nacular: "Don't you understand this principle? If you don't know this principle, then how will you understand all Kingdom principles?" He said, *"This is the principle upon which the entire Kingdom of God is based and oper-ates. If you don't grasp this principle, you will not be able to grasp how the rest of the Kingdom Laws function and hence you will miss the entire purpose, function and op-eration of the Kingdom of God."*

If one misses this point, one will never be able to understand anything that Jesus was saying about how the Kingdom of God works. Mark chapter four, is *the Master parable* that unlocks the mystery of the Kingdom of God. *Perhaps* this is the reason why Hanegraaff seems to have so much difficulty with grasping the message of the Word of Faith?

Jesus continues by saying, *"Take heed what ye hear.* **with what measure ye mete, it shall be measured to you....**" In other words, the amount (30-, 60-, 100- fold) of understanding that we give to our hearing the Word of God determines the increase of understanding (finances etc,) that God will be able to measure back unto us. We choose the measuring receptacle with which God is able to measure back to us. This is why He told us to be careful what we hear and how we give. Remem-ber, we reap what we sow.

Here is the pivotal point of how the Kingdom of God functions, based upon the principle of sowing and reaping. Jesus said, *"**So is** the kingdom of God, as if a man should cast seed into the ground....*" In plain

English, He was saying *"On this account or Because of this,* **this** is how the Kingdom of God functions in the same manner as a man would cast seed (sowing) into the ground." But, wait a minute, Jesus reiterates this Law once more.

> **Mark 4:30-32 Emphasis Added**: "And he said, **Whereunto shall we liken the kingdom of God? or *with what comparison shall we compare it?*** It is like *a grain of mustard seed, which,* **when it is sown** *in the earth, is less than all the seeds that be in the earth:* **But when it is sown,** *it groweth up, and becometh greater than all herbs....*"

In order to be absolutely sure that we comprehended *exactly* what He was saying, Jesus repeated His explanation of how the Kingdom of God functioned in comparison to this natural realm. The principle of sowing and reaping in this natural realm functions the way it does because the Master Law of the Kingdom of God is its spiritual prototype. The master law of farming, which says a seed must be sown, is a natural duplication of the Master Spiritual Law of the Kingdom of God.

To illustrate that this Law is consistent with a whole Bible context, the prophet Isaiah prophesied the heart of this teaching which is found in Mark chapter four:

> **Isaiah 55:10, 11**: "For as the rain cometh down, and the snow from heaven, and returneth not thither, but watereth the earth, **and maketh it bring forth and bud**, that it may give *seed to the sower, and bread to the eater.* **So shall my word be** that goeth forth out of my mouth: it shall not *return unto me* void, but shall accomplish that which I please...."

According to the book of Isaiah, the Word of God is *not only* Seed that functions in line with the Master Law of the Kingdom, but it is also the spiritual "water" which causes or **forces** production of sown seed in the spiritual realm. God's Word is compared to or likened to natural water which forces the production of natural seed. God's Word, when believed and spoken, forces the spiritual seed that we have sown into production and increase. I call this *God's Law of Reproduction and Increase.*

Thus as a result, Hanegraaff *apparently* does not understand the Master Law of the Kingdom and, hence, is unable to comprehend that the principle of sowing & reaping **is** the Master Law of God's Kingdom.

Therefore, the principle of Seed-Faith giving is completely Bible-based, and is the *principle Law* of the Kingdom of God.

Moreover, God said through Isaiah (speaking about His Word), "it shall not return unto me void…" What did God mean? How was His Word "returning" unto Him? Every time a person speaks God's Word in faith, that individual is *returning* God's written Word to Him. God promises that His Word will not return unto Him void, or without accomplishing that which He has already spoken. Now, let us return to the hundredfold return principle once more.

The Hundredfold Return & The NU

As I began to do more intensive research on the hundredfold return principle, I discovered something that was very interesting. In *Christianity in Crisis*, Hanegraaff made a comment that seemed to hold some weight:

> "To take Jesus literally in Mark 10:30 is to reduce this passage to a logical absurdity. It would be one thing for Christ to promise a 100-to-1 return when it came to houses; it would be quite another to promise a 100-to-1 return on wives and children."[14]

At first, this seemed like a very valid point, until I researched verse 29 of this Scripture passage from *The Spirit-Filled Life Bible*. Below is what I found.

"NU **omits** *or* wife"[15]

I was unfamiliar with the acronym "NU," so I researched further for the definition of this term and found it listed under the "Special Abbreviations" section.

> "NU *the most prominent modern* Critical Text of the Greek New Testament, published in the twenty-sixth edition of the Nestle-Aland Greek New Testament and in the third edition of the United Bible Societies' Greek New Testement."[16]

Therefore, the word *wife* is not even included in the translation of these two Greek New Testaments. Thus proving that Jesus can indeed be taken literally when He said that all who give to the Gospel can believe for a *hundredfold blessing* in return. It is not abnormal to have spiritual children, fathers, mothers, as well as brothers and sisters in Christ. There-fore, Jesus is referring to both spiritual and material blessings.

Points of Contact: Should They Be Used?

As usual, Hanegraaff finds the practice of sending supporters "points of contact," (clothing, oil, etc.) as an unscrupulous *tactic*.[17]

> "Oral Roberts once referred to the 'point of contact' as the 'great-est discovery' he had ever made. And well he should! In conjunction with the seed-faith strategy, Roberts has used this tac-tic to raise more money than Tetzel ever dreamed of."[18]

After reading the above quotation, I'm saddened in my heart. Why? Because Hanegraaff assumes that Roberts and others who use this practice are really using a tactic or strategy to deceptively separate people from their money. Hence, the title of this chapter: PTL: [P]ass [T]he [L]ute?

However, I believe with all that is within me that neither Roberts nor any other Faith teacher is using this principle as a "tactic or strategy" to fleece the flock of God. Yes, this has happened in the past, but please remember that those who have done these things God has allowed to be exposed. What's more, I believe that if there are those who still have this sort of deception in mind, then they too will be exposed—*It's just a matter of time*! On the other hand, I can understand Hanegraaff's concern involv-ing this practice. Although this principle is taught in the Bible, I question sometimes if some ministries aren't cheapening it by using it so often and so glibly. There's no doubt this is a solid Biblical practice, but in today's times I wonder if we have robbed it of its *power* by almost making it a tradition.

From various passages in the Word of God, it seems quite clear that people in the days of the apostles, would almost carry on in a frenzy to lay sick out in the streets just so one of the apostles' shadows could fall upon the sick and they would be healed. That seems to some like almost "apostle worship," or that these people were reaching to desper-ate levels. But we *must* not misunderstand something.

These people were desperate—desperate for a miracle in their lives. Desperate to have their family members be restored to health. One will never know how desperate one can get, until one is in need of help that only a miracle can bring!

Kenneth Hagin made a profound statement that I believe relates to the practice of using "points of contact" and other controversial ministerial methods.

"God doesn't ask us to understand His Word. All He asks us to do is believe it. I don't understand how a lot of things work. But thank God they do. **And they work because we believe**....I can't tell a person just how divine healing works. But I know what makes it work. It's faith! Faith makes it work."[19]

The reason many of these seemingly bizarre methods bring about the miracle we need is not because we have faith in the cloth or the oil, but that we have faith in God and His Word Who said that *these* methods would work. People often misunderstand these methods because they have simply forgotten how to believe with child-like faith. Often times we become so "educated" that we are "too smart" to understand how God uses the *foolish things* to confound the "wise." And Jesus said, "We must become like a little child (opened to learn), in order to enter God's Kingdom."

His Word *Never* Fails

Like clock-work, Hanegraaff again accuses John Avanzini of "twisting facts," when in reality he, himself, is guilty of such contortion.

"In his book *It's Not Working, Brother John!* Avanzini uses every strategy imaginable to lead hapless followers to believe that a failure to receive means that something is wrong with them. He writes, 'The problem is, *something is wrong with the saint*...Without fail I find something wrong in their lives.'"[20]

As we have seen so many times before, Hanegraaff is really the contortionist. He quoted Avanzini completely out of context. The section that he quoted was not an attack upon the saints of God, but rather a *defense* of the Word of God. Below is the quotation of Avanzini in its entirety.

"The Problem Is Not With the Word of God—The longer I live, the more convinced I am that **absolutely nothing is wrong with the Word of God**. The problem is, *something is wrong with the saint*. Whenever I investigate *those who claim God's promises are not working*, without fail I find something wrong in their lives.

Not once in over thirty years of ministry have I ever found any-thing wrong with the Word of God. *The Word never fails.*"[21]

In the short number of years that I have been "in the ministry," I have also seen so-called believers doing their *gut level best* to find fault with the Word of God. They would rather complain or side against God's Word than admit that they had failed. Please remember, God never fail—people fail!

They will violently fight to prove that God's Word did not de-liver what He promised, rather than admit that they themselves have somehow violated the God-given guidelines for whatever promise they sought. Job made much the same mistake. He refused to acknowledge that he had done something to cause his trial, but only after he repented was God able to intervene and restore double.

It amazes me how so many supposed *believers* can consistently proclaim that they "believe" the Word of God and yet **challenge** its au-thority and integrity. Such action is a negation of terms. If one truly believes God and His Word, then they will not constantly question and argue (*in their favor*) against the Word of God. If I believe, then **I believe**. If I always question, then I don't really believe. The word *believe* in the Bible does not denote the same thing as today's English meaning. The Biblical definition for the word *believe* is as follows:

> "…the Greek word *pisteuo*, which the vast majority of versions render 'believe.' That simple translation, however, hardly does jus-tice to the many meanings contained in the Greek *pisteuo*: 'to adhere to, cleave to; to trust, to have faith in; rely on, to depend on.'"[22]

Therefore, if I truly believe the Word of God *as the infallible ex-pression of God Almighty*, then I will adhere to, cleave, trust and depend upon it regardless of whether or not I understand its line of reasoning. Why? It's because His ways are much higher than my ways! Thus, **this** was the point that Avanzini was attempting to make. Again it seems that Hanegraaff was completely oblivious to that fact.

Still Publishing The Gospel

In this chapter we have investigated many negative issues in the Body of Christ today, and rightly so. We must not avoid valid areas that need improvement. Nonetheless, I desire to close on a positive note, one that can bring real praise and glory to God for His patient, mercy or *hesed* in the lives of men.

In *Christianity in Crisis*, Hank Hanegraaff did his best to make Oral & Richard Roberts look like two absent-minded morons. However, since the scandal of 1987, God has truly restored much of what *the devil* has stolen. In my opinion, if the Roberts' were not doing their best to live for Jesus, their work for the Lord would have been eradicated after the 1987 8 million dollar scandal. In spite of that, they are still around preaching the Gospel of the Kingdom of God (Seed-Faith giving). In *Charisma Magazine*, Ken Walker, a free-lance writer, wrote an encouraging article, called "Richard Roberts: The Legacy Continues," which discussed the progress that Richard Roberts has had since he became president of ORU. I wish to share portions of this article because it shows God's favor!

"...since 1993, when Richard Roberts assumed the presidency of Oral Roberts University, he's taken the struggling school to a new level of success. A new fire of the Holy Spirit burns brightly at Oral Roberts University. You can see it in students' faces...In the three years since Richard Roberts became president, ORU has gone from the edge of catastrophe to the brim of hope...The City of Faith, the shuttered medical facility that used to symbolize financial failure, has become City Plex Towers. Leased to more than 100 businesses...it recently broke into the black after once losing $2.5 million a year."[23]

"What's behind the turn around? Richard points to one thing: the grace of God...He has endured a long string of tragedies—the deaths of two siblings and his first son, Lindsay's miscarriages, and a barrage of criticism aimed at his family...when someone raises the subject of modern critics who say Oral's 'seed-faith' theology treats God like a vending machine, Richard erupts into hearty laughter. As long as the earth remains there will be seed harvests, he says; the university's climb out of debt because of tithing is proof of the Word's promise that giving leads to results. 'You have got to be brain dead not to know what the Bible teaches about seed time and harvest,' he says."[24]

"In his 1995 autobiography, Oral Roberts said his own strength was in building, but his son's was in managing...Were he the chief financial officer of a Fortune 500 company, Roberts would merit acclaim as a turnaround genius for his financial reversal of

ORU...Although bankers, accountants and creditors warned him against it, Richard reinstated tithing at ORU. His first test of faith came 30 days later through a $500,000 shortfall on a $1.2 million obligation. On the due date, a check arrived for $1 million...The fact that ORU has experienced a turnaround brings up the obvious: There were problems during the end of Oral's presidency. But Richard won't comment on them, saying he always wants to give honor to his father...He advises other sons of ministers not to cast off their fathers' trailblazing days."[25]

Thus as a result, it is fair to say that God is the God of the turnaround. He's a God of forgiveness and a God of grace. Despite whatever mistakes that have been made, God's loving favor is still upon their lives.

I would like to also add that the above quotations from *Charisma* have painted an entirely different picture than that of *Christianity in Crisis*. People who love and worship money are not faithful tithers and givers. People who love money don't give large sums of it away along with expensive property.

Today, ORU has experienced a miraculous financial and spiritual turnaround, all because of the faithfulness of a man to tithe and give seed-faith offerings as led by the Spirit. If the principles of tithing and seed-faith giving were not valid, I do not believe that there would even be an Oral Roberts University today. Yet, ORU is still *much* alive and *much* involved in the publishing of the Gospel through its students, books, and TV programs. Again I say, *"Judge nothing before its' time."*

14

A COVENANT *IS*
A BIBLICAL CONTRACT!

What is a covenant? According to *Christianity in Crisis*, the Faith teacher's interpretation of God's Covenant is cultic, rather than Christian.[1]

> "If you still have lingering doubts as to whether the Faith movement is cultic or Christian, its concept of 'covenant-contract' should forever settle the issue in your mind. The Faith teachers' notion that all Christians have a divine right to wealth and prosperity...He [God] is also...forced into playing a game called 'Let's make a deal.' That is essentially what the Faith movement's concept of covenant-contract is all about."[2]

However, what exactly is a covenant and how does the Bible define the practice of covenant making? In order to answer this question, it is appropriate that we do some research from several different sources, so we can better comprehend what *precisely* a covenant is. According to the dictionary, *covenant* is defined as "a usu. formal, solemn, and binding agreement: compact; a written agreement or promise usu. under seal between two or more parties...."[3]

The concordance defines *Covenant* in (Ps. 89:34,39) as, "sense of cutting; a compact (because *made by passing between pieces of flesh*):— confederacy, [con]-feder [-ate], covenant, league."[4] And in (Heb. 10:16) it means, "a disposition, i.e. (**spec.**) a contract (*espec. A devisory will*):— covenant, testament."[5] The Bible dictionary defines *Covenant* as the following: "primarily signifies 'a disposition of property by will or otherwise.' In its use in the Sept., it is the rendering of a Hebrew word meaning a 'covenant' or agreement (from a verb signifying 'to cut or divide,' in allusion to a sacrificial custom in connection with 'covenant-making...')."[6]

Another Bible dictionary defines Covenant as, "*a mutual agreement between 2* or more persons to do or refrain from doing certain acts; sometimes the undertaking of one of the parties."[7]

191

Finally, another Bible dictionary gives us a long, but very powerful eye opening understanding of what the Covenant really means.

"**Covenant** [is] A pact, treaty, *alliance or agreement between two parties of equal **or** of unequal authority*...God's covenants can be understood by humans because they are modelled on human covenants or treaties...Noah received God's first covenant (Gen. 9:9-17). This was a divine oath or promise not to repeat the flood...God made His second covenant with Abraham (Gen. 15:18; 17:2). As the covenant with Noah involved a righteous man (Gen. 6:8-9), so the covenant with Abraham involved a man of faith...The covenant with Abraham, like Noah, involved divine promises, not human obedience...Abraham did not walk through the divided animals. Symbols of God's presence did...God's covenant is not simply the selfish demands of a victorious, powerful overlord placing unreasonable demands on His subjects. God works for His covenant people. He protected them in the wilderness, gave them the land, and gave 'power to get wealth' (Deut. 8:18; 29:9). The blessings of the covenant are more than part of a ceremony. They become reality in the life of His people...God's covenant has a future. It was not limited to a brief period of human history. God's covenant with Israel was a covenant pointed to all the earth, to the Gentiles (Isa. 42:6; compare 49:8)...In the New Testament only Hebrews makes covenant a central theological theme. The emphasis is on Jesus, the perfect High Priest, providing a new, better, superior covenant (Heb. 7:22; 8:6)...Christ's blood established an everlasting covenant (Heb. 13:20)."[8]

Having just examined all of this pertinent information, I believe that it is fair to say that *the Covenant* involves a "blood cut" in the flesh or spirit. It is an agreement **or contract** between two individuals of *equal or unequal authority*. Hence, despite Hanegraaff's determination to twist the Faith teacher's words, the preceding definitions define a covenant almost identical to their own teaching from their audio/video tapes and books.

The Blood Covenant

One could say that the most predominant teacher of the Covenant among the Faith teachers today would be Kenneth Copeland. In his series, *Covenant Made By Blood*, Copeland clearly explains how he interprets the meaning of a covenant.

"...Without a revelation of the covenant, it is nearly impossible to grasp the strength and integrity of God's promises to His children. Because His is in covenant with us, God will keep His Word even if He has to swear to His own hurt to do it...The blood covenant demands absolute, unwavering loyalty...To seize the real meaning of the word covenant, you need more than just a definition. You need a revelation from Almighty God...Webster's Ninth Collegiate Dictionary defines the word covenant as 'a usually formal, solemn, and binding agreement: COMPACT, a written agreement or promise usually under seal between two or more parties especially for *the performance of some action.*' These definitions could very well describe our modern use of the term contract."[9]

Copeland continues in his explanation of the Covenant by saying:

"The Bible is a book of covenants; therefore, covenant terminology is threaded all the way through it from Genesis to Revelations...Since the covenant agreement was entered based on difference and not similarities, their strengths and weaknesses balanced each other out. This union made both tribes strong...They agreed upon a blessing for keeping the terms as well as a curse for breaking them...The purpose of a covenant is to establish a relationship which is impossible to break...In God's covenant, His motivation for keeping His Word is *His love*, **not the fear of a curse**. *His integrity is completely dependent on His own character.* God's love entails a loyalty that is true even toward those who are disloyal to Him. In other words, God is faithful to His Word even when we are unfaithful to Him."[10]

"Many in the Body of Christ have said that *we are not meant to arbitrarily stand on a promise that applies to the situations of our lives.* They believe if God doesn't give it to you that faith cannot produce the end result. Those who believe this way do not understand that God has entered a covenant with us *specifically* so that we will believe and trust the integrity of His promises. **Understanding covenant relationship removes the doubt as to whether God wants us to take His promises and stand on them**. Those who do understand the covenant know that God is eager to keep His Word. The covenant is at the forefront of His thinking all of the time...*He has told us to meditate it day and night, talk about it, and think on it continually.*"[11]

Without a doubt, from Copeland's own writing, one can **clearly** see that he does not believe nor teach a distorted, *cultic* viewpoint of the Abrahamic & New Covenant. He merely believes and teaches exactly what the Word of God says about the Abrahamic & New Covenant. Contrary to Hanegraaff's interpretation of his teaching, Copeland is truly teaching the Biblical viewpoint of God's Covenant with man. As Copeland has profoundly stated, we must have a revelation from God in order to really obtain a proper understanding of what God's Covenant actually means.

Perhaps you are still wondering why I have used so many long quotations. Again, the *purpose of this book* is not merely to write what *I* think the Faith teachers are teaching, but rather to clearly display, from their own words, exactly what they believe and teach. I believe it is best to allow their teachings to speak for themselves.

Another Faith teacher who has been *severely* criticized for his teaching on the blood Covenant is E.W. Kenyon. Robert W. Tozier, in his article *The New Inquisition*, points out some other important details concerning Kenyon's teaching of the Covenant.

> "Hanegraaff twists the meaning of Kenyon regarding the Abrahamic Covenant when he flippantly states that Kenyon wrote that God and Abraham became 'blood brothers.' Anyone that's read Kenyon's book, *The Blood Covenant*, knows that Kenyon was simply pointing out the seriousness of covenant to primitive people...Hanegraaff differs in the understanding of the covenant contract that God made with Abraham...Hanegraaff differs in the understanding of the covenant that God mad with Abraham. God is sovereign but He is not a forceful God. Abraham was free to turn down the offer. I really cannot agree with Hanegraaff that Abraham had no choice (I don't see it to be heresy to believe either way). This is like saying that man has no free will. Hanegraaff does not recognize that God had a need in this covenant contract as well. God's need was to fulfill his eternal plan. However, you could agree that our all knowing God knew that Abraham would choose to accept his part in God's plan. Even in a situation where a superior party imposes an agreement on another *the weaker party still has the choice to decline....*"[12]

Tozier continues his comments on Kenyon by also referring to Kenneth Copeland's teaching on the Abrahamic Covenant.

"The contract was part of God's plan from the beginning. The problem seems to be if Kenneth Copeland or E.W. Kenyon comments on it. Hanegraaff will restate their words as if the idea of a bilateral covenant was ludicrous. I disagree totally with Hanegraaff on this issue. This was certainly a bilateral agreement. God would honor His promises if Abraham honored his part of the bargain...Hanegraaff's reference to Copeland regarding God needing to 'destroy himself' if he ever broke his covenant with Abraham is in reference to the seriousness of covenant to early primitive people. God cannot break His promise, but man can and does...To break covenant between covenant partners to these early people was to forfeit ones life...God swore 'by himself' since there was no higher authority...There is nothing blasphemous or heretical in the teaching of Copeland in this regard. The heresy is in the mind of Hanegraaff. In his zeal to root out heretical ideas he fails to comprehend the meanings intended by those he chooses to attack.[13]

Tozier and I see the same sort of twisted interpretations coming through Hanegraaff's writing. As we have already noted, there is, in fact, no heretical teaching in the writings of Copeland and Kenyon. I am not attempting to imply that they are *infallible*, but rather that they have *never* attempted to propagate erroneous doctrine. They are simply pointing out the seriousness of the Abrahamic and New Covenant; *nothing more, nothing less*. It is clear to me that if Hanegraaff had *really* done his homework, before he took his pen in hand, he would have been able to comprehend what the Faith teachers are really teaching, and hence would have had no need of writing the distorted assumptions that he has written. Hanegraaff has a zealous desire, but the Bible says, Proverbs 19:2 (TAB): "Desire *without knowledge* **is not good.**"

As previously noted, Hanegraaff contends that the Covenant between Abraham and God was not bilateral.[14] However, what does the word bilateral really mean? According to the dictionary, *bilateral* denotes "having two sides; affecting reciprocally two nations or parties, a treaty, trade agreement."[15]

For one to say that the Abrahamic Covenant *was not* bilateral, a **voluntary** agreement between two parties is to contradict the very reality of man possessing a free-will, which is repeat throughout the Word of God. To challenge this Scriptural fact, in my opinion, is a serious violation of the written Word of God. The devil <u>orders and dominates</u>, but God leads and guides by His Righteous character. I have never read *any-*

where in the Bible where God forced anyone to believe or even act on His commands and promises. He has always revealed His will to us and then left the choice up to us. Without question, obedience incurs blessing, and disobedience *always* carries with it a curse. God says, "You choose!"

Wealth And The Covenant

In his usual manner, Hanegraaff challenges the teaching that wealth for the believer is part of the Covenant.

"The 'good news' of Faith theology is that we, like Jesus, are Abraham's seed and therefore heirs to the covenant...How foreign to Scripture is all of this! The Bible is not a mere contract we can use to command God."[16]

In part I agree with Hanegraaff. It is true that the Bible *is not* merely a contract with which we can "order" God around. However, as we have seen throughout this chapter, this indeed *is not* the sort of doctrine which the Faith teachers embrace. No one has the right to "order" God around, as if He *owes* us "the world" on a platter. On the other hand, God tells us in the Word that we are to put Him in *remembrance* of His Word. He also says that we can ask for whatever *we* desire and He will do it. There is a delicate balance between the two. God *longs* to give us the desires of our hearts, **but** He *will not* give us the things that we ask for *if* we are asking with improper motives (James 4:3).

This is the delicate balance that Hanegraaff seems to not discern. The Bible clearly teaches that God has given us the *right*, by promise, to ask for whatever *we* desire. However, *the key thought* behind this promise is that we abide in His Word and His Word in us. Hence, we will *naturally* ask only for those things that are in His Word/will. The Word will change *our* desire to be like His.

Again, Robert W. Tozier imparts some additional insightful commentary concerning the Covenant of God.

"**Covenant Means Wealth?**...Hanegraaff would lump everyone together and have you believe that Faith teachers teach 'Cadillac Faith' or 'name it and claim it.' I believe the message is clear, if God has said it's yours, you can have it. Hanegraaff mistakenly interprets the Faith message of prosperity to mean that the Abrahamic Covenant assures that we as heirs may command wealth, this is simply not so. Jesus said that if we seek the Kingdom first then our needs would be met...Now if you understood the message that I have tried to convey, you understand prosperity teaching. You can have the needs you ask for, provided you are self disciplined and that whatever you ask for are included in God's promises (Mark 11:22-26/John 14:12-15)."[17]

It is the will of God that we have all our needs met and have plenty left over **to give to the needs of others**. The Bible is clear concerning why God has given us the power to receive wealth: "*That we may help to establish His Covenant in the earth!*" This is saying that God wants us to be blessed *so that* we can be a blessing. Everyone knows that one cannot be *much* of a blessing if one is not blessed. Prosperity is much more than mere money. It is a lifestyle of giving and receiving, which God's Word clearly teaches.

The Establishment of The Abrahamic Covenant

Galatians 3:18-23: For if the inheritance *be* of the law, *it is* no more of promise: but God gave *it* to Abraham *by promise*. Wherefore then *serveth* the law? It was added because of transgressions, *till the seed should come* **to whom the promise was made**; *and it was* ordained by angels in the hand of a mediator. Now a mediator is not *a mediator* of one, but God is one. *Is* the law then against the promises of God? God forbid: for if there had been a law given which could have given life, verily righteousness should have been by the law. But the Scripture hath concluded all under sin, that *the promise by faith of Jesus Christ might be given to them that believe*. But before faith came, we were kept under the law, shut up **unto the faith which should afterwards be revealed**.

Hanegraaff has claimed that the Abrahamic Covenant could not possibly be bilateral, but rather a unilateral promise.[18] However, he ignores the obvious fact that Abraham always had the opportunity to refuse the agreement. Abraham had *full authority* over his will to say yes or no, the same as God had *full authority* to never initiate the promise in the first place. Therefore, *in this sense*, God and Abraham were on equal ground. Despite the fact that Abraham was unregenerated, God honored him and gave him His promise by faith. God gave him *Jesus'* promise until He came into the earth! God allowed Abraham to stand in the promise that He originally made to Jesus. Therefore, the promise was indeed bilateral in two senses. *First*, Abraham was a free will agent, with the right to choose, the same as God is a free will agent. *Second*, the promise was originally made to our Lord Jesus Himself. This **is not** to say that Abraham had *the exact same* "bargaining" power as God had. *In this sense*, the Covenant was also unilateral—God blessing Abraham!

Nonetheless, God imparted the promise to him because he believed (had faith) in God's Word. This gave him credit with God in order to receive the manifestation of the promise, until Jesus was born into this earth, **the One to Whom the promise was originally made**. Without a doubt, Abraham and the rest of the world, were the recipients of the greatest benefits of the Covenant but God the Father also benefited from this Covenant. Why did He benefit? He gained back His people who were Spiritually Dead (separated) from Him.

As in most human covenants, each party of the agreement benefited from the promise, *they shared in everything*. Abraham received prosperity: spirit, soul, body and financially, plus God was reunited with His creation. This reunification culminated in the Death of Jesus, and was officially finalized when He poured out His blood in heaven. When I said that *"they shared in everything,"* I do not mean that man has or will become a *god*. At this point in our investigation, such a notion should be perfectly clear.

God gave (sowed) His only Son, **expecting** to reap sons and daughters back unto Himself. God did not just give Jesus for the sake of giving Him up. He had something on His mind. He had a motive—**the restoration of His family**. Yes, God gave *expecting* to receive something in return. He **is** our example, and the Bible says that we are to "be imitators of God [*copy Him and follow His example*], as well-beloved children [*imitate* their father]" (Ephesians 5:1 TAB). It *is not* selfish to give expecting to receive. Nonetheless, it is also improper to give **only** expecting to lavish the return upon ourselves. God, when He gives, always does so with the *sole purpose* of being a blessing to families of the earth. That's a part of the nature of God.

Hanegraaff contends that "the Faith teachers insist that prosperity signifies spiritual favor while poverty is a sign of spiritual failure."[19] He uses a defrocked Faith preacher as his proof. However, this in no way is the true picture of the majority of today's Faith preachers. Prosperity is not the *only* "sign" of God's favor, as well as poverty is not the main "sign" of failure either.

On the other hand, prosperity, at times, is an indication of the favor of God. *Abraham is a prime example of this*. Poverty is also a part of the curse in Deuteronomy 28. Despite what some may say, poverty is a curse according to the Bible. That does not mean that all who are poor are poor because they are "in sin." Poverty *can be* a result of one's sin, but it is not always the cause. For every rich sinner, there are thousands of poor sinners. Sin touches all financial classes.

Moreover, Hanegraaff attempts to **bolster** his position by centering in on the *misfortune* of former P.T.L. Club founder and President, Jim Bakker. He implies that the Faith message is cultic because Bakker was supposedly a victim of the "Prosperity Gospel." What you are about to read is an edited letter that I wrote to *Charisma Magazine* in September 1996, after having read an article concerning Bakker's decision to turn against the message of faith. This letter is not meant to be an indictment against Jim Bakker. He has the right to believe whatever he desires! However, he **does not** have the right to blame his mistakes on the "Prosperity Gospel" as the origin of his fall. God's Word is never the cause of our sinfulness. The Word of God does not instill greediness or the love of money. God's Word instills His character and fruit in us, not sinful ungodly desires!

With this finally explained, please read the following letter, knowing that it is not intended to attack or slander Bakker. Rather, it's intended to show the *true* reason behind Bakker's misfortune.

A Letter To The Editor of Charisma

Dear Letters To The Editor,

I recently purchased your Sept. '96 issue of *Charisma*, and I would like to comment about the article: "Jim Bakker Rejects 'Prosperity Gospel.'" First of all, I am glad to see that Mr. Bakker is out of prison and can start his life over again. I believe he is a repentant man; however, I also see some important inconsistencies in his life due to the writing of "*I Was Wrong.*" In the 1970's and 80's, he preached the Gospel with an emphasis on prosperity, but now due to his "fall from grace," he has totally turned his back on the same message that made the P.T.L. Club *so successful in preaching the Word of God world-wide*. I find this almost as disturbing as all of the scandal that caused him to enter prison in the first place.

See, Bakker has stated, "...the 'prosperity message' is **bunk** from the devil."[20] I perceive that he is implying this because of his *new found knowledge* based on his personal experience which landed him in prison. I would like to remind Mr. Bakker that what happened to him has **no** reflection on the "Prosperity Gospel," as to whether or not it is "*bunk from the devil*".

In (2 Chron. 26:1-5), the Bible tells us about a man named Uzziah, who "as long as he sought (*inquired of, yearned for*) the Lord, God made him to prosper" (TAB). As many know Uzziah was a young king and *God prospered him greatly*. However, there came a time where **Uzziah** stopped seeking the Lord (he did his own thing), and *because of this*, he ended up with *leprosy*! **His own disobedience** brought, the leprosy, not the fact that he was wealthy. If wealth would have corrupted him, God would not have been *the One* Who prospered him.

Another powerful revelation is found in Deuteronomy 8:10-19. God strictly warned the people not to forget the Lord their God, **after He had** prospered them. In verse 19 He says, "...if thou do **at all** forget the Lord thy God, and walk after other gods, and serve them,...I testify against you this day that *ye shall surely perish*." There is no doubt in my mind that Jim Bakker's fall was brought about by his looking to his own "*wisdom and abilities*," which gave him **a false sense** of superiority. Hence, **he** forgot the Lord his God, and started to follow self. Therefore, *the love of money* became his primary over-riding emphasis, *rather than* the accurate principles which the vast majority of the "Prosperity teachers" teach. Sad to say, Bakker's life turned out much like Uzziah's. He too walked into *leprosy*.

Now, *thank the Lord*, Bakker has been restored from the old leprosy, **but** it is apparent that, at the moment, he is walking toward *another form of leprosy*. I sense that he is subconsciously trying to shift the blame for his fall onto the "Prosperity Gospel" instead of taking the responsibility for his own sinful actions. Bakker *used to live* the life of a sinful man and now he is looking for someone or something to blame for his past lifestyle. This grieves my heart, *and, I believe, the heart of God as well*. Prosperity didn't destroy him, *foolish actions* **did**!

In Proverbs 1:32, it says; "...the prosperity **of fools** shall destroy them." Thus, foolish actions can easily destroy a person's life. The Bible also *doesn't* say that money is the root of all evil, but rather it says **the love of money** is the root of all sorts of evil. Finally, in Proverbs 28:26, it says, "He that trusteth in his own heart **is a fool**...." We all, at times, act in a foolish manner, but we are equally as foolish if we do not take *responsibility* for our own actions. I'm **not** saying Bakker is a fool, but rather that he *acted* in a foolish manner.

Jim Bakker was not "deceived" into the things that he did. He knew what he was doing. He was being corrected by the Holy Spirit all those years, but instead he "trusted in his own heart...." And therefore, he lived foolishly. The *"Prosperity Gospel"* was his scapegoat to avoid the painful truth of who caused this fall...*Jim Bakker*. Praise the Lord, it's now *under the Blood of Jesus* so you can move on to bigger and better things in God, and please consider where you are now heading?

Please, Jim, don't let past mistakes cause you to swing over to the other side of extremism. **This is where I am concerned** *the most*. You were once an extremist with the message of prosperity, and now you are *fast becoming an extremist* on the other side.

Please don't throw out the baby with the bath water, just because you were once over-balanced on the prosperity message. Remember this verse: "The Lord delights [takes pleasure] in the prosperity of His servants." It is God's will to prosper His people...Let God be true and **every** man a liar!!! Gregg N. Huestis — *Frankfurt, Germany* — 28 Sept. 1996

Any one of us can fall to the same things that Bakker did, **no one is untouchable**. But the choice is still up to us. The decision to sin always lies within our own power. It is improper for any one to imply that someone or something else is the cause of our error. We are the ones who must make the choices in our lives.

In reality, we are *the source* of our own success or failure. God has given us all we need to be successful in this life: spirit, soul, and body, but we are the ones who must choose to obey His Word. God cannot help those who will not obey the instructions that he has already given. God's Word never motivates one to sin He always leads us into repentance and restoration with Himself. It is a sin to accuse God's Word of causing one to act in a sinful manner. This sort of logic simply does not add up. It is illogical and spiritually dangerous for anyone to imply that God's Word caused Him to sin! Only a **worldly** interpretation of God's Word could cause one to error. But, this *is not* the Word's fault—it's ours!

It is time for the Body of Christ to stop blaming God and His Word for all our problems. God is **never** our problem. His Word is also **never** our problem. We are our own worst enemies. We are the ones who make the choices in our life. No one else can make us do that which we do not desire to do. It's time to wake up, people of God, and accept responsibility for our own actions. He who has an ear to hear...**hear!**

15

SICKNESS—SUFFERING, SYMPTOMS; SATAN AND SOVEREIGNTY

In *Christianity in Crisis*, Hank Hanegraaff relates the real life testimonies of people who said that they *believed* God and His Word for healing, and confessed the Promises, but nonetheless, they or their family member still died.[1] Hanegraaff wrote about the subjects of Sickness, Suffering, Symptoms, Satan, and Sovereignty separately in his book, but I intend to address these issues all in one chapter, because I believe that they are all *very* intimately entwined. Thus, they are difficult to divide up and still discuss accurately.

Having read these testimonies, I must admit that they are truly *emotionally* compelling. Therefore, I wish in no way to *degrade* or *mock* the emotional reactions of those who have related them. As I read their stories, I could honestly empathize with the pain that they went through. So please understand that I am not attempting to condemn them for experiencing the various emotions that one experiences in difficult times such as these.

My Personal Experience With Death

I can relate to the emotional gamut that one encounters due to the death of a loved one. My grandmother, whom I loved very dearly, died on 28 March 1993 of complications due to *hepatitis*. I was extremely upset particularly because I had prayed with her over the phone approximately one week earlier. When we prayed together she said she could "feel the power of God all over her and that her body was feeling better." So you can imagine how I felt about her death, knowing that we had believed God *together!* I was torn inside out and was very angry about the whole situation. I did not understand why my grandmother died.

You see, some years earlier, she had emphysema. Together my parents, myself, and our church believed God for her healing. She received her miracle, stopped smoking, and was doing fine. My grandmother was a born-again Christian. Yet, despite this fact, she was still in bondage to addiction by cigarettes. Eventually she gave into the cry of her body for nicotine and she began smoking again. However, my grandmother ended up needing an operation, a *colostomy* or a resection of the bowel to another area to continue elimination. While she was in the hospital she received a blood transfusion, and shortly after she left the hospital she developed hepatitis. My family and I believe she caught Hepatitis from the blood transfusion she received during this operation.

Without expounding on the many details, I was very hurt inside. I wanted to know why! The Lord suddenly reminded me that my grandmother was tired and just wanted to go home to be with Him—she had mentioned this to me a number of times. He said, *"She lost her will to live and submitted to the course of that disease."* My mother also reminded me of the fact that grandma had a difficult time maintaining her focus on God's Word. She spoke *more* about the problems of the disease, rather than her victory in Christ. Unfortunately, she glorified the illness more than *the Cure*!

Although this experience was very painful and confusing to me, I *never one* time doubted the Word of God. I know that what God said in His Word is true **regardless of the circumstances**. God and His Word are first place and the final authority in my life. Moreover, it became obvious to me that all the prayer in the world would not heal a sick person who had already determined to die. No one can win a war *if they* **refuse** *to fight* in some manner. I could believe only so far for my grandmother, but she would have to be the one to fight on and win for her. Despite this seemingly contrary situation (to God's Word), I determined not to cast away my confidence in God and His Word. God doesn't fail—people fail!

Death is a part of this life, but no where in the Bible does it say that we have to contract some horrible physical disease in order to die and go be with the Lord. When it is our time, at 120 yrs.—Gen. 6:3, He could simply *call* the spirit man home to be with Him. Furthermore, we cannot allow someone else's bad experience, of which we could not possibly know all the *intimate* details, to dictate to us whether or not God and His Word are true. Let God be true—and everything else a lie!

Thus as a result, whenever I read testimonies such as those included by Hanegraaff, I have to ask myself a few questions. *Did this person truly "believe" as they have said? Were they confessing the Word of God, rather than "I'm going to die," when they were experiencing difficulties physically?* The reason I say this is because all that anyone knows about someone **is what they tell them**. I can speak the Word in the presence of other believers, *but* *what am I speaking when I am under attack? Who am I glorifying the most in my everyday speech* (confession)? We can never rely or put our absolute faith in anyone's experiences. God's Word is the basis for our faith. Anything that contradicts the Word is not the truth! That's His Word—*not* mine!

It is important to note that the Greek word for "*believe*," means far more than what the average person understands. *Believe*, according to *the Amplified Bible* means "to trust in, cling to and rely on [something]."[2] Therefore, when one says *"I believe the Word of God more than the circumstances I'm experiencing,"* they mean that they trust in, cling to and rely on God's Word instead of their circumstances. Faith people do not flat out "deny" their symptoms exist, but rather they have made the decision to consider God & His Word **over** their circumstances. It all boils down to this one thing. **Where is my faith?** Is my faith founded in the knowledge of my physician or is it founded in the knowledge of the *GREAT* Physician? Do I really trust God? Do I really believe **and act** upon His Word?

At this point I need to clarify something. I *am not* saying that all those who die of illness are faithless. I am simply pointing out that it is not the will of God for a child of His to leave this earth under the bondage of sickness or disease. God does not need to use sickness or disease in order to welcome home one of His children. God is not dependent upon those things for us to leave here and go be with Him! We all have times where we are being attacked and we sometimes struggle, no one is denying that. However, we also have the choice to not allow that attack to gain victory over us! Every person is "subject" to being *attacked* by sin, sickness, disease and poverty, because we live here on earth. But, no where in the Bible does it say that we must lay down and allow these enemies to conquer us without a fight.

It has become apparent to me that Hanegraaff *literally* believes that the Faith teachers teach that we **should never have attacks of sickness** and if we do, we are in some secret sin or something.[3] That's a lie straight out of the pit of hell! I have never heard one of them ever make such a foolish statement. Kenneth E. Hagin makes this senseless notion perfectly clear with the following statement:

"I **do not** want to leave the impression, however, that the majority of Christians are sick *because they have sinned*. I think the majority of Christians are sick because of two reasons: *First*, they do not know what belongs to them under the covenant; and, *second*, if they begin to get a little inkling of it, they don't know how to take advantage of it and walk in the light of the New Covenant. Thus, Satan takes advantage of Christians and destroys some of us."[4]

All humans, including believers, are in the possible reach of sickness and disease. Sickness can come against us because of "Sin" as a whole in this world. The believer **is** redeemed from the curse. However, since this world is still under the effects of the curse and we live here, we can sometimes be affected by these attacks. Consequently, this is part of the reason why various people of God, such as: Hagin Copeland, Roberts, the Price's, have experienced *attacks of Satan* in the area of sickness. Consider the insightful words of Hagin on why healing isn't always instant.

"Why doesn't the manifestation always come instantly? There are a variety of reasons. One is that healing is by degree, based on two conditions. First, the degree of healing virtue ministered. Second, the degree of the individual's faith that gives action to that healing virtue. If there is no faith to give action to it, it will not be manifested at all, even though the healing virtue is actually ministered...Someone said, 'I thought it was that healing power that flowed out of Him.' Jesus said her faith [Mark 5:24-34], did it. It was a combination of the two—her faith activated the healing power. It was there all the time, but those other people who touched Him received nothing because there was no faith. We need to realize that this power is passive and inactive until faith is exercised. It will not operate on its own."[5]

Sickness could *never* be a blessing. Why? It's because the purpose of sickness and disease is to act *as a parasite* in the body to destroy the life of that body. Sickness and disease **are selfish in nature**, and hence could never be caused by God. They're selfish in the sense that they desire to grow and expand as much as possible *to the benefit of self* and to the disadvantage of the host. God's nature is righteousness, love, peace and selfishness **is not** a characteristic of God! Jesse Duplantis calls cancer—**rebellious cells**,[6] because they rebel (act on their own selfish will) against the original plan and purpose of God. That is cancer's *nature* in a nut shell.

Without question, every member of the human race has the possibility of being attacked by some form of disease. Some family lines are more prone to it than others. However, this is not to say that God has not given us a way to overcome the world—*even the world of sickness and disease.*

Dealing With Symptoms

Hanegraaff writes with much sarcasm, "According to Faith mythology…Ever since then [the fall], mankind has been susceptible to sin, sickness, suffering, and death."[7] With a statement such as this, it appears that he is ignorant of the fact that these four conditions of human life were non-existent before man's fall from grace. Man never experienced any of these destructive forces prior to Sin. Thus, if any of them *were* the perfect will of God for man, then God would have seen to it that man had more than his share of these diabolical *blessings*. Jesus was anointed by God to heal, not destroy, through *selfish* means.

Amazingly, Hanegraaff challenges Galatians chapter 3:13, 14, 29, in which Paul tells us that we are redeemed from the curse of the Law, we are Abraham's seed, and we are heirs according to the promise. I do not believe that Paul could have made the truth of our status more evident than that. We are exactly what Paul said we are! I must admit that I do understand how Hanegraaff could misinterpret Benny Hinn saying, **"No sickness should come your way**."[8] Nevertheless, I do not believe that Hinn meant this in *the way* Hanegraaff heard it. If he did, then why is he still traveling the world preaching healing *to believers*? More likely than not, Hinn was referring to Psalm 91, which makes a proclamation very similar to his. Still, God protected the children of Israel for forty years from sickness and disease while in the desert. If God did this for them, then why wouldn't He do the same for the redeemed?

Hanegraaff and others who think like him have a very difficult time with the idea of what they would call "denying symptoms." But, is that really what the Faith teachers teach? Do they teach people to flat out deny all physical symptoms as if they didn't even exist? You be the judge!

"Some have misunderstood this type of teaching, thinking I tell people *to deny all symptoms and go on as if they weren't even there*. They think I am teaching Christian Science. However, this is not Christian Science; this is Christian sense. **We do not deny pains and other symptoms**, for they are very real. Instead, *we look beyond them* to God's promises. Real faith in the Word says, '*If God says it is so, it is so*'…real faith simply says about one's self what the Word says."[9]

"*I don't deny the existence of the mountain [problem]. I deny the right of it to exist in my way*…THE WORD SAID IT. REMOVED…No, it's not Christian Science. *I don't deny the existence of disease. I deny the right of that disease to exist in this body, because I'm the Body of Christ.*"[10]

"If you and I are going to receive the promises of God by faith as effectively as Abraham did, we must follow his example and 'consider not.' What exactly must we not consider? *The things in this natural world that appear to contradict the Word of God.* In Abraham's case he considered not his circumstances. **That doesn't mean he denied the reality of them. It means he didn't give them primary importance in his thinking.**..If you consider what your body says **over what the Word says, it will dominate you**...'But Brother Copeland, I can't help what my body does. After all, it has a nature of its own.' No it doesn't. Your body does what it is trained to do...If your body didn't have the ability to receive training, you'd still be trying to button your shirt the way you did when you were 4...In that same way, you can train your body to line up with the Word of God. Hebrews 5:14 says **you can actually teach your senses to discern good and evil**...To successfully *consider not* your body and your circumstances, you must *consider Jesus.* [Heb. 12:1-3]...if you fail to consider Jesus, you will get mentally weary and faint before your faith brings results...*To consider Jesus you must consider His Word*...To consider Jesus means to constantly keep in mind that fact that He is working on your behalf 24 hours a day."[11]

Are Faith Teachers *Against* Doctors?

According to Hanegraaff, the Faith teachers teach against doctors and all forms of medicine.[12] Although he admits that they do not *overtly* proclaim this prohibition to their followers. Again, is this really what's taught by these people?

"Let me show you what I mean. Suddenly the pressure hits there's two books lying on the counter—one of them is the phone book, one of them is the Bible. **Which one are you going to grab first under pressure?** Now, right now you think you're going to grab the Bible, but some of you are just going to run out the door...in times of death and hard places. *You wanna call the One that has Life. Get your prayer done* **first.** *Get your Scripture your standing on first*...**Don't you go to the hospital *without* standing on the Word of God.** Do that first!...**You might not need to go to the hospital**."[13]

"Now I'm not fighting doctors, **don't misunderstand me**. If you haven't learned to operate in this, go on to your doctor. He is your very best friend. *Doctors are fighting* **the same evil** *with medical means.* **There is nothing wrong with going to your doctor.** *But learn to operate in the* ABILITY OF GOD…If you have not developed your faith in the Word to the level where you can receive your healing **through the Word**, then *use medical science's healing,* **but don't allow sickness and disease to lord it over you. Use whatever means you must to get rid of it, but don't let it dominate you.** If you have to take pills to get your healing, then every time you have to take one, say 'I take this pill in the name of Jesus.' You will find the Name of Jesus will make your pills work twice as good. *Don't let Satan condemn you over taking medicine. God wants you well…***don't suffer 39 years and say I trusted the Lord…Get some medical help**, get back on your feet, then get in the WORD of God and find out where you missed it. *Learn to control circumstances, instead of allowing them to control you.*"[14]

I believe, without a doubt, that we have addressed the questions of whether or not the Faith teachers believe in denying physical symptoms or the use of doctors. They, in fact, are not teaching either. In reality, they are teaching that we are to look to God as *the Source* of our healing and health. Meaning that we are to consider not our circumstances, but rather consider what the Word of God *says about our circumstances.* There is a tremendous difference between the two. Even Charles Capps acknowledged that if you need healing but have not been able to receive it by faith, then by all means go to your doctor—**"don't suffer 39 years and say I trusted the Lord…Get some medical help."**[15]

Benny Hinn takes the brunt of Hanegraaff's criticism concerning his interpretation of Ephesians 5:23. He quotes Hinn as saying, "*the Bible says in Ephesians 5:23 that Jesus Christ is the savior of the body…If Jesus Christ is the savior of the body, then your body ought to be made whole.*"[16] Hanegraaff then concludes, "The actual Bible text has **nothing to do with** the physical body...the 'body' referred to…is…'the church.'"[17]

Let's examine these *interesting* words. Hanegraaff is correct in saying that Paul is *literally* referring to the Church or Body of Christ. On the other hand, what is the Body of Christ composed of? What does Paul mean when he says the Body? The Body of Christ is an institution set up by Jesus Himself, but the Body of Christ *is also* an institution made up of people who, in turn, have physical bodies. If the physical bodies of the members of the Body of Christ are not well, then Christ's institution is also not well, and, hence, unable to produce physical or spiritual results.

By His Stripe We *Were* Healed

Hanegraaff continues by saying, "One of the Faith movement's favorite proof texts is the wonderfully true Isaiah 53:5...Contrary to Faith teachings, it is common knowledge that the Hebrew word *raphah* often refers to spiritual rather than physical healing."[18] Is this really true? According to *The New Strong's Exhaustive Concordance*, the word *healed* [Raphah] is defined as "to mend, cure, heal, physician, repair, make whole."[19] This definition, without a doubt, denotes that of physical healing. As far as Hanegraaff is concerned, this passage of Scripture has little to do with physical healing but rather "salvation—spiritual healing,"[20] Hanegraaff's line of reasoning is bizarre, confusing, and warped.

Spiritual healing—who invented such a concept! Is salvation *merely* a form of spiritual healing? When we were born-again, *were we* actually healed (repaired) as Hanegraaff would lead us to believe, or did something **much** greater take place? The Bible is clear that when we were born-again we were made new creatures all together.

> **2 Corinthians 5:17 (TAB)**: Therefore if any person is [ingrafted] in Christ (the Messiah) he is a new creation (**a new creature altogether**); the old [previous moral and spiritual condition] has *passed away*. Behold, the fresh *and* new has come!

Seeing that Second Corinthians 5:17 clearly teaches that we are a new creation—**a new creature altogether**, then why in the Name of Jesus would we need to be spiritually *healed* (at conversion) when we were completely re-created in the first place. We were re-created by God to be a creature that never existed before that time.

This is one of the main differences between traditional and non-traditional understanding of salvation. Traditionalist Christians cling to **salvation** merely in terms of the *Atonement*. Non-traditional believers embrace the Atoning blood of Christ, but they go one step further by looking toward *Eternal Redemption*. *Atonement* denotes "**a covering** of Sin,"[21]but Eternal Redemption means "a separation from Sin."[22] New Covenant believers are not only forgiven, but their Sin has been **blotted (wiped) totally out**. We have been freed and separated from our <u>old</u>

nature and way of living. Sin and the old man (sin nature) no longer rule over us. The old man has died and has been buried with Christ.

Kenneth Hagin sheds some light on *spiritual healing* with the following thought provoking quotation.

"I was reading after another supposedly outstanding Bible exponent (he must not have read the same Bible I'm reading), who said, 'First Peter 2:24 doesn't mean physical healing; *it refers to spiritual healing*: 'By whose stripes you were healed *spiritually*.' Well, if he had ever read the Bible, he should know that a sinner does not get healed spiritually. The human spirit of the lost man or woman is not healed—it's *reborn*. The person becomes a new creature in Christ Jesus. Old things are passed away. **All things become new.** So First Peter 2:24 does not refer to spiritual healing...*If your spirit was healed, you would still have the same spirit, too, except it would just be healed*...In only one sense of the word could divine healing be called spiritual healing: Our body is healed by God, and He is a Spirit. So divine healing is the Spirit's healing us, or spiritual healing. (We are not talking here about the healing of the human spirit.)"[23]

Hagin's statement confirms that of 2 Corinthians 5:17. We are totally new creations in Christ. The human spirit wasn't healed at conversion, but was *literally* re-created. Therefore, when we accepted Jesus, we became a totally new person in the spirit man! Hence, the healing that is referred to in First Peter 2:24 could *only* allude to healing of the physical body and soul (mind, will, and emotions). Jesus died to save us from anything that we might need saving from. *Salvation* encompasses physical, spiritual, and financial healing.

Hanegraaff claims that Isaiah 53:4 was *fulfilled* in the ministry of Jesus, as if to say that "the day of miracles" was done away with after the life of Jesus and the Apostles. Therefore, *in his mind*, healing is not guaranteed through the cross to a believer today.[24]

However, Isaiah chapter 53:4, 5, in *the Amplified Bible*, clearly shows us that Hanegraaff has missed it's meaning almost completely.

Surely He has borne our griefs (**sicknesses**, **weaknesses**, and *distresses*) and carried our sorrows *and* **pains** [*of punishment*], yet we [ignorantly] considered Him stricken, smitten, and afflicted by God [as if with leprosy]. But He was wounded for our transgressions, He was bruised for our guilt *and* iniquities; the chastisement [**needful** *to obtain*] peace *and* well-being for us was upon Him, and with the stripes [that wounded] Him we are healed *and* made whole.

However, **the Curse of the Law;** is another of many festering sores in the side of the Bible "Answer" Man. He *jests* that Galatians 3:13 and Deuteronomy 28 have little or nothing in common.

"Another example of text abuse is found in their correlation of Galatians 3:13 with Deuteronomy 28...This argument can be dispensed with quickly...there is not even the slightest possibility that he [Paul] is referring to the 'curses' described in Deuteronomy 28."[25]

Nonetheless, according to the Bible Dictionary, Galatians 3:10, 12, 19, 21 are all referring to the Mosaic Law.[26] And Deut. 28 is a list of the blessings and curses that one will experience for either obeying or disobeying *that* Law. The curse and blessing of the Law is multifaceted. The Mosaic Law can either be a blessing or a curse, depending on which way one operates in it. The good news is that **we** are the ones who can choose how the curse of the Law will affect us. If we live according to God's Word, we'll be protected from failure. There are several different blessings or curses that become evident as we either obey or disobey the Law. Hanegraaff is really arguing a small point in order to *prove* his traditional interpretation of orthodox Christianity. Furthermore, he gives **absolutely no proof** to back up his claim that Gal. 3:13 and Deut. 28 have nothing in common.

Satan's Role In Sickness

What influence do Satan and demons have when it comes to sickness? Can a demon really cause illness in a human being? "Are [demons] behind every disease?"[27] Hanegraaff claims the Faith teachers have taught this. The Bible is clear that demons **do** have a certain involvement in causing disease. However, this is not to say that a demon is behind every sickness or disease known or unknown to man. On the other hand, this is also not to say that Satan and demons do not play a significant role in sickness and disease. Also, we by obedience or disobedience have *a huge affect* on our health.

Hanegraaff claims that "binding and loosing" in Matt. 18:18 has "nothing to do with demons."[28] He says, "The context...involves *church discipline.*"[29] In its literal sense he has a point. However, when one realizes that there are two *different* realms of existence (natural & spiritual), one can easily see the spiritual application of this Biblical principle.

Remember that we're really in a battle against principalities and powers and spiritual wickedness (Eph. 6:12). All principles in the Word of God have at least two points of view—one in the natural realm, and one in the spiritual realm. So in this sense, we have been given the keys of the Kingdom to discipline natural rebels as well as spiritual rebels (Satan & demons). Also, consider Jesus' words in Matt. 16:16-19.

"And Simon Peter answered and said, Thou art the Christ, the Son of the living God. And Jesus answered...Blessed art thou...for flesh and blood hath not revealed *it* unto thee...upon this **rock** [Christ the Anointed], I will build my church; and the **gates** [satanic authority], **of hell** shall not prevail against it. And I give unto thee the keys of the kingdom...whatsoever thou shalt bind...shall be bound...whatsoever thou shalt loose...shall be loosed...."

These verses of Scripture are the basis for the teaching of binding & losing spiritual forces and one can easily see that they are referring to our spiritual authority *in Him*.

Consequently, Jesus was teaching His disciples that they literally would soon be given spiritual authority in order to bind (demons) and loose (call upon) godly spirits (love, joy, and peace) to triumph over the realms of darkness. Like it or not, we have been given authority to bind demonic spirits, and Jesus told us to **act** upon it! Too many believers are willing to allow the enemy to destroy their lives with no resistance.

Demons and deliverance are a spiritual reality. This sort of ministry may not be the most comfortable or welcomed ministry in many churches today, but, nevertheless, it is still a valid, important ministry within the Body of Christ. In my experience with working in the deliverance ministry, *the one who screams the loudest against its operation is usually the one who needs this ministry* **the most**. Demonic spirits will motivate individuals to rebel against the ministry of deliverance in order to keep themselves from being discovered and evicted from the one they control!

Hanegraaff asks the question, "Is it true that the author of sickness is always Satan and never God?...While Scripture makes it clear that

Satan is often the agent of sickness, he is certainly not always its author."[30]

Hanegraaff's Slant On *Who* Makes People Sick

Having read through Hanegraaff's book, I have gained a good picture of his Biblical perspective concerning who is the *author* of sickness and disease. There are some very interesting statements on health found in Scripture. Consider, for example, Exodus 4:11 NIV, which Hanegraaff's used to reinforce his peculiar point of view on who makes us sick.

Exodus 4:11 (NIV): "The Lord said to him, 'Who gave man his mouth? Who **makes** him deaf or mute? Who gives him sight or **makes** him blind? Is it not I, the Lord?'

Notice how this verse **seems** to make God out to be a God who makes people sick, deaf, and mute, as if it was *God's will* for some to remain in that condition. First of all, the context is not one of a proclamation of God's ability or willingness to inflict sickness and disease on His people. Here God is simply giving Moses *no excuse* for not going and doing what he was told. If this verse was saying what it *appears* to be saying, then Hanegraaff would have a case against the Faith teachers. Now, second of all, look at how this verse reads in the KJV, NKJV, and TAB versions.

"And the LORD said unto him, Who hath made man's mouth? or who *maketh* **the** *dumb*, or deaf, or the seeing, or the blind? have not I the LORD?

(NKJV): So the LORD said to him, "Who has made man's mouth? Or who *makes* **the** *mute*, **the** deaf, **the** seeing, or the blind? Have not I, the LORD?

(AMP): And the Lord said to him, Who has made man's mouth? Or who **makes the dumb**, or the deaf, or the seeing, or the blind? Is it not I, the Lord?

God makes the dumb—**NOT** *makes* them dumb. By this I mean that He created all flesh, but He did not **actively** cause someone to be deformed or diseased. There is a major difference in interpretation between the NIV and the other three translations, isn't there? In these other three translations, God is stating that He is the maker OF ALL **and** *has the ability to change all of these conditions*. Moses' problem was stuttering, wasn't it? God was simply telling Moses that his problem was no problem for God Almighty. Unfortunately, the NIV is not the only version that translates this verse of Scripture in a way that makes God appear as *a torturer of His own people*. Traditional religious translators help them along by translating the Word of God so that it makes God look like some sort of assassin.

Scientifically educated theologians write book after book on this bogus doctrine preaching that "God doesn't heal all **and some He even gives cancer....**"

It is obvious that Hanegraaff is oblivious to the fact that the Old Covenant was written from a **permissive** rather than *causative* perspective concerning God's role in many of the affairs of men. Kenneth Copeland addresses this controversial issue with the following statement:

"One thing that has led people to believe that God is the One Who inflicts sickness on us is the wording of the King James Version of certain Scriptures. For example, Deuteronomy 28:61 states, 'Also every sickness, and every plague, which is not written in the book of this law, them will the Lord **bring** upon thee, until thou be destroyed.' Dr. Robert Young, author of *Young's Analytical Concordance to the Bible*, sheds some crucial light on that and other similar Scriptures in his book *Hints to Bible Interpretation*. There he explains that the Hebrew language contains **idioms which cannot be translated into the English language and properly understood**. Also, there was little understanding of permissive and causative verbs. In other words, according to Dr. Young's studies, Deuteronomy 28:61 should have been translated with a permissive verb [meaning]—allow to ascend."[31]

Who is to blame for sickness and disease? Is it all Satan's fault? Is it our fault, or is it rather a combination of the two? Gloria Copeland sheds some acute light upon these interesting questions.

"All the authority and dominion the church does not **actively** enforce is under the sway and power of Satan, not because it is God's will, but because man originally gave Satan dominion over him. Even though *Jesus has taken that dominion away* from Satan, **man still has to enforce his authority** in the earth. Because of our enemy, this authority does not operate passively. It will not work automatically, but it must be *enforced*. In ignorance of God's

Word, the church has allowed Satan to steal her authority, and for the most part, to control the earth"[32]

"God is good. *He could not be the source of any sickness.* It is an abomination to His nature of love for people to believe God made them sick. There are those who say they know God does not make people sick, **but they believe He allows Satan to put sickness on them to teach them or to get them into His will.** God does not have to allow Satan to do his evil work. Satan is quick to bring disease to Christians *if they will allow it.* It is *you* who must govern Satan in your life and circumstances. *If you are not walking in God's Word, you have no defense against Satan and his fruit of sickness.* **Your lack of knowledge of God's Word or your lack of diligence to act on that Word allows disease to fill your body.** God is *never* the source of sickness."[33]

Jesus has given the Church His authority in order to *enforce* the victory that He won for us. The victory is ours, but it won't come to us automatically. We will have to fight for it. Just as God gave the promise land to Israel, they nonetheless, had to be the active agents of enforcing God's promise of receiving the promise land. Healing of our bodies is no different. Gloria Copeland also comments on how healing does not always come *as an instant miracle manifestation*, but that we often must possess "the land" of our healing.

"**Q**: Recently, I prayed and asked God to heal me of a physical problem I've been suffering with for some time. I thought I prayed in faith, but haven't seen any improvement in my condition. I'm confused. What's happening? **A**: YOU'RE IN THE MIDST OF POSSESSING the 'land' called healing!—If you are a believer, it *already* belongs to you.—As far as God is concerned, healing is yours. Jesus has already paid the price for it. But for you to receive it, you have to put your foot on it. You have to go in and possess the land!--Because the manifestation of healing doesn't always come instantly."[34]

Moreover, Morris Cerullo addresses this issue by challenging the Church to not continue in blaming God for their failure to receive healing.

"Why am I not healed? It has caused much unnecessary hurt and wounding in the Kingdom of God in the lives of people who have not been able to get healed. I have had people come crying to me,

216

literally shaken to the core, saying, 'Brother Cerullo, I believe. Why am I not healed?' *Their struggle is real and evident,* **but it attempts to make God vulnerable.** *The blame for the failure is put on God. God will not be vulnerable to any man.*"[35]

Cerullo brings up a very important point. Why is it that we blame God whenever *we* have failed to receive the things we have believed? As he said, "God will not be vulnerable to any man."[36]

It's time for the Church to get a revelation concerning this immense problem within the Body of Christ. God is good! God gives good gifts; not evil, selfish, addictive ones. He is not our problem. He is the answer to any of our problems in life.

Furthermore, Robert W. Tozier sums up this subject appropriately:

"The most blasphemous thing I've read in Hanegraaff's book is his implication that God Himself is the author of sickness. '**All suffering of whatever nature, arises from violated law.** The violation may indeed be *unintentional,* but the result is inevitable; nevertheless, if we violate law, **suffering must come…**Disease or accident may be the cause, suffering the result.' 'Man has no power to originate either good or evil. God is the author of all good, and Satan is the originator of all evil'…Sickness, therefore, is a consequence of sin, whether personal or original…God was not the author of sickness. 'Sin was not part of the original creation.'"[37]

Sickness—*the Glory* of God?

Hanegraaff, like many of his peers, believes that God gives us sickness and disease in order to bring Him glory among men. He quotes David in Psalm 119:71, 75 in an attempt to reinforce his perplexing train of thought.

"It was good for me to be afflicted so that I might learn…."[38]

I have ascertained that Hanegraaff used this passage of Scripture in order to imply that the word *afflicted,* which David referred to, was involving *sickness and disease.* However, upon closer examination via the concordance, one plainly sees that sickness and disease had **nothing** to do with David becoming afflicted, but rather it was a time of abasement, humbling, or a period of chastening (correction) that he went through.[39] Neither sickness nor disease could be *remotely* denoted from this Bible concordance definition. What's more, does God **really** give us sickness and disease in order to receive glory, or to teach us some *deep* "spiritual" meaning of the Kingdom? If one were to ask Hank Hanegraaff this question, most likely he would give a "resounding Yes," and point one to a real life example such as Joni Erickson Toda.

Nevertheless, the question *still* remains: "Does God really give us these *presents* of destruction and evil?" Many Faith teachers have spoken out to address this issue. I want you, the reader, to decide:

"Another tradition is that we can glorify God more by being patient in our sickness than by being healed. **If** sickness glorifies God more than healing, **then** any attempt to get well by natural or divine means would be an effort *to rob God of the glory*...**If** sickness glorifies God, **then** we should rather be sick than well. **If** sickness glorifies God, Jesus robbed His Father of all the glory that He possibly could by healing everyone, and the Holy Spirit continued doing the same throughout the Acts of the Apostles...Another tradition is that while God heals some, it is not His will to heal all. But Jesus, Who came to do the Father's will, did 'heal them all.' **If** healing is not for all, why did Jesus bear our sicknesses, our pains, and our diseases? **If** God wanted some of His children to suffer, **then** Jesus relieved us from bearing something which God wanted us to bear. But since Jesus came to do the *will of the Father*, and since He *has borne our diseases*, it must be God's will for all to be well."[40]

"Sometimes it amuses me when people accuse faith preachers of saying the Christian life shouldn't include any suffering. *Think about it for a moment.* Let's say you wake up one morning *with all the symptoms of the flu*—You lie there in your bed, moaning and groaning all day...*suffering for Jesus*—Let me ask you, **how does the Lord get any glory out of your having the flu?**...But now, let's set up another scene. Say you wake up one morning with all those symptoms—But instead of **cowering** in bed, you throw the covers aside and say, 'No, devil! I'll not submit to this sickness. Jesus paid a high price for me to be healed'—The last thing you feel like doing is reading your Bible. But you don't care what your body feels like doing—You walk around the room **declaring the Word of God**, determined to *talk* in faith, *act* in faith and resist the devil until he runs—**Now you tell me, which of those** [models] **is the higher**

kind of suffering?...There's *far more suffering* **in resistance** than there is **in submitting** *to that sickness*. What's more, when you suffer by resisting and **you defeat the devil. You truly do bring glory to God!**...There is no comparison between burning at the stake because you refuse to deny the Name of Jesus *and suffering from sickness or poverty*—some people have mistakenly decided sickness and disease are their part of Jesus' suffering."[41]

"Many Christians have *never* read the Bible...Then, the devil brings them that other lie and they accept it. *'Well, now, you are sick to glorify God.'* They just go along and accept sickness because, *'I'm glorifying God now.'* **Nowhere** in the Bible can you find that God got any glory out of anybody *being sick*. I'll tell you when He did get glory — **when they got** *well*."[42]

"When Jesus said, *'the Father...doeth the works,'* it meant that he did *all* of the works that Jesus did. For example, when Jesus was aboard that tiny boat in the Sea of Galilee and rebuked the storm (Mark 4:39), **it actually was the Father rebuking the storm through Jesus**. Well, if God *caused* the storm, God would be working *against* Himself if He *rebuked* it! The same holds true with healing. If God is the author of sickness and disease, yet God healed people through Jesus, **then God would be working against Himself!** (And Jesus said in Mark 3:24, 25 that a house divided against itself cannot stand.)"[43]

It is plain to see from the previous quotations that God *does not* receive **any** glory by our *being sick*; however, He does receive glory among all when He has *healed* a person from the bondage of Satan through sickness. He gets the glory through healing, because natural medicine cannot bring about these same sorts of results in the same fashion—many times *they are* **instant** *results*! Sickness is not what causes the glory to be given to God, but rather it is when the power of God comes and drives out the sickness that He receives true glory!

If I am suffering with illness, I *am not* suffering for Jesus. Jesus has already suffered sickness *for me*; thus, my suffering is a suffering of *ignorance* of the will of God. Hanegraaff contends that Jesus said a man was blind merely so that God could heal him and receive glory.[44] He cites John 9:2, 3 as his "proof" text. However, does his interpretation truly line up with the *whole context* of the Bible. Is he merely attempting to build a doctrine on one isolated verse of Scripture?

John 9:2-4: And his disciples asked him, saying, Master, who did sin, this man, or his parents, that he was born blind? Jesus answered, Neither hath this man sinned, nor his parents: **but that the works of God should be made manifest in him**. I must *work the works of him* that sent me, while it is day: the night cometh, when no man can work.

When one reads these verses of Scripture, it *appears* that Jesus was saying that **God** made this man blind just so He could *show off* by healing him, hereby obtaining glory from the crowds. In reality, however, Jesus never addressed why or how this man became blind. He simply focused on the **answer** to the man's problem—*the works of His Father.*

Here we have a prime example of what Kenneth E. Hagin was illustrating in a previous quotation. If God the Father *caused* this man's blindness and Jesus were to come and heal him, then Jesus would be working *against* His Father and, thus, God's Kingdom could not stand. Jesus said, "*If Satan cast out Satan, his kingdom is divided against itself, and cannot stand.*" **Any** kingdom that is divided cannot stand.

Moreover, Jesus called healing "*the works* of Him Who sent Him," because He was implying that His Father's works were healing (not blindness). It makes *absolutely* no sense to say that God made someone sick *just* so that He could heal them. That sort of behavior is the exact **opposite** of His very character and nature. No matter how one views these verses, the *work* that caused God to get glory was not a *work of illness,* but God's work *of healing that illness.* **Healing** brought the glory…not the sickness!

Here is something interesting to consider. Hanegraaff believes that our bodies will not change or be able to be free from sickness until Christ comes.[45] He uses 1 Cor. 15:42-44 as the basis for his assumption. However, what does 1 Cor. 15:42-44 have to do with healing in this present life?

So also *is* the resurrection of the dead. It is sown in corruption; it is raised in incorruption: It is sown in dishonour; it is raised in glory: it is sown in weakness; it is raised in power: It is sown **a natural body**; it is raised **a spiritual body**. There is a natural body, and there is a spiritual body.

This passage of Scripture is referring to the rapture of the Church, when we all will receive a *glorified* body—one that is natural and spiritual all at the same time. Without question, we *have not* yet received this kind of body. Nonetheless, this in no way proves that our bodies can't live free from illness. It is referring to how our bodies will become at the resurrection.

In this earth we will never be 100% free from the *attacks* of the enemy, because we live in a fallen world. But, Jesus said, "Be of good cheer for I have overcome the world." And Revelation 12:11 says, "And **they** overcame *him* by the blood of the Lamb **and by** the word of their testimony...." We overcome the enemy (Sin, Sickness, Death, and Fear) because Jesus overcame the world. Our victory over all of our enemies has been made possible by the blood of the Lamb—Yes! On the other hand, *we're* the ones responsible for adding our testimony *of faith to* **His blood** so that we can walk in the overcoming power of Jesus.

Sovereignty—If It Be Thy Will?

The Faith teachers have been openly criticized again and again for teaching people that they should not *continually* pray *"If it be Thy will"* prayers to God. The Bible "Answer" Man implies that they have overtly insulted Jesus because He prayed such a prayer.[46] However, are these teachers really insulting Jesus when they teach people not to *continually* pray in this manner? Out of all the prayers Jesus prayed He **only** prayed "If it be Thy will" **one time**. This was during His hour of temptation in the Garden when He was struggling with be separated from His Father by going to the cross.

Now, what are they *really* saying when they teach these things? Hanegraaff takes Fred Price to task more than the other Faith teachers, so we'll begin addressing this issue by establishing what Price actually teaches on this subject.

"There are certain Biblical rules and principles regarding prayer...I used to think praying was praying. But I found out there are different kinds of prayer for different kinds of circumstances, and each kind of prayer has its own spiritual rules that govern it [i.e.]...you can not play baseball with track and field rules...there are spiritual rules that govern different kinds of praying...1. *Prayer of Agreement*. 2. *Prayer of Faith Petition Prayer*. 3. *Prayer of Intercession*. 4. *The Prayer of Praise and Worship*. 5. *Prayer of Consecration and/or Dedication*. **This** is a prayer whereby you place yourself in a position to be used of God. **You have to use** *"If it be Thy will" in this type of prayer*, **because you cannot find God's will in the Bible**...This is the type of prayer that Jesus prayed before He went to the cross...But you *never* use a dedication and consecration prayer when you are trying to pay your bills. If you tack an *"if it be Thy will"* onto **a petition prayer**, you are praying in doubt."[47]

Dr. Price's comments clearly illustrate that he *is not* opposed to one praying "If it be Thy will," providing that one **does not** already know the 100% will of God on the matter.

Furthermore, he instructs people not to pray "If it be Thy will" when one desires to receive *the promises* of God. He says that a petition prayer is the same as the prayer of faith. When one prays the prayer of faith, one must already *know* the will of God on the matter, or else their prayer will be one of doubt.

Mark 11:22-25 *clearly* teaches that one must pray in faith, **knowing** what is the will of God; and believe that one has *received* the request—**When we pray**! According to the Bible, Jesus *never* prayed "If it be Thy will" when He was healing or interceding on the people's behalf. Jesus Christ is *our example* of how **we** need to be constantly praying.

Similarly, Kenneth Copeland echoes the teaching of Jesus in Mark 11:22-25:

> "The only people who pray 'If it be Thy will' are those who don't have any hope or expectancy. If you've been praying that way, stop it! **Go to the Word and find out what God's will is. The Word of God is His will**. It is His will for you to be well. It is His will for you to be prosperous. It is His will for you to lay hands on the sick and it is His will for them to recover."[48]

Here, Copeland is once again referring to receiving the promises God has already given to us in His Word. Nothing more—nothing less!

Hanegraaff's distorted version of events, again, does not pass the test of scrutiny. I find it difficult to understand why he did not recognize Price's teaching while reading the *Word Study Bible*. Price's teaching on prayer and the various spiritual rules involved, was openly written for all who are *willing* to see "Why didn't Hanegraaff seem to see this?"

The Bible *only* teaches us to pray "If it be Thy will," when we do not know the 100% will of God on the matter, or when we are submitting to do His will despite our own. These are the only reasons why Paul,

James and the others prayed such a prayer. Paul prayed that we would be filled with the knowledge of the will of God with all wisdom and understanding.

Therefore, it is the will of God that we know and understand His will for our lives! If we don't know the will of God regarding something, we had better pray until He reveals it to us. God's will for our lives is not always spelled out in the Bible; therefore, we must take time with God and find out what His will is concerning these areas that aren't covered by the promises.

God is sovereign the Bible clearly supports this teaching. He can do whatever He pleases. However, God cannot violate His own Word? Can He promise something only to turn around and do the exact opposite, without violating His character and not be a liar? Absolutely not! His Word is His character and His character is His Word.

Psalm 89:34: My covenant will I not break, nor alter the thing that is gone out of my lips.

Psalm 119:89: For ever, O LORD, *thy word is* **settled** *in heaven.*

God spoke to us through David in the Palms that His Word is *already* established in heaven and that He will **never** break or *alter* anything that has gone out of His mouth. Did the Word of God come out of God's mouth? No doubt! Therefore, He will **never** break or *alter* the words that He has spoken unto us. In other words, the Word of God (the Bible), is the indestructible, unchangeable *will* of the living God.

Someone might say, "But He changed from the Old Covenant to the New Covenant." Yes, He did, but He told us about the continuation (changes) of the Covenant from the very beginning. In Genesis chapter 3 verse 15, God tells us that it has always been His will and number one priority to bring to pass the New Covenant. This *could not* be accomplished without Jesus' Death, burial, and resurrection into heaven.

Evangelist Jesse Duplantis makes some *very* notable observations concerning the sovereignty of God and how it relates to the Word of God.

"God Is Only Sovereign Outside of His Word. The problem a lot of people have including Christians, is that they don't understand the sovereignty of God. God is 100 percent sovereign. Webster's

Dictionary defines sovereign as 'possessed of supreme power; unlimited in extent; absolute' Those things are all true of God. *But God is only sovereign* **outside** *of His Word.* He is not sovereign inside of His Word. Follow me carefully now. *Outside* God's Word He is unlimited. **But God sovereignly chose to limit Himself, absolutely, to His Word.** Let me give you an example. God sovereignly put in the Bible, 'By His stripes ye were healed.' Putting those words on the written page of the Holy Cannon was a sovereign act of God. That means if you release faith in those words, and you **act** on that faith, then God has *sovereignly* **obligated** Himself to heal you. Why must He? Because the Bible says, *God is not a man, that He should lie.* (Num. 23:19). Would you like to see a sovereign act of God? Read about Saul on the road to Damascus in Acts nine. God sovereignly slapped him off his donkey! Paul fell to the ground and said 'Lord!' Jesus was mad...I mean He was hot!...Paul had been persecuting Christians, but Jesus never said, 'Why are you persecuting them?' He said, 'Why are you persecuting Me?' He took it very personal. I need to warn you*, Jesus* **hasn't changed** *in the past two thousand years.* If you start talking bad about Christians or persecuting them, **He takes it very personal.**"[49]

The church has been using the fact that God is sovereign for to long *as an excuse for its own laziness.* Whenever destructive things take place, in *which they have met with little or no resistance*, it is typical of them to put the **blame** on God because He is sovereign. Insurance companies, for example, call natural disasters "acts of God," even though God had **little or nothing to do with them.** Traditional *minded* Christians fall right in line with this sort of contorted logic. Anything that takes place that is not understood becomes *enshrined* in the doctrine of the sovereignty of God. God is sovereign—*without question.* But, He will not force Himself on anyone who is unwilling to yield their lives to His protection and influence. God **always** honors His Word. Moreover, God *always* honors our right to choose. Because of our own irrational rebellious choices, we have, many times, reaped the destructive consequences of our own foolishness. All the while attempting to *pawn off the results* of these irresponsible choices *on to the sovereignty of Almighty God.*

A Closing Thought On God's Sovereignty

"So many believers wring their hands and worry about whether or not they're praying according to God's will. Many of them have been taught a wrong view of God's sovereignty. *They think that His ways are past finding out, and it is more spiritual to pray, 'God, whatever Your will is in this situation, You just go ahead and do it.'* Just think what kind of confusion that causes. Whatever results from that kind of praying is credited to God—good or bad! To really honor God's sovereignty, we must pray what He has already declared to be His will...We just need to grab our Bibles and find out what the will of God is. God's Word IS His will. He has made some very specific promises in it. And it's His will to fulfill every one of them. [*A perfect example*] Think about what you did when you prayed for salvation. You didn't pray, 'God, I'm sick and tired of this life under Satan's control, and I want You to be my Lord and Savior. **But I don't want to tell You what to do. Whatever Your will is**—*to set me free or to keep me in this miserable condition, to send me to heaven or to send me to hell*—**No**! You prayed for God to save you just like His Word **said** He would...You prayed **expecting** results **according to the promise**. These same principles work in any area of prayer. Do you need healing in your body...Do you have financial needs...God wants His will to be done on earth *as it is done in heaven*. Find the promise that applies to your situation and ***pray the answer*** instead of the problem...let's start with His Word and finish with His Word."[50]

Again, Copeland makes a valid point. Why is it that one would pray *according to the Word of God*, believing that he will receive what God said regarding salvation, but yet this same person is **unwilling** or *unable* to believe God for the salvation of his soul, physical body and finances? **How sad!**

16

SOME CLOSING REMARKS

As I began work on this book, I realized that the Lord wanted me to add a chapter in which I would deal with some unexplored issues that Hanegraaff did not overly address and clarify them in a proper fashion. Perhaps there are several issues that I have not even dealt with as of yet, however, in this final chapter I will *only* address those particular subjects that the Lord lays on my heart.

As I write this chapter, God still has not revealed to me *all* of these issues which He desires for me to address. Nevertheless, He did instruct me to deal with a number of particular topics of importance. We will start with these issues and see where the Lord leads for there.

In *Christianity in Crisis*, Hank Hanegraaff addressed the subject of sickness and suffering by opposing some of the Faith teachers, who have experienced attacks of sickness and disease, as if to say *they* think they are untouchable to attacks of sickness. One notable incident involved Dr. Betty Price, who was attacked by the enemy with cancer. According to Hanegraaff, this proves the Faith message to be cultic.

> "As we proceed through this section on sickness and suffering, we will draw a clear line *between the cultic concepts of the Faith movement* and those of the *historic* Christian faith…Sickness and suffering are indeed the common denominator of a fallen world. We all get sick and eventually we all die—including every single person committed to the Faith movement. *As much as the Faith teachers would have you believe otherwise*, there are no exceptions to the rule. Fred Price may proudly proclaim, 'We don't allow sickness in our home,' but the reality is that his wife has been stricken with cancer and has profusely thanked her doctors for the painful radiation and chemotherapy she has received from them."[1]

First of all, I want to say that I agree with Hanegraaff that **all** sickness and suffering is the result of a fallen world; however, Jesus clearly told us that we are not of this world (John 15:18, 19). Also, Paul said in Galatians 3:13 that we have been redeemed *from* the curse of the

Law: Sin, sickness, disease, poverty. Meaning we've been freed from anything that brings death or destruction into our lives. Now that *does not* mean that we are incapable of being attacked by sickness or that we'll never die, but that Jesus has made the way for us to live free *from the cruse's effect* upon our lives.

Next, I would like to point out some important details concerning Betty Price's assault from the enemy. The first and most obvious detail that Hanegraaff seems to have overtly missed is the fact that Dr. Price *is still alive* despite being assailed by cancer. In fact, she has made a **full** recovery from this attack of illness. In a television program that the Prices produced, they revealed many details about what happened to Mrs. Price and how they discovered the reason why she was open to the attack by cancer. The conclusion that the Prices came to was that Mrs. Price wasn't taking proper care of her body and, hence, *she* opened the door to the enemy.

Dying For A Lack of Knowledge!

It is true that she went through chemotherapy and radiation in order to win against the cancer. However, despite the fact that her condition was very poor, her treatment was fast and successful because she began to take proper care of her body, as well as prayed in faith believing for her healing. In her case, she needed to realize that she wasn't taking proper care of herself in order to get well. She did not realize this until after her condition became critical. The Bible says, "My people parish for the lack of knowledge," and in Mrs. Price's life this was precisely what was taking place. Because of her lack of knowledge about proper nutrition, she was *literally* dying.

Nonetheless, God in His grace and mercy revealed to Mrs. Price where she had opened the door to the enemy, and once she shut that door, the treatments she was receiving began to work at an *extremely* fast pace (previously her treatments were not working very well). Today, Betty Price has been living, **cancer free** for approximately five years. As far as Mrs. Price was concerned, she needed the assistance of medical treatment to get well. Perhaps you're wondering, "*Why did she need medical help? Why didn't she just use faith?*" Sometimes, one can end up so weak that one is unable to fight, physically or spiritually, and this *may* have been the case.

However, this still **does not** negate the fact that faith in God's Word works. She used four things in order to reclaim her health: prayer, faith in God and His Word, a proper diet *with adequate amounts of water*, and, finally, medical treatment through chemotherapy and radiation. *Hence, she is alive and cancer free!* Medicine was not her only resource for the restoration of her health—God was still her Source of healing!

Hanegraaff also opposed Kenneth E. Hagin because he went through multiple symptoms of heart trouble as a youth. Concerning Hagin, he makes this unflattering remark:

> "Kenneth Hagin may brag that he has not had a headache, the flu, or even 'one sick day' in nearly 60 years, yet he has suffered at least four cardiovascular crises, including one full-scale heart stoppage and another episode persisting for six weeks. Although Hagin claims his 'rights' and literally stands on his Bible when illness comes, his six-week bout with heart trouble defies his 'positive confession.'"[2]

Concerning this quotation, I would like to add a simple point. Hagin may have had a few bouts with the enemy in the area of heart trouble, but nevertheless, at the ripe *young* age of **80**, he is *still* alive and preaching two services a day! Regardless of Hanegraaff's disdain for Hagin's successes in living free from sickness and disease, in spite of the attacks he has encountered during his life. Also, he would have to admit that it is truly *a miracle* that Hagin has lived past the age of 16, (especially when all his doctors said he wouldn't). Hagin has relied upon God has his Source of healing since the age of 16, and because of that he is still out preaching the Gospel at the age of 80! ***That's not bad folks***!

Another Faith teacher who has been denounced by Hanegraaff because of his attacks of illness is Oral Roberts. Concerning Roberts, he makes the following comment:

> "Most ironic of all, veteran faith healer Oral Roberts suffered a heart attack just hours after supposedly being healed of chest pains by Paul Crouch on TBN's live television show on October 6, 1992...."[3]

It is not possible for me to prove whether or not Roberts had a *literal* heart attack. However, despite whatever it was that took place, I can *verify* that he is *still* alive and preaching the Word of God.

This quotation speaks loud and clear of Roberts' faith in God and His Word which has seen him through the good times, as well as the not so good! Despite whatever attacks of illness that Roberts has experienced, he has kept his faith in God (and His Word), and God has honored His Word in his life!

Symptoms v. God's Word

Hanegraaff makes a point that is important in the natural world concerning symptoms of physical illness or disease, and rightly so, because the body was created by God to work in this manner.

> "The danger of denying symptoms or pawning them off as devilish decoys can hardly be overstated. With diseases like cancer, early detection and diagnosis are crucial to effective treatment and recovery...symptoms are often a divine demonstration of *God's sovereign healing power* in progress...Despite these well-documented medical facts [symptoms], Faith teachers continue to convince their followers that symptoms are tricks of the devil designed to rob them of divine health and healing."[4]

I believe that symptoms *can be* a divine demonstration of God's sovereign healing power; however, I also know that the Bible says the enemy is a liar *and the father of **all** lies*. Satan can bring symptoms against our bodies that are a lie according to the Word of God. Moreover, it appears to me that Hanegraaff has *more faith* in the medical facts (*symptoms*) than he does in Scriptural **truth** (*God's Word*). My body says, "I hurt! I must be sick." But, the Word of God says, "By His stripes you **were** healed." Now don't misunderstand me! I'm **not** saying that we should never listen to the messages that our bodies send to us. I'm saying that we should take the symptoms that appear, go to the Word of God, and pray *the answer* into our physical need.

This is *precisely* what the Faith teachers have endeavored to impart. Pray the answer (God's Word) instead of reinforcing the problem that already exists in your body. Telling God about how sick we are *does absolutely nothing* about getting rid of that illness. If the truth be known, whenever we do this sort of thing, all we are really doing is throwing ourselves a private "pity-party." We are simply feeling sorry for ourselves—which is a cowardly act.

However, praying *in line* with His Word will not only heal our bodies, it will also help keep us well in the future. Take God's Word daily, like you would a prescribed medication—It's health to *all* our flesh (Prov. 4:22).

Physical symptoms in our bodies may be a fact, but God' Word is the **ultimate** Truth, and Truth always overrides a fact! Why? It's because facts *are not* always true, especially when they concern the Kingdom of God. I like what a Christian *brother* of mine often says, "*Our circumstances that attempt to contradict God's Word are a lie in heaven.*" Perhaps if Hanegraaff would apply more faith in the Truth of God's Word, he wouldn't have to always rely upon a fact—a physical manifestation. This was Thomas' problem and the Lord Jesus called such action **faithless**! I didn't say it—Jesus did. Again, ***don't*** deny physical symptoms, but instead take them as a sign that there *may be* a problem and pray according to God's Word—which is *always* the answer!

If you have children, would you ever give them cancer in order to make them better people? Perhaps your thinking, "You need your head examined fellow!" Of course not, then *why* would any one think that a loving, compassionate God would give His children some form of disease in order for instruction. Teaching is the purpose of God's Word and the Holy Spirit—He is our Teacher.

I like what I heard one preacher say, "God—*good!* Devil—**bad!**" God gives good gifts. Sickness or disease is *never* a good gift, because its *primary purpose* is to kill and destroy the one it lives in. God isn't the author of death. Death and disease came as a result of Sin!

John 5:24: Verily, verily, I say unto you, He that heareth my word, and believeth on him that sent me, hath everlasting life, and shall not come into condemnation; **but is passed from death unto life**.

We have passed from Death to Life. This does not mean we will never die physically, but rather that Death does not *reign* over us any longer. It's important to note that no where in the Bible has God promised that we wouldn't die **physically**—apart from His promise to Rapture those who are alive. Therefore, we have no Scriptural basis for using our faith to believe God to live forever *physically*. However, God has promised to satisfy us with long life (Ps. 91:16).

Furthermore, He has also said that the length of man's days will be **120** years (Gen. 6:3). Therefore, we do have *a promise* from God to live at least 120 years. But someone said, "*Get real! Most people don't live past 70.*" This may be *a fact* of life, but God's Word is *the Truth*. I believe most people do not live to, at least, 120 simply because *they believe* that 70 years is the average life span of a man— statistical facts tell us this. However, I have searched through the Bible many times and no where have I ever found a verse of Scripture that says a man's life is limited to 70 or so years.

Nevertheless, it is time for the Body of Christ to stop giving more credibility to their *symptoms* (facts) than they do to *the Word of God* (the Truth). God cannot lie; therefore, what He says is **always** true!

Hermeneutics: The Science of Studying *God*

According to Hanegraaff, the Bible *hence God* can be conveniently studied in a similar manner that a scientist would study bugs or ancient dinosaur bones. This science called *Hermeneutics* is Hanegraaff's answer to eradicating all forms of whatever he calls heresy.

> "The best antidote to heretical teaching is good hermeneutical training. Hermeneutics is the science and art of biblical interpretation. Hermeneutics is a science in that it is regulated by rules and an art in that it involves intuitive and analytical acumen. The rules can be remembered easily with the help of the acronym L-I-G-H-T-S...**L**iteral Interpretation, **I**llumination by Holy Spirit, **G**rammatical Principle, **H**istorical Context, **T**eaching Ministry, **S**criptural Harmony."[5]

According to Hanegraaff's definition, hermeneutics is the science of Biblical interpretation, and it is governed by specific rules. However, I would like to pose an important question, "*Who is responsible for creating these 'rules' of interpreting the Bible?*" Seeing that I have never read any such rules in chapter and verse, I question the point and validity of using them. Therefore, since these "rules" are not specifically outlined in Scripture, I can only come to one conclusion: *they are the creation of* **mere** *men*. We all know how man is at creating anything. I mean, he can't even write a dictionary without having to update it every 3-5 years to make sure it is "current" and with the times. Moreover, such an idea as studying God or the Bible by a set of *man-made* rules is probably the most *egotistical* thing that man has ever done. Since when is God or His Word limited to a set of rules invented by humans? Give me break guys! God is greater that any so-called doctrinal rules for studying His Word.

Also, seeing that this form of study is done in a scientific manner, the Scientific Method seems to be a great part of its creation. Again, the Scientific Method is a creation of man, invented in order to uniformly study the universe. It is absurd to attempt to apply such circumscribed regulations to an infinite God. Especially, when the Bible says, "My ways

are not *your* ways, *neither are* My thoughts *your* thoughts (Jn. 1:1-3; 14)." Neither God, nor His Word could ever fit into our finite religious box, because He is the Word.

It is time for the theologically minded Christians to get off their high intellectual horse and repent of their *intellectual idolatry*. Much of the intellectual religious community has made a "god" out of their own rules and regulations for studying God & His Word. In the same fashion as *the Pharisees* made a "god" out of the Talmud—*traditional* writings created by man. There is nothing wrong with studying and being intelligent; however, there is a major problem when intellectualism becomes more meaningful and powerful in our lives than God or His Word. *Intellectualism* reasons away the simplicity of all that God has clearly stated in His Word. It looks to its own finite understanding, instead of opening itself to God's infinite Wisdom!

Returning To The Faith of God

As we have already noted in Chapter 4, Hank Hanegraaff contends that God doesn't have faith, He's the object of our faith.[6] Similarly, in Chapter 2, we defined *faith* as "confidence or assurance." Therefore, the faith that we possess is not confidence or assurance *in ourselves*, but rather we have faith (assurance, confidence) *in God*. Seeing that faith is actually confidence or assurance *in something*, why couldn't God have confidence (faith) in Himself and in His ability to perform what He has promised?

If the average human being were to have an overabundance of confidence or assurance in himself, one would call him egotistical, and rightly so, **if** he were unable to make good on his claims. However, in the case of God Almighty, He *can* make the boldest of claims and not be egotistical, because *He not only has the power to back up His claims,* **but** *He also cannot lie*. Hence, when God says, "I am the Lord God of all flesh, *is there anything too hard for me*?" Jeremiah 32:27.

He actually is proclaiming His confidence and assurance (faith) in His own ability to do anything that needs to be done. Why does He proclaim His confidence in Himself? So that we His people would also receive **and act** in faith, knowing that He can do whatever He said! This is how He imparts faith to us—He infuses it into us **by His Word**. This is the only way we receive faith (Rom. 10:17). It *never* comes by praying or begging for it!

Since faith is confidence or assurance in something and God proclaims His faith or confidence in His own ability, God *indeed* does have faith. However, His faith is not in something higher in authority or more powerful than He. His faith (confidence) is in His own ability to bring to pass whatever He chooses. God believes in Himself. He believes what He says is true. He **knows** He can do whatever He's said—that's what faith **actually** is in its purest sense.

More On Faith Filled Words

We have also seen that Hanegraaff, with much sarcasm, contests the notion that words are like containers that can be filled with whatever we choose. However, I believe the Lord has shown me how to prove this.

Whenever one has a hateful argument with another, what is the result? Many times those involved end-up hating each other simply because they refused to apologize. How could this happen? The spirit of hate was transferred and counter-transferred to those involved in the argument. Words are filled with whatever spiritual force (*active ability*) that we allow. Words filled with love create a loving atmosphere and feeling in a relationship. Why is that? It's because, there is transference of love within one's words when one speaks loving words. Words really are *like a container* that can be filled with whatever we choose and then released toward the intended person or thing. They carry whatever we allow them to convey!

For example, in the Unites States of America, one can be arrested and charged with murder. Unfortunately, it actually makes no difference if he is guilty or not, because when the jury hands down their verdict, this man will *still* be subject to their judgment (words). If they hand down a ruling of "Not guilty," his fate will be *freedom*, but if their verdict is "Guilty," his fate is *punishment*. He will be forced to endure whatever punishment fits the crime. Their words can only carry (be filled with) one thing for that man's life: freedom or punishment (life or death). This same principle functions in the realm of the Spirit. We **always** reap good or bad consequences from the seeds that we have sown with our words and corresponding actions! This *is* a Spiritual Law that God set in place from the beginning.

Another astute example is when a couple decides to get married, before they say, "I will" in the presence of the minister, they are free to go their own separate ways. But once they say, "I will" as far as they, their families, the government and God are concerned—**they did**! In all of their eyes (especially God's), they have entered into a one-flesh covenant. They have joined themselves together, in the spirit, by their words of *commitment*. Their words were filled with the power (ability) to join them spiritually, socially, financially, emotionally, and also physically. Why? It's because their words were filled with a spiritual force (love, faith, peace), one of lifetime **commitment**.

I want to give one *final* example of how words are containers of blessings or curses. Words have creative abilities about them. They form or create pictures within the mind. Therefore, if I were to say, "flower," instantly a picture of some kind of flower would form in your mind. The more I defined that picture, the more your mind would create the kind of picture that I perceived.

Thus if I said, "long stemmed flower" or "long stemmed red flower" or, even more detailed, "a long stemmed red rose," then one would know exactly what kind of flower I was thinking about.[7] My words *created* a picture of a red rose within your mind. I used my words as a *carrier* (container) of my thoughts, so that you would see what I am seeing.

Moreover, seeing that God does in fact have faith, one can also easily *see* that His Word is *impregnated* with faith. Why? It's because every statement that God makes is a statement of confidence (faith) in His own ability to do what He already said and assurance that whatever He said will come to pass. Every word of God is filled with confidence (faith) that He has the ability to carry out what He says. Whatever God said will take place—then it will take place—**and He's *confident* that it will**!

This is the way that He set up this planet. He decided that everything in the natural and spiritual realm would respond to spiritual forces (good or bad) within the words of the one who is speaking. God does this, and we must also (Prov. 18:20, 21).

What Is The Word of Faith?

The Faith message has been given many different titles from various religious groups within the Body of Christ, such as: the Faith *Movement*, the Authority *Movement*, the Blab It And Grab It Group, and even the Name It And Claim It Bunch, among others. Furthermore, according to Hanegraaff, "There is no denying that *much* of Faith theology is **derived directly from** metaphysics."[8] Of course, Hanegraaff is *assuming* that the Word of Faith acquired its initial inspiration from E.W.

Kenyon alone. However, where did E.W. Kenyon and the modern-day Word of Faith teachers actually obtain their inspiration and basis for the message of Faith? Moreover, what exactly *is* the Word of Faith and where did they get their name?

> **Romans 10:1-11**: Brethren, my heart's desire and prayer to God for Israel is, that they might be saved. For I bear them record that they have *a zeal of God*, **but not** *according to knowledge* [God' Word]. For they being **ignorant** *of God's righteousness*, and going about to establish **their own righteousness**, have not submitted themselves unto the righteousness of God. For Christ *is* the end of the law for righteousness to every one **that believeth**. For Moses describeth *the righteousness which is* **of the law**, That the man which doeth those things **shall live by them**. But *the righteousness which is of faith* **speaketh** *on this wise*, **Say not** in thine heart, Who shall ascend into heaven? (that is, to bring Christ down *from above*:) Or, Who shall descend into the deep? (that is, to bring up Christ again from the dead.) But what saith it? *The word is nigh thee, even* **in thy mouth**, *and* **in thy heart**: that is, **the word of faith**, *which* **we** *preach*; That if thou shalt *confess* **with thy mouth** the Lord Jesus, and shalt *believe* **in thine heart** that God hath raised him from the dead, thou shalt be *saved* [Sozo]. For with the heart man **believeth** unto righteousness; and *with the mouth* **confession** is made unto salvation. For the Scripture saith, **Whosoever believeth on him shall not be ashamed**.

Contrary to what some traditional Christians believe and preach, Romans Chapter 10 Verses 1 through 11 is *undeniably* where the teaching and name of the Word of Faith *originated*. This **is** the message of the Word of Faith in a nut-shell! Not only that, but the apostle Paul even preached the Word of Faith, because he said, "which **we** preach." Let us examine these verses of Scripture in order to see how they relate to the modern message of faith.

Paul, in these verses, speaks of how Moses compared two kinds of righteousness: *the righteousness of God* (or the righteousness which is of faith), and *the righteousness which is of the Law* (or going about to establish *our own* righteousness). Consequently, Paul is saying that there are **only** two kinds of righteousness—God's or our own. Moreover, Paul also gives a detailed explanation of how both of these types of righteousness believe **and** speak. He said that the righteousness which is of faith, **does not** say someone bring Jesus to me in the flesh, so that I can see Him, and receive whatever I may need. How does the righteousness that's of faith speak?

> "*But what saith it?* **The word** is nigh thee, *even* **in thy mouth**, and **in thy heart**: that is, the word of faith, which we preach...."

What did Paul want to communicate to us today from this verse? He was saying that those who live by *their own righteousness* **always** need to see, feel, and touch something *before* they will believe they've received it. These are those who are **carnal** "believers" or those who are controlled by their circumstances. On the other hand, *the righteousness which is by faith believes* **and** *speaks* the Word of Faith (faith in God's written Word) *without* depending upon seeing, feeling or touching the results of that Word in the natural realm. *The righteousness which is of the Law* operates by a fickle Faith because it's always based upon *circumstances* which are **always subject to change**. However, *the righteousness which is by faith* operates with a constant, firm, unwavering faith *in the written Word of God* because he knows that His Word is near him and that all he has to do is proclaim (*speak*) his faith in that Word.

Unfortunately, *most* Christians believe that these verses of Scripture *merely* deal with one receiving salvation of his spirit. Is this really all it refers to or is it telling us how to receive **everything** we need from God? I believe it is teaching us how to receive everything we need! Why? It is because the word *saved* in verse 9 is the Greek word *Sozo*. According to the concordance, the word *Sozo* denotes: "*to save*, i.e. *deliver* or *protect* (lit. or fig.):—**heal**, preserve, save (self), do well, **be (make) whole**."[9] Some have said that this is only referring to our spirit being saved—"spiritual healing."

However, of all the times that the word *saved* is used in the New Covenant, *sozo* is also used, except for two times. *Sozo* literally means to the believer that we are saved (delivered, protected, healed etc.) from **anything** that we need saving from: *spirit, soul, body, and financially*. This means God has *saved* (**sozo**) us from everything that we need to be saved from.

Now, without a doubt, you know what the origin is of the Word of Faith and its teaching. So forget about all the childish myths, created by carnal-minded people, circulating regarding the Word of Faith. These fabrications are all based upon religious tradition and misinterpretation. God's Word is *clear* about how we are to receive from Him. We must **believe** God's Word, **confess** our faith in that Word, and **act** according to what He has already told us (in His Word). When we do these things, the Bible says that we will **never** be ashamed.

It is time for the Body of Christ to stop acting upon the various traditional (*man-made*) doctrines and start believing, speaking and acting upon God and the Word of God only. If we will simply put our faith in God and His Word, He will do exactly what He said He *would* do. **Because God is not a man that He should lie!**

Another Side of the Coin

End Notes

END NOTES

Chapter 1: Hanegraaff's Cast of Characters & Beyond

1. Hank Hanegraaff, *Christianity in Crisis*, (Eugene, OR: Harvest House, 1993), 32.
2. Ibid., 32.
3. Ibid., 35.
4. Ibid., 38.
5. Ibid., 47.
6. Ibid., 43-45.
7. *Charisma &Christian Life Magazine*, (May 1995), 48.
8. Ibid., 49.
9. Ibid., 49.
10. Ibid., 49.
11. Ibid., 49.
12. Ibid., 50.
13. Robert W. Tozier, *The New Inquisition*, (25 July 1994), 1, 2. [Author & Publisher unable to locate].
14. *Charisma & Christian Life Magazine*, (July 1995), 108.
15. *Charisma & Christian Life Magazine*, (May 1995), 47.
16. Ibid., 25.
17. Hank Hanegraaff, *Christianity in Crisis*, Study Guide (Eugene, OR: Harvest House,1994), vi.
18. *Charisma & Christian Life*, Magazine, (July 1997), 62.

Chapter 2: The Force of Faith!

1. By permission. From Merriam-Webster's Collegiate® Dictionary, Tenth Edition ©1997 by Merriam-Webster, Inc.
2. Hank Hanegraaff, *Christianity in Crisis*, (Eugene, OR: Harvest House, 1993), 65.
3. Ibid., 65, 66.
4. Ibid., 67.
5. William DeArteaga, *Quenching the Spirit*, (Altamonte Springs, FL: Creation House, Second Printing, 1992), 203, 204.
6. Ibid., 204.
7. Kenneth Copeland, *Kenneth Copeland Reference Edition*, (Fort Worth, TX: Kenneth Copeland Ministries, Inc., 1991), 305.
8. Kenneth Hagin, *New Thresholds of Faith*, (Tulsa, OK: Kenneth Hagin Ministries), 5.
9. Frederick K.C. Price, *How To Obtain Strong Faith*, (Tulsa, OK:

Harrison House, Seventeenth Printing, 1977, 1980), 97.

10. Benny Hinn, "The Faith of God," *This Is Your Day*, (Orlando FL: World Outreach Center, Inc./Benny Hinn Media Ministries (Spring 1996), 3, 4.

11. Jim Kaseman, *Another Dimension To Faith*, (Willmar, MN: The Print House, 1994), 13.

12. Paul Yonggi Cho, *The Fourth Dimension*, Vol. 1 (So. Plain field, NJ: Bridge-Logos Publishing, Inc., 1979), 24.

13. Kenneth Copeland, *Freedom From Fear*,(Fort Worth, TX: Kenneth Copeland Publications 1980, 1983 reprint), 13.

14. Gloria Copeland, "The Unbeatable Spirit of Faith," *Believer's Voice of Victory* (July 1995): 29, 30.

15. Lynn Hammond, *The Master Is Calling: Discovering the Wonders of Spirit-Led Prayer*, (Minneapolis, MN: Mac Hammond Ministries, 1995), 63.

16. Morris Cerullo, *Proof Producers*, (San Diego, CA: World Evangelism, Inc., 1984), 105, 106, 104.

17. Hank Hanegraaff, *Christianity in Crisis*, (Eugene, OR: Harvest House, 1993), 69.

Chapter 3: The Formula of Faith?

1. Hank Hanegraaff, *Christianity in Crisis*, (Eugene, OR: Harvest House, 1993), 73.

2. Ibid., 73.

3. Ibid., 73.

4. Ibid., 74.

5. Kenneth Hagin, *New Thresholds of Faith*, (Tulsa, OK: Kenneth Hagin Ministries, 1985, 1994, Second Edition, Twelfth Printing), 34.

6. Kenneth Hagin, *Your Faith In God Will Work*, (Tulsa, OK: Kenneth Hagin Ministries 1991, 1994, Revised from *Having Faith In Your Faith*), 5.

7. Hank Hanegraaff, *Christianity in Crisis*, (Eugene, OR: Harvest House, 1993), 76.

8. Kenneth Hagin, *How To Write Your Own Ticket With God*, (Tulsa, OK: Kenneth Hagin Ministries 1979, 1989 Sixth Printing), 6, 32.

9. Ibid., 6.

10. Ibid., 6.

11. Ibid., 27.

12. Paul Yonggi Cho, *The Fourth Dimension* Vol.1, (So. Plainfield, NJ: Bridge-Logos Publishing, Inc., 1979), 21, 22.

13. Hank Hanegraaff, *Christianity in Crisis*, (Eugene, OR: Harvest House, 1993), 76.

14. Ibid., 79.

15. Ibid., 81.

16. *The New Strong's Exhaustive Concordance of the Bible*, (Nashville, TN: Thomas Nelson Publishers, Inc., 1990; word # 3049), 863.

17. Ibid., (Set before him: word # 4295), 945.

18. Hank Hanegraaff, *Christianity in Crisis*, (Eugene, OR: Harvest House, 1993), 82.

19. Paul Yonggi Cho, *The Fourth Dimension* Vol.1, (So. Plainfield, NJ: Bridge-Logos Publishing, Inc., 1979), 21.

20. Ibid., 24.

21. Ibid., 31.

22. Ibid., 87, 90; 91; 93.

23. Ibid., pg. 96, 97; 113.

24. William DeArteaga, *Quenching the Spirit*, (Altamonte, Springs, FL, Second Printing, 1992), 161,162.

25. Ibid., 162, 163.

26. Gregg N. Huestis, *When The Holy Spirit Reveals*, (Ticonderoga, NY: Blessed To Be A Blessing Publishing, 1997), 4.

27. Gregg N. Huestis, *Speak The Word Only*, xii-xiii. (presently an unpublished work).

28. Hank Hanegraaff, *Christianity in Crisis*, (Eugene, OR: Harvest House, 1993) 85.

29. Ibid., 85.

30. Ibid., 85.

31. Ibid., 85.

32. *The New Strong's Exhaustive Concordance of the Bible*, (Nashville, TN: Thomas Nelson Publishers, Inc., 1990; word # 2388), 1017.

33. John Garlock, *The Spirit-Filled Life Bible*, (Nashville, TN: Thomas Nelson Publishers, Inc., 1992), 908. Used by permission. All rights reserved.

34. Hank Hanegraaff, *Christianity in Crisis*, (Eugene, OR: Harvest House, 1993), 85.

35. Frederick K.C. Price, "Prayer: Do You Know What Prayer Is…and How to Pray?" *The Word Study Bible*, (Tulsa, OK: Harrison House, 1990, 1994), 1177, 1178.

36. Ibid., 1177.

37. *The New Strong's Exhaustive Concordance of the Bible*, (Nashville, TN: Thomas Nelson Publishers, Inc., 1990; word # 5414), 401.

Chapter 4: The Faith of God

1. Hank Hanegraaff, *Christianity in Crisis*, (Eugene, OR: Harvest House, 1993), 90.
2. *Young's Analytical Concordance of the Bible*, [Faith # 4] (Word Inc., Publisher), 32.
3. *The Compact Bible Dictionary*, (Zondervan Publishing House,1967), 601.
4. *The Vine's Expository Dictionary of Old & New Testament Words*, (Nashville, TN: Thomas Nelson Inc., 1984, 1996), 661.
5. Hank Hanegraaff, *Christianity in Crisis*, (Eugene, OR: Harvest House, 1993), 89.
6. Charles Capps, *God's Creative Power*, (Tulsa, OK: Harrison House, 1976), 2.
7. Ibid, 2.
8. Hank Hanegraaff, *Christianity in Crisis*, (Eugene, OR: Harvest House, 1993), 89, 90.
9. Ibid., 93.
10. Kenneth Copeland, *Freedom From Fear*, (Fort Worth, TX: Kenneth Copeland Publications 1980, 1983; Reprint), 11, 12.
11. Hank Hanegraaff, *Christianity in Crisis*, (Eugene, OR: Harvest House, 1993), 93.
12. Kenneth Copeland, *Freedom From Fear*, (Fort Worth, TX: Kenneth Copeland Publications 1980, 1983; Reprint), 11.
13. Robert W. Tozier, *The New Inquisition*, (25 July 1994), 5. [Author & Publisher unable to locate].

Chapter 5: The Hebrews Hall of Fame

1. Hank Hanegraaff, *Christianity in Crisis*, (Eugene, OR: Harvest House, 1993), 97.
2. Gregg N. Huestis, *When The Holy Spirit Reveals*, (Ticonderoga, NY: Blessed To Be A Blessing Publishing, 1997), 8-17.
3. *The Spirit-Filled Life Bible*, (Nashville, TN: Thomas Nelson Inc., 1992), 711. Used by permission. All rights reserved.
4. *The New Strong's Exhaustive Concordance of the Bible*, (Nashville, TN: Thomas Nelson Publishers, Inc., 1990; Word # 2009), 119.
5. Ibid., (Word # 2005), 633.
6. Ibid., (Word # 7200), 930.
7. *The New Strong's Exhaustive Concordance of the Bible*, (Nashville, TN: Thomas Nelson Publishers, Inc., 1990; Word #'s 572, 571), 219.

8. Hank Hanegraaff, *Christianity in Crisis*, (Eugene, OR: Harvest House, 1993), 100.
9. Hank Hanegraaff, *Christianity in Crisis*, (Eugene, OR: Harvest House, 1993), 97.

Chapter 6: Who's Deifying Man?

1. Hank Hanegraaff, *Christianity in Crisis*, (Eugene, OR: Harvest House, 1993), 108.
2. Ibid., 108.
3. Kenneth Hagin, *Zoe: The God-Kind of Life*, (Tulsa, OK: Kenneth Hagin Ministries, 1981, 1995 Reprint), 36-38; 6.
4. Ibid., 6.
5. Kenneth Copeland, "Believer's Voice of Victory" program (26 February 1995).
6. Hank Hanegraaff, *Christianity in Crisis*, (Eugene, OR: Harvest House, 1993), 109.
7. Ibid., 109.
8. Charles Capps, *Authority in Three Worlds*, (Tulsa, OK: Harrison House, 1980, 1982 Ninth Printing), 17.
9. Kenneth Copeland, "Believer's Voice of Victory" program (8 Jan. 95).
10. Hank Hanegraaff, *Christianity in Crisis*, (Eugene, OR: Harvest House, 1993), 110.
11. *The New Strong's Exhaustive Concordance of the Bible*, (Nashville, TN: Thomas Nelson Publishers, Inc., 1990; word # 430), 423.
12. Kenneth Copeland, "1993 South West Believer's Convention," Video #3/G-63-0307 (Fort Worth, TX: Kenneth Copeland Ministries), (3 Aug. 1993)
13. Hank Hanegraaff, *Christianity in Crisis*, (Eugene, OR: Harvest House, 1993), 116.
14. *The New Strong's Exhaustive Concordance of the Bible*, (Nashville, TN: Thomas Nelson Publishers Inc., 1990; word # 2844), 800.
15. *Young's Analytical Concordance*, [Partakers] (Word Inc., Publishers,), 731.
16. *The Vine's Expository Dictionary*, (Nashville, TN: Thomas Nelson Inc., 1984, 1996), 178.
17. *The New Strong's Exhaustive Concordance of the Bible*, (Nashville, TN: Thomas Nelson Publishers, Inc., 1990; word # 2304), 277.
18. *Young's Analytical Concordance of the Bible*, [Divine] (Word

Inc., Publishers), 261.

19. *The Vine's Expository Dictionary*, (Nashville, TN: Thomas Nelson Inc., 1984, 1996), 427.

20. *The New Strong's Exhaustive Concordance of the Bible*, (Nashville, TN: Thomas Nelson Publishers, Inc., 1990; word # 5449), 736.

21. Kenneth Copeland, "1993 South West Believer's Convention" Video #2 (Fort Worth, Tx: Kenneth Copeland Ministries), (2 Aug. 1993).

Chapter 7: How Would Someone Demote God?

1. Hank Hanegraaff, *Christianity in Crisis*, (Eugene, OR: Harvest House, 1993), 121.
2. Ibid., 121.
3. Robert W. Tozier, *The New Inquisition*, (25 July 1994), 8. [Author & Publisher unable to locate].
4. Hank Hanegraaff, *Christianity in Crisis*, (Eugene, OR: Harvest House, 1993), 122.
5. Ibid., 123.
6. Ibid., 124.
7. Benny Hinn, *Good Morning Holy Spirit*, (Nashville TN: Thomas Nelson Publishers, 1990), 71.
8. Ibid., 72-74.
9. Hank Hanegraaff, *Christianity in Crisis*, (Eugene, OR: Harvest House, 1993), 125.
10. Kenneth Copeland, "The Just Shall Live By Faith," (Fort Worth, TX: Kenneth Copeland Ministries, 1996), audiotape 1, side # 1.
11. Hank Hanegraaff, *Christianity in Crisis*, (Eugene, OR: Harvest House, 1993), 125, 126.
12. Kenneth Copeland, "Believer's Voice of Victory," program (29 January 1995)
13. Kenneth Copeland, "1993 South West Believer's Convention," Video #3/G-63-0307 (Fort Worth, TX: Kenneth Copeland Ministries), (3 Aug. 1993)
14. Hank Hanegraaff, *Christianity in Crisis*, (Eugene, OR: Harvest House, 1993), 129
15. Ibid., 129, 130
16. Kenneth Copeland, *The Power of The Tongue*, (Fort Worth, TX: Kenneth Copeland Publications 1980,1983), 6, 7
17. Kenneth Copeland, *Freedom From Fear*,(Fort Worth, TX: Kenneth Copeland Publications 1980, 1983 reprint), 4

18. Hank Hanegraaff, *Christianity in Crisis*, (Eugene, OR: Harvest House, 1993), 134
19. *The New Strong's Exhaustive Concordance*, (Nashville, TN: Thomas Nelson Publishers, Inc., 1990; word # 4991), 907.

Chapter 8: Who Has Authority To Demote Christ?

1. Hank Hanegraaff, *Christianity in Crisis*, (Eugene, OR: Harvest House, 1993), 137.
2. Ibid., 137.
3. Kenneth Copeland, "Believer's Voice of Victory" program (1 January 95)
4. Hank Hanegraaff, *Christianity in Crisis*, (Eugene, OR: Harvest House, 1993), 138.
5. Kenneth Copeland, "Question & Answer," *Believer's Voice of Victory* (April 1996), 17.
6. *The Vine's Expository Dictionary of Old & New Testament Words*, (Nashville, TN: Thomas Nelson Inc., 1984, 1996), (NT) 101.
7. Kenneth Copeland, "Taking An Offense," *Believer's Voice of Victory*, (July 1995), 5.
8. Kenneth Hagin, *The Healing Anointing*, (Tulsa, OK: Kenneth Hagin Ministries, 1997), 9-11.
9. *The New Strong's Exhaustive Concordance*, (Nashville, TN: Thomas Nelson Publishers, Inc., 1990; "Son of God"), 991,992.
10. Ibid., ("Son of Man"), 991, 992.
11. Hank Hanegraaff, *Christianity in Crisis*, (Eugene, OR: Harvest House, 1993), 138.
12. Ibid., 139, 140.
13. Ibid., 140.
14. Ibid., 141.
15. Ibid., 140.
16. Charles Capps, *Authority in Three Worlds*, (Tulsa, OK: Harrison House, 1980, 1982 Ninth Printing), 189.
17. Hank Hanegraaff, *Christianity in Crisis*, (Eugene, OR: Harvest House, 1993), 141.
18. *The New Strong's Exhaustive Concordance*, (Nashville, TN: Thomas Nelson Publishing, 1990; word # 3056), 1231.
19. Kenneth Hagin, *Healing Belongs To Us*, (Tulsa, OK: Kenneth Hagin Ministries, 1969, 1984), 5.

Chapter 9: Spiritual Death & The Cross

1. *The New Strong's Exhaustive Concordance*, (Nashville, TN: Thomas Nelson Publishing, Inc., 1990; word # 1459/2641), 375.
2. *The Amplified Bible Expanded Edition*, (The Zondervan Corporation and The Lockman Foundation,1987; See: footnote), 800.
3. Ibid., 800.
4. *The New Strong's Exhaustive Concordance*, (Nashville, TN: Thomas Nelson Publishing, Inc., 1990; word # 8438), 1237.
5. *The Spirit-Filled Life Bible*, K. R. "Dick" Iverson, (Nashville, TN: Thomas Nelson, Inc., 1992), 770. Used by permission. All rights reserved.
6. *The New Strong's Exhaustive Concordance*, (Nashville, TN: Thomas Nelson Publishing, Inc., 1990; word # 4148/3256), 186.
7. Ibid., (word #'s 6115 & 6113), 844.
8. Ibid., (word # 4941), 576.
9. *The Vine's Expository Dictionary of Old Testament & New Testament Words*, (Nashville, TN: Thomas Nelson Inc., 1984, 1996), (NT) 300.
10. Ibid., (NT), 455.
11. Ibid., (OT), 237.
12. *The New Strong's Exhaustive Concordance of the Bible*, (Nashville, TN: Thomas Nelson Publishing, Inc., 1990; word # 5999), 1115.
13. Ibid., (word # 7646), 912.
14. *The Vine's Expository Dictionary of Old & New Testament Words*, (Nashville, TN: Thomas Nelson Inc., 1984, 1996), (NT) 385.
15. *The New Strong's Exhaustive Concordance of the Bible*, (Nashville, TN: Thomas Nelson Publishing, Inc., 1990; word # 4221), 235.
16. Ibid., (word # 2983), 862.
17. Morris Cerullo, *Proof Producers*, (San Diego, CA: World Evangelism, Inc., 1984), 127, 128.
18. *The Vine's Expository Dictionary of Old & New Testament Words,,* (Nashville, TN: Thomas Nelson Inc., 1984, 1996), (NT) 149.
19. *The New Strong's Exhaustive Concordance of the Bible*, (Nashville, TN: Thomas Nelson Publishing, Inc., 1990; word #'s 4416, 4413; 5088), 364.

20. Ibid., (word # 3825), 23.
21. Ibid., (word # 1325), 383.
22. *The Vine's Expository Dictionary of Old & New Testament Words*, (Nashville, TN: Thomas Nelson Inc., 1984, 1996), (NT) 513, 514.
23. Ibid., (NT), 493.
24. *The New Strong's Exhaustive Concordance of the Bible*, (Nashville, TN: Thomas Nelson Publishing, Inc., 1990; word # 859), 869.
25. Ibid., (word # 1344), 578.
26. Ibid., (word # 591), 870.
27. *The Vine's Expository Dictionary of Old & New Testament Words*, (Nashville, TN: Thomas Nelson Inc., 1984, 1996), 523,524 (NT).
28. *The New Strong's Exhaustive Concordance of the Bible*, (Nashville, TN: Thomas Nelson Publishing, Inc., 1990; word # 2227), 856.
29. By permission. From Merriam-Webster's Collegiate® Dictionary, Tenth Edition ©1997 by Merriam-Webster, Inc. [Identification].
30. Ibid., [Identify].
31. *The New Strong's Exhaustive Concordance of the Bible*, (Nashville, TN: Thomas Nelson Publishing, Inc., 1990; word # 3908), 215.
32. Ibid., (word # 5055), 361.
33. Ibid., (word # 3860), 393.
34. Kenneth Hagin, *Zoe: The God-Kind of Life*, (Tulsa, OK: Kenneth Hagin Ministries, 1981, 1995, Sixth Printing), 44.
35. Hank Hanegraaff, *Christianity in Crisis*, (Eugene, OR: Harvest House, 1993), 140.

Chapter 10: He Who Knew No Sin *Became* Sin

1. Hank Hanegraaff, *Christianity in Crisis*, (Eugene, OR: Harvest House, 1993), 155.
2. Ibid., 155, 156.
3. Kenneth Copeland, "Believer's Voice of Victory," program (1 Jan. 1995)
4. Hank Hanegraaff, *Christianity in Crisis*, (Eugene, OR: Harvest House, 1993), 156.
5. Ibid., 157, 158.
6. Kenneth Copeland, "Believer's Voice of Victory," program (9 April 1995)

7. Hank Hanegraaff, *Christianity in Crisis*, (Eugene, OR: Harvest House, 1993), 159.
8. *The Vine's Expository Dictionary of Old & New Testament Words*, (Nashville, TN: Thomas Nelson Inc., 1984, 1996), (NT), 743..
9. *The New Strong's Exhaustive Concordance of the Bible*, (Nashville, TN: Thomas Nelson Publishing, Inc., 1990; word # 1096), 667.
10. *The Vine's Expository Dictionary of Old & New Testament Words*, (Nashville, TN: Thomas Nelson Inc., 1984, 1996), (NT), 322.
11. Hank Hanegraaff, *Christianity in Crisis*, (Eugene, OR: Harvest House, 1993), 161.
12. Robert W. Tozier, *The New Inquisition*, (25 July 1994), 10, 11. [Author & Publisher unable to locate]
13. Kenneth Copeland, "The Just Shall Live By Faith," (Fort Worth, TX: Kenneth Copeland Ministries, 1996), audiotape 1, side # 14. Charles Capps, *Authority in Three Worlds*, (Tulsa, OK: Harrison House, 1980, 1982 Ninth Printing), 125, 126.
15. Ibid., 127, 128.
16. Ibid., 128, 131, 132; 142.
17. Ibid., 132, 134.
18. Hank Hanegraaff, *Christianity in Crisis*, (Eugene, OR: Harvest House, 1993), 162.
19. Kenneth Hagin, *Zoe: The God-Kind of Life*, (Tulsa, OK: Kenneth Hagin Ministries, 1981, 1995, Sixth Printing), 44.
20. Hank Hanegraaff, *Christianity in Crisis*, (Eugene, OR: Harvest House, 1993), 165.
21. *The New Strong's Exhaustive Concordance of the Bible*, (Nashville, TN: Thomas Nelson Publishing, Inc., 1990; word # 305), 80.

Chapter 11: The First Born From Among The Dead

1. Hank Hanegraaff, *Christianity in Crisis*, (Eugene, OR: Harvest House, 1993), 171.
2. Ibid., 169.
3. Kenneth Copeland; "Believer's Voice of Victory," program (16 April 1995).
4. *The New Strong's Exhaustive Concordance of the Bible*, (Nashville, TN: Thomas Nelson Publishing, Inc., 1990; words # 4416/4413), 364.
5. Hank Hanegraaff, *Christianity in Crisis*, (Eugene, OR: Harvest

House, 1993), 174.

6. Kenneth Copeland, "Believer's Voice of Victory," program (16 April 1995).

7. Hank Hanegraaff, *Christianity in Crisis*, (Eugene, OR: Harvest House, 1993), 172.

8. *The New Strong's Exhaustive Concordance of the Bible*, (Nashville, TN: Thomas Nelson Publishing, Inc., 1990; word # 5315/5314), 998.

9. Hank Hanegraaff, *Christianity in Crisis*, (Eugene, OR: Harvest House, 1993), 172.

10. Ibid., 161.

11. E.W. Kenyon, *What Happened From The Cross To The Throne*, (Kenyon Gospel Publishing Society, 1993, Fifteenth Edition), 19, 20.

12. Adele Pillitteri, Ph.D., RN, PNP, *Maternal & Child Health Nursing*, Second Edition (Philadelphia, PA: J.B. Lipppincott Company, 1995), 195.

Chapter 12: Who's "Conforming" To Culture?

1. Hank Hanegraaff, Christianity in Crisis, (Eugene, OR: Harvest House, 1993), 192.

2. *Charisma & Christian Life Magazine*, (May 1995), 49.

3. Ibid., 49.

4. Ibid., 49.

5. Hank Hanegraaff, *Christianity in Crisis*, (Eugene, OR: Harvest House, 1993), 187.

6. Ibid., 188.

7. Ibid., 188.

8. Ibid., 189.

9. Ibid., 191, 192.

10. John Avanzini, *Financial Excellence*, (Fort Worth, TX: His Image Publishing), 22, 23.

11. Ibid., 77-79.

12. Frederick K.C. Price, *How To Obtain Strong Faith*, (Tulsa, OK: Harrison House, 1977, 1980 Seventeenth Printing), 28,29.

13. Frederick K.C. Price, *The Spirit-Filled Life Bible*, (Nashville, TN: Thomas Nelson Publishing, 1992), 267.

14. Ibid., 1539.

15. Hank Hanegraaff, *Christianity in Crisis*, (Eugene, OR: Harvest House, 1993), 37.

16. Jerry Savelle, "1993 South West Believer's Convention," Video #3/W-63-0323 (Fort Worth, TX: Kenneth Copeland

Ministries), (6 Aug. 1993)

17. Jerry Savelle, "The Believer's Voice of Victory," program (30 Jan. 1995)

18. Jerry Savelle, "Practicing Patience" (Crowely, TX: Jerry Savelle Ministries International, 1995), audiotape, side #1.

19. Ibid., side # 2.

20. Kenneth Copeland, "Prosperity Why Should You Prosper?" *The Word Study Bible*, (Tulsa, OK: Harrison House Publishing, 1990,1994), 1133,1134.

21. Kenneth Copeland, "The Law of Increase (Mark 4:24,25)" P-2 (Fort Worth, TX: Kenneth Copeland Ministries 1995), audiotape, side #1.

22. Kenneth Copeland, "The Blessing of Twice-Sown Seed," *Believer's Voice of Victory*, (March 1996), 17.

23. Jay Sekulow, "The Only Message That Counts," *Believer's Voice of Victory*, (Nov. 1997), 26.

24. Kenneth Copeland, "Kenneth Copeland Ministries 30th Year Celebration," *Believer's Voice of Victory*, program on [C.C.E.], (29 Dec. 1997)

25. Jerry Savelle, "Practicing Patience," (Crowely, TX: Jerry Savelle Ministries International, 1995), audiotape, side #2.

Chapter 13: PTL: [P]ass [T]he [L]ute

1. *Charisma & Christian Life Magazine*, "Jim Bakker Rejects 'Prosperity Gospel'" (September 1996), 16.

2. Hank Hanegraaff, *Christianity in Crisis*, (Eugene, OR: Harvest House, 1993), 193, 195.

3. Ibid., 194, 195.

4. Barry Segal, *Good Morning Europe*, Interview conducted by Rory Alec, program on "The Christian Channel Europe" (10 Dec. 1997)

5. Hank Hanegraaff, *Christianity in Crisis*, (Eugene, OR: Harvest House, 1993), 193.

6. Ibid., 195.

7. Ibid., 196.

.8. Ibid., 196.

9. Ibid., 199.

10. Ibid., 199, 201.

11. Ibid., 204.

12. Ibid., 205.

13. Ibid., 205.

14. Ibid., 206.

15. *The Spirit-Filled Life Bible*, (Nashville, TN: Thomas Nelson Publishing, Inc., 1992), 1490. Used by permission. All rights reserved

16. Ibid., li..

17. Hank Hanegraaff, *Christianity in Crisis*, (Eugene, OR: Harvest House, 1993), 203.

18. Ibid., 201.

19. Kenneth Hagin, *God's Medicine*; (Tulsa, OK: Kenneth Hagin Ministries, 1977, 1995—twenty-first Printing), 8, 9.

20. Hank Hanegraaff, *Christianity in Crisis*, (Eugene, OR: Harvest House, 1993), 208.

21. John Avanzini, *It's Not Working Brother John!*, (Fort Worth, TX: His Image Ministries, 1992), 13.

22. *The Amplified Bible*, (Zondervan Publishing & The Lockman Foundation,1987), vi.

23. *Charisma & Christian Life Magazine*, (March 1996), 37, 38.

24. Ibid., 38, 39, 42.

25. Ibid., 39, 41.

Chapter 14: A Covenant *Is* A Biblical Contract!

1. Hank Hanegraaff, *Christianity in Crisis*, (Eugene, OR: Harvest House, 1993), 211.

2. Ibid., 211

3. By permission. From Merriam-Webster's Collegiate® Dictionary, Tenth Edition ©1997 by Merriam-Webster, Inc. [Covenant]

4. *The New Strong's Exhaustive Concordance of the Bible*, (Nashville, TN: Thomas Nelson Publishing, Inc., 1990; word # 1285 OT), 229.

5. Ibid., (word # 1242 NT), 229.

6. *The Vine's Expository Dictionary of Old & New Testament Words*, (Nashville, TN: Thomas Nelson Publishing, Inc., 1996 NT), 135. Used by permission.

7. *The Compact Bible Dictionary*, (Zondervan Publishing House, Grand Rapids, MI 1967), 118.

8. *Holman's Bible Dictionary* software for Windows on CD-ROM (by Parsons Technology, Inc. 1994), [Covenant], 1, 4-7; 9. Used by permission.

9. Kenneth Copeland, *Covenant Made By Blood*, (Fort Worth, TX: Kenneth Copeland Publications 1987, 1989, reprinted August 1989; #90-1752), Introduction—1, 2.

10. Ibid., 1, 2; 8.

11. Ibid., 14.
12. Robert w. Tozier, *The New Inquisition*, (25 July 1994), 12. [Author & Publisher unable to locate].
13. Ibid., 12, 13.
14. Hank Hanegraaff, *Christianity in Crisis*, (Eugene, OR: Harvest House, 1993), 212.
15. By permission. From *The Merriam-Webster's* Tenth, Collegiate Dictionary, (G. & C. Merriam Company, Springfield, 1997), [bilateral].
16. Hank Hanegraaff, *Christianity in Crisis*, (Eugene, OR: Harvest House, 1993), 213.
17. Robert W. Tozier, *The New Inquisition*, (25 July 1994), 13, 15. [Author & Publisher unable to locate].
18. Hank Hanegraaff, *Christianity in Crisis*, (Eugene, OR: Harvest House, 1993), 212.
19. Ibid., 214.
20. *Charisma & Christian Life Magazine*, "Jim Bakker Rejects 'Prosperity Gospel'" (September 1996), 16.

Chapter 15: Sickness—Suffering, Symptoms; Satan And Sovereignty

1. Hank Hanegraaff, *Christianity in Crisis*, (Eugene, OR: Harvest House, 1993), 235-237.
2. *The Amplified Bible*, (Zondervan Publishing & The Lockman Foundation, 1987), x.
3. Hank Hanegraaff, *Christianity in Crisis*, (Eugene, OR: Harvest House, 1993), 237.
4. Kenneth E. Hagin, *A Better Covenant*, (Tulsa, OK: Kenneth Hagin Ministries, 1980, 1993 Fifth Printing), 29.
5. Kenneth E. Hagin, *Healing Belongs To Us*, (Tulsa, OK: Kenneth Hagin Ministries, 1969, 1984 Fourteenth Printing), 22-25.
6. Jesse Duplantis, "1993 South West Believer's Convention," Video #2/H-63-0308 (Fort Worth, TX: Kenneth Copeland Ministries), (3 Aug. 1993)
7. Hank Hanegraaff, *Christianity in Crisis*, (Eugene, OR: Harvest House, 1993), 241.
8. Ibid., 242.
9. Kenneth E. Hagin, *New Thresholds of Faith*, (Tulsa, OK: Kenneth Hagin Ministries, 1985, 1994 Twelfth Printing), 8.
10. Charles Capps, *The Tongue A Creative Force*, (Tulsa, OK: Harrison House, 1976, Thirty-sixth Printing), 27, 43.
11. Kenneth Copeland, "Taking Flight," *Believer's Voice of Victory*, (November 1993), 3,4.

12. Hank Hanegraaff, *Christianity in Crisis*, (Eugene, OR: Harvest House, 1993), 247, 248.
13. Kenneth Copeland; "1993 South West Believer's Conven tion," video #4/J-63-0310 (Fort Worth, TX: Kenneth Cope land Ministries), (3 Aug. 1993).
14. Charles Capps, *The Tongue A Creative Force*, (Tulsa, OK: Harrison House, 1976), 49, 59; 60.
15. Ibid., 60.
16. Hank Hanegraaff, *Christianity in Crisis*, (Eugene, OR: Harvest House, 1993), 248.
17. Ibid., 248
18. Ibid., 249, 250.
19. *The New Strong's Exhaustive Concordance of the Bible*, (Nashville, TN: Thomas Nelson Publishing, Inc., 1990; word # 7495), 480.
20. Hank Hanegraaff, *Christianity in Crisis*, (Eugene, OR: Harvest House, 1993), 250.
21. *Young's Analytical Concordance of the Bible*, [Atonement], (Word Inc., Publishers), 62.
22. Ibid., [Redemption], 800.
23. Kenneth E. Hagin, *How To Keep Your Healing*, (Tulsa, OK: Kenneth Hagin Ministries, 1980, 1995, Seventeenth Printing), 3-5.
24. Hank Hanegraaff, *Christianity in Crisis*, (Eugene, OR: Harvest House, 1993), 251.
25. Ibid., 251.
26. *The Vine's Expository Dictionary of Old & New Testament Words*, (Nashville, TN: Thomas Nelson Publishing, Inc., 1996), (NT), 355.
27. Hank Hanegraaff, *Christianity in Crisis*, (Eugene, OR: Harvest House, 1993), 257.
28. Ibid., 257.
29. Ibid., 257.
30. Ibid., 258, 259.
31. Kenneth Copeland, "Questions & Answers," *Believer's Voice of Victory*, (January 1995), 23.
32. Gloria Copeland, *God's Will For Your Healing*, (Forth Worth, TX: Kenneth Copeland Publications, 1972, 1991 Reprint), 17.
33. Ibid., 23.
34. Gloria Copeland, "When Healing Takes Time, *Believer's Voice of Victory* (Nov. 1992), 15.
35. Morris Cerullo, *Proof Producers*, (San Diego, CA: World

Evangelism, Inc., 1980), 104.

36. Ibid., 104.

37. Robert W. Tozier, *The New Inquisition*, quoted Hanegraaff, T. McClung, R. Shepherd (25 July 1994), 18. [Author & Publisher unable to locate]

38. Hank Hanegraaff, *Christianity in Crisis*, [quoted Psalm 119:75], (Eugene, OR: Harvest House, 1993), 267.

39. *The New Strong's Exhaustive Concordance of the Bible*, [Afflicted] (Nashville, TN: Thomas Nelson Publishing, Inc., 1990, word # 6031), 16.

40. T.L. Osborn, "Healing," *The Word Study Bible*, (Tulsa, OK: Harrison House, 1990, 1994), 1188.

41. Kenneth Copeland, "The Power of Resistance," *Believer's Voice of Victory*, (June 1997), 6, 5.

42. Frederick K.C. Price, *How To Obtain Strong Faith*; (Tulsa, OK: Harrison House, 1977, 1980 Revised Edition, Seventeenth Printing), 30, 31.

43. Kenneth E. Hagin, *Don't Blame God*, (Tulsa, OK: Kenneth Hagin Ministries, 1979, 1996 Sixteenth Printing), 19.

44. Hank Hanegraaff, *Christianity in Crisis*, (Eugene, OR: Harvest House, 1993), 267.

45. Ibid., 268, 269.

46. Ibid., 271.

47. Frederick K.C. Price, "Do You Know What Prayer Is…and How to Pray?," *The Word Study Bible*, *Prayer*, (Tulsa, OK: Harrison House, 1990, 1994), 1179-1182.

48. Kenneth Copeland, "Don't Give Up Hope," *Believer's Voice of Victory*, (January 1995), 4.

49. Jesse Duplantis, "The Language of War," *Voice of the Covenant*, (January 1998), 7, 8.

50. Kenneth Copeland, "Pray Like Harvest Depends on It," *Believer's Voice of Victory*, (January 1998), 18, 19.

Chapter 16: Some Closing Remarks

1. Hank Hanegraaff, *Christianity in Crisis*, (Eugene, OR: Harvest House, 1993), 237.

2. Ibid., 237.

3. Ibid., 238.

4. Ibid., 246.

5. Ibid., 219, 220.

6. Ibid., 90.

7. Gregg N. Huestis, *When The Holy Spirit Reveals*, (Ticonderoga,

NY: Blessed To Be A Blessing Publishing, 1997), 4.

8. Ibid., 30.
9. *The New Strong's Exhaustive Concordance of the Bible*,
   (Nashville, TN: Thomas Nelson Publishing, Inc., 1990, word
   # 4982), 914.

An Important Message

Dear Reader,

We believe it was no accident that you have come across this book. We want you to know that the Lord Jesus loves you and wants to bless your life <u>in every area possible</u>. He wants to give you **peace** and **joy** like you have never experienced before. If you desire to accept His free gift, we invite you to pray the following prayer:

"Dear Heavenly Father, I come to you in the Name of Jesus, I admit that I am a sinner in need of a Savior. I ask you to forgive me of all of my sins. You said in Romans 10:9&10, that if I confess with my mouth the Lord Jesus and believe in my heart that You raised Jesus from the dead, that I would be saved (born a new).

I believe in my heart that Jesus is the Son of God. I believe He died on the cross for my freedom from sin and evil. I believe that You raised Him from the dead so that I would have a right relationship with You. I accept Jesus as my personal Lord and Savior. Jesus come into my heart and change me into the person You want me to be. I give you my life today.

Father, I thank You for accepting me as a member of Your family. Thank You for giving me Your peace and joy. I thank You for blessing every area of my life. Help me to live for You. I ask all these things in Jesus Name. Amen!"

If you have just prayed this prayer, accepting Jesus as your Lord and Savior, please email us at: **info@b2bablessing.org.** We would love to hear from you and help you grow in your new faith in Christ.

—Gregg & Emily Huestis
Blessed To Be A Blessing Ministries

www.ingramcontent.com/pod-product-compliance
Lightning Source LLC
Chambersburg PA
CBHW030918090426
42737CB00007B/232